DUE DATE	RETURN DATE		DUE DATE	RETURN DATE

WARS, PLOTS AND SCANDALS IN POST-WAR FRANCE

PHILIP M. WILLIAMS

CAMBRIDGE at the University Press 1970

Published by the Syndics of the Cambridge University Press
Bentley House, 200 Euston Road, London N.W. 1
American Branch: 32 East 57th Street, New York, N.Y. 10022

This selection © Cambridge University Press 1970

Library of Congress Catalogue Card Number: 77–96105

Standard Book Number: 521 07741 9

Printed in Great Britain
at the University Printing House, Cambridge
(Brooke Crutchley, University Printer)

Contents

Preface

This collection brings together a dozen articles on French political subjects, mostly concerned either with the plots and scandals which arose out of the long struggle for decolonisation, or with the culmination of that struggle in the long Algerian war. Chapter 1, written as an introduction to this volume, shows the close connection between the two themes. Chapter 2 traces the bitter divisions in French domestic politics, exacerbated by the decline of French external power, which the dying Third Republic bequeathed as a poisoned heritage to its successors. Chapters 3 to 6 deal with the major political scandals and conspiracies of the fifties and sixties; and chapters 7 to 10 with the Algerian crisis and the army's challenges to the Fourth and Fifth Republics. Chapter 11 discusses the use President de Gaulle made of his new diplomatic freedom once decolonisation was complete, and chapter 12 (a lecture given in the United States in 1968) suggests an analogy on the other side of the world. My articles on the regular political process in France in these years have been included in a companion volume, *French Politicians and Elections, 1951–1969*.

In this collection chapters 1, 6 (the longest in the book) and 12 have not previously been published. The rest are reproduced exactly as they first appeared, except for the correction of misprints, and changes consequent on the omission of references to books in chapter 11, which was originally a review. Some titles have been changed, some explanatory (lettered) footnotes have been added, and new material is included in the Appendices to chapters 5 and 7. Each article specifies the original place and date of publication and I am grateful to Methuen & Co. (chap. 2), *The Cambridge Journal* (chap. 3), *Occidente* (chap. 4), the BBC (chap. 5), *French Historical Studies* (chap. 7), *Encounter* (chaps. 8 and 10), *The Guardian* (chap. 9) and Basil Blackwell Ltd (chap. 11) for permission to reproduce them.

I am indebted also to the Warden and Fellows of Nuffield College, Oxford, under whose auspices I have followed French politics for most of the last twenty years; to Jean Brotherhood for efficient and patient secretarial help and proof-reading; to Christine Woodland for preparing the index; and to David Goldey, Laurence Whitehead and Frank Wright for useful advice in the selection of material. They have no responsibility for my errors of fact or judgment.

P. M. WILLIAMS

Oxford, 1969

PART I

THE BURDEN OF HISTORY

1 The politics of scandal

The mechanism is always the same: in the beginning a genuine fact; the opposition seize upon it; embroider it; create a whole theory; incriminate parliamentarians and ministers. The judicial authorities become involved; the enquiry lasts for months and months and most of the prominent figures are found innocent, but public opinion, 'brainwashed' by the campaign of slander and insinuation launched when the Affair blew up, is not going to be fooled by that. Because of a well-known tendency to latent anti-parliamentarianism, it is delighted in its certainty of the dishonesty, meanness or corrupt behaviour of the powers that be, it wants to retain its certainty of their guilt—and if courts or parliamentary committees decide they are innocent it only sees in that a new scandal. 'Slander, slander—something will always stick.' The phrase does not date from the Fourth Republic.[1]

This passage was written three years before the murder of Stefan Marcovitch which opened the Paris scandal of 1969, the Delon affair.

France is the classic land of political scandal. Other countries have had their famous sensations involving Wilma Montesi or Christine Keeler, the journalists of *Der Spiegel* or the bishops of the Greek Church. But in no capital is the Affair so hallowed a part of the national political tradition as it is in Paris. For there an over-centralised, over-bureaucratic administration inherited from Napoleon rules over 'the most fickle and unmanageable people on earth'.[2] Thoroughly suspicious of rulers who seem remote and inaccessible, Frenchmen are deeply prone to see corruption, conspiracy and treason everywhere. This credulity is delightedly exploited by an unscrupulous opposition of the extreme Right, never reconciled since the great Revolution to a liberal or democratic regime yet rarely able to triumph over the hated Republic in a contest of ideas and policies before the electorate. Finding slander and scandal its most effective weapons, over the decades the extreme Right has bred leaders—journalists or lawyers by profession, nihilists rather than conservatives by temperament—who have specialised in these methods of political combat.

Their opportunity was rarely far to seek. Always under challenge since the Revolution, French regimes have felt the need of a politically reliable police organisation to protect them against subversive activities. The police, being politically committed, have consequently been perpetually suspected

---

[1] G. Elgey, *La République des illusions* (Paris, Fayard, 1965), p. 189: referring to the wine scandals of 1946. Translations are by the author.
[2] C. de Gaulle, *Mémoires de Guerre: III, Le Salut* (Paris, Plon, 1959), p. 28.

by opponents of the government of abusing their functions to serve not merely the security of the regime but the convenience of the politicians in office. These in turn had friends who inevitably included, along with honest supporters of the existing order, a proportion of careerists, hangers-on and self-seekers who covered their personal political or financial operations by an ostentatious devotion to the ideological principles of the regime: Republicanism no less than patriotism can be the last refuge of a scoundrel. Scandal flourished amid the weakness of cabinets, the arbitrary behaviour of the bureaucracy, the irregular conduct of individuals in high administrative or political positions; and governments frequently found themselves tempted to cover it up. Thus a former director of the 'CID' in Paris—where senior police officers are as likely to publish books on politics as on crime—wrote in 1958: '"Politics", a distinguished Belgian moralist has said, "is the art of finding scapegoats." In France it is not an art. It is a tradition, of which the petty official and the policeman are usually called to pay the price.'[3]

This French propensity to scandal does, of course, contain an element of optical illusion. When people are contented, even a major and proven scandal may have no visible political effects—witness the total indifference of the electorate of the United States to Teapot Dome and the many other misdeeds of Harding's Administration—and minor ones are easily smothered and rapidly forgotten. Similarly, financial scandals caused little concern in France in the 1920s, but the manipulations of a very minor crook, Stavisky, were enough to shake a regime which had become unpopular by 1934. The rarity of recent periods in which Frenchmen have seemed politically satisfied helps to explain the propensity to scandal, as we shall see that the dramas of decolonisation help to account for its special efflorescence in the years since 1945.

Nevertheless the propensity goes far back into French history—at the very least as far as the Queen's Necklace in the period just before the Revolution. Ever since those days, the form of the French political order has been called into question by some important section of opinion. After Sedan, Jules Ferry hopefully announced (in what must rank high among the least successful historical predictions ever made): 'France, delivered from the corruptions of the Empire, has entered into the period of the austere virtues.' But some of the monarchists continued to regard the Republic as *la gueuse* and remained eager to believe—or invent—the worst that could be said of her and her friends. They were to be given ample material. In the eighties a President was driven to resign by the revelation that his son-in-law had been selling official decorations. In the nineties large-scale bribery

---

[3] L. Ducloux, *From Blackmail to Treason: Political Crime and Corruption in France 1920–1940* (London, Deutsch, 1958), p. 132.

of deputies to pass a law to save the insolvent Panama Company 'opened a breach which has never been repaired in the people's confidence in its elected representatives'.[4] At the end of the decade, in the greatest Affair of them all, Military Intelligence resorted to forgery and perjury to discredit an innocent junior officer and so protected a traitor; in reaction to the army's excesses the Republicans then attempted a military purge, using the masonic lodges to spy on officers who went to Mass (*l'Affaire des Fiches*).

In this century, the major Affairs have been of four types. A surprisingly small number have concerned the private lives of politicians, like the killing of the editor Gaston Calmette by Madame Caillaux in 1914, and the Ballets Roses scandal in 1958. Then there have been several financial cases of the Panama variety, though of smaller magnitude; among them those centred round Stavisky's operations and the extensive political and judicial protection he apparently enjoyed until his eventual suicide in 1934; alleged corruption over import licences for Algerian wine in 1946; mysterious deals by Joanovici during and after the Liberation; and the profitable traffic in over-valued Indo-Chinese piastres up to 1953. Next, there have been plots to overthrow the Republic, mounted by the extreme Right or by elements in the army (such as the Left believed were involved either as cause or consequence in both the Dreyfus and the Stavisky affairs). In 1937 the Cagoulards—who certainly were plotting counter-revolution—blew up the offices of the Employers' Confederation, intending the Communist Party to get the blame. In the 'Blue Plan' of July 1947 and the 'Whitsun Plot' of 1949 the government of the Fourth Republic claimed to have exposed Gaullist conspiracies against it which had complicities in the army. In the 'bazooka plot' of January 1957, fascists in Algiers, with links to the survivors of the Cagoulards, fired a shell into the office of the Commander-in-Chief, General Salan, and killed his ADC. In May 1958 the Gaullists demonstrated that they had no hostility in principle to the kind of subversive activities which later, in 1960 and 1961, were directed against them by their recent allies of the extreme Right (see chapters 7 and 10).

Finally, there are the accusations of betraying the nation. These are occasionally launched by the Left—as in 1950 against René Hardy, a Resistance hero who was alleged to have turned Gestapo agent—but habitually by the Right. In the nineties Dreyfus was charged with espionage, and his sympathisers with subversive intentions. In the First World War, journalists and politicians suspected of lukewarmness were denounced for much worse offences, and the campaign culminated in the arrest and suicide of an editor, Almereyda of the *Bonnet Rouge*, the banishment of a minister, Malvy, and the imprisonment of an ex-premier, Caillaux. In 1936 Blum's

[4] M. Blocq-Mascart, *Du Scandale* (Paris, Bouchet-Chastel, 1960), p. 144.

Minister of the Interior, Salengro, committed suicide when falsely accused of having deserted under fire twenty years before. After 1940, political leaders were charged with responsibility for the military defeat; the more fortunate, like Blum, were merely put on trial by the Vichy regime, but others, like Mandel and Zay, were assassinated by Vichy's collaborationist militia. Since the war, in the Generals' Affair of 1950 and the Leakages Case of 1956, there have been campaigns against soldiers or journalists supposed to have passed information to France's opponents in Indo-China and Algeria, and against politicians who were thought to have sympathised with and covered up for them (chapters 3 and 4). Often these charges had only the shakiest foundation and some can hardly have been believed by those who spread them. Their object was not to save the Republic but to ruin it by discrediting its defenders. For the reactionaries, denounced by the Left for treason against a regime they regarded as illegitimate, were naturally tempted to retaliate by accusing their enemies of treason to the nation itself.

Out of these repeated conflicts both sides have developed their own presumptions and their own folklore. Colonel Fourcaud at once saw a new Almereyda case in the Affair of the Generals, and when the Leakages occurred, Colonel Dides referred to *L'Express* as a lineal successor of the *Bonnet Rouge*. *Carrefour* in the first case, *Rivarol* in the second, played the scandalmongering role of *Gringoire* in the campaign against Salengro. Indeed André Baranès, the villain (or hero) of the Leakages Affair, was exonerated by the same judge who had recently acquitted *Gringoire*'s publisher, Horace de Carbuccia (the contributors to his journal had been given heavy sentences after the war, but Carbuccia had prudently retired to Switzerland for some years before facing a French court). Thus the scandals themselves display a familiar pattern, and the behaviour of the participants offers constant reminders of history. Their attitudes are set by the conflicts of the past, and forecast those of the future.

Moreover, these cases have a common feature: they all involve some branch of the State machine. Occasionally another type of sensation attracts attention; in the early Fifth Republic there was one concerning a former President of the Assembly, another over the private inheritance of a millionaire. But the true political scandal involves the State and usually, though not invariably, ends in the courts—to be exploited effectively by publicity-conscious lawyer-politicians. Many characters indeed reappear in successive cases in different roles: François Mitterrand from minister and victim to central figure of a mysterious plot (chapter 5); J. B. Biaggi from riot leader to deputy and defence counsel; Raoul Salan from Republican general and victim to military putschist and leader of the right-wing terrorist OAS; Roger Frey from

6

conspirator to Minister of the Interior; J. L. Tixier-Vignancour from political lawyer to presidential candidate (though he still defiantly attended a requiem mass for Bastien-Thiry who had failed to assassinate de Gaulle).

The State or parts of its apparatus may figure in a scandal, either as the intended victim of a conspiracy, or as itself the plotting agency, or—far more commonly—as the supposed protector of the guilty party. In different circumstances either the Left or the Right may be inclined by their political prejudices to suspect the misdeeds of men in power. For in France, unlike Britain or the United States, a powerful and highly centralised State machine was created long before liberal or democratic institutions had developed, and therefore was and remains an object of suspicion by the Left; at the same time the historic champions of authoritarian rule have usually in recent decades been excluded from power in Paris, and therefore, despite their theoretical attitude, have a deep mistrust and contempt for the current holders of political authority. So when police chiefs or secret servicemen or judges or generals are accused of misusing their positions, it is sometimes— as over Dreyfus—the Left which seeks to uncover the scandal and expose those responsible, while the Right leaps to defend the established social, administrative or military order and denounce its critics. But on other occasions, as over Stavisky, an attack is launched by the Right against some Republican political institution which finds its defenders on the Left. In either case the political scandal focuses on the alleged abuse of power by its holders for some personal or partisan end. As counsel for Ben Barka's family (chapter 6) put it in his closing speech in court, the Dreyfus affair acquired its historical significance because it exposed the influence of the army, the Stavisky scandal because it demonstrated the subordination of the State to the money power, Ben Barka's own case because it revealed the political role of the police.

There are several domestic reasons for France's propensity to political scandal. The deep divisions in the country explain the mistrust of the political leaders of the other side. The long history of sensational Affairs has fed the scapegoat-hunting mentality of the public. Meanwhile, within the official machine, the structure of government makes it difficult to establish respon- sibilities and therefore facilitates the misdeeds which arouse public indigna- tion. Outside the governmental service, the ordinary Frenchman feels no sense of participation in the vast centralised official hierarchy, which neither inclination nor experience leads him to view as concerned with his own needs or wishes.

In a time of domestic discontent and foreign humiliation, there are thus many reasons why he is disposed to view his political leaders with a mixture of suspicion and contempt. Once, indeed, there was good ground for doing so: Wilson, Panama, Dreyfus, the *Bonnet Rouge*, Stavisky were all of them genuine scandals, however outrageously they were exploited by one side or the other. The peculiarity of the post-war Affairs—though signs were to be found in the 1930s, with the Salengro case or the Cagoulards' attempt to blame the Communist Party for their own crimes—lies in the enormous exaggeration (as in the Generals' Affair), or total perversion (as in the Leakages Case), or deliberate provocation (as in the Mitterrand business) of incidents to use against the regime. This was only possible because, under a veneer of sophistication, the French voter is remarkably credulous and eager to believe the worst of his public men. But it also required a high degree of skill and a low degree of scruple among the spokesmen of some extremist groups.

Institutional factors have facilitated this exploitation of scandal: a venal press, weak libel laws, lax court procedure, judges who were underpaid and therefore sometimes of poor quality. Repeated challenges to the Republican regime have obliged it to keep its police force highly involved in politics, with all the justified and unjustified suspicion that situation can provoke. Above all, the political system in the Third and Fourth Republics was one of a highly centralised state with fragmentation of power at the top. The Jacobins had always feared that institutions with a genuine local base would endanger national unity, splitting the country on political or religious lines by creating new La Rochelles or Vendées. Their Orleanist successors insisted on the primacy of indirect democracy through Parliament. Combining both principles, the Republicans rejected referendum and direct election as firmly as locally elected institutions with real powers. Thus, decisively separating the people of France from their masters in Paris, the Third Republic ensured that when bad times came after 1930, the State would operate in a political vacuum in which it could not count on the active loyalty of its citizens in crises. But at the same time it failed to secure effective authority at the top because Parliament, all too representative of a deeply divided country, was never able to establish a united majority or coherent government. Civil service expertise proved inadequate when there was no popular base for real political authority. Instead the centralised power was dissipated among rival parties, ministers and state services. (Internecine conflicts were particularly frequent in the police force, perhaps out of an instinctive cautionary tendency of the Republican politicians to self-preservation by dividing and ruling.) This dissipation of authority ensured that no one was ever responsible: and political morality is low where responsibility is diffused.

If responsibility were not so diluted, if a decision did not depend on so many services or individuals, if the regulations did not present so tangled a thicket, if [political] interventions were not so insistent, if supervisory checks were less slow and were followed up by sanctions, if, in a word, it did not seem so simple to escape from the consequences of one's acts, there would be fewer abuses.[5]

But this structure, of centralisation in Paris without central control of the government, was not—as was and is widely believed—merely the consequence of a parliamentary republic in which majorities were hard to find and harder still to retain. The system of fluctuating groups and frequently changing governments was already highly developed in the July Monarchy. It re-appeared in the later stages of the Second Empire, it characterised the Vichy regime from the start and, below the surface, some of its features live on in the obscurity cast by the long shadow of President de Gaulle. The French State, so imposing in appearance, is highly vulnerable in reality. Where else in the world has the State machine so nearly withered away on three or four different occasions in this century? In 1917 it almost did so, in 1940 it did so completely, and twice recently—in May 1958 and ten years afterwards—it has collapsed without having suffered the impact of war on its home soil.

The fragility of the State in Paris marks an obvious and enormous contrast with Washington. Yet there are also some striking resemblances between political life in the two countries.[6] In the matters here discussed, scandal features more prominently in the politics of France and the United States than in other major countries (Italy perhaps excepted). In both, domestic struggles and resentments are projected into foreign policy and predispose the aggrieved citizen to mistrust his leadership: 'nous sommes trahis' is an all too familiar cry on both sides of the Atlantic. In both, political power in the nineteenth and early twentieth century flowed not from the ports and industrial areas but from the distant rural regions; if their representatives could not always exercise the authority of the State, they could at least prevent its being used against their interests. For to the rural voter in both countries the big city seemed remote, cosmopolitan and suspect; it was provincialism that made him distrust the metropolis, the source of subsidies but also of taxes, scandals and foreign wars.[7] The peasants and small bourgeoisie who had benefited from the Revolution had little to hope and much to fear from a strong government in Paris. When a working-class uprising seemed dangerously close, they might turn to the lesser evil of a strong authoritarian ruler, but in normal times they preferred to keep political authority diffused, and therefore safe, by sending a querulous and mistrustful body of parliamentary representatives to watch and control the men in office. 'The true power of the voters should be defined, I believe, rather by resistance

---

[5] Blocq-Mascart, *Du Scandale*, pp. 192–3.

[6] See the companion volume to this work, *French Politicians and Elections*, chap. 7, for a comparison.

[7] The common feature of provincialism was suggested to me by David Goldey.

to the authorities than by reformist action...The important thing is to construct every day a little barricade...'[8] So wrote Alain, the most influential intellectual spokesman of the Radicals—not a frustrated opposition sect but the political party which held or shared power almost continuously from 1900 to 1940.

In the United States too political authority was diffused. But different methods were used to keep in check the possible ravages of 'big government': the separation of powers, the federal system, and decentralised political parties, so weak that they sometimes seemed to be held together by nothing but 'the cohesive power of public plunder' (a characteristic shared by governing parties in France—and elsewhere—if not by opposition ones). But the United States has compensations lacking in France. Though below the presidential level responsibility is dissipated, with conflicts and confusions similar to those in Paris, at the top the nation's political head is elected as the choice of the people, and thus enjoys a popular mandate denied to French leaders before 1958. When public confidence in his subordinates is shattered, they can usually be replaced without the President's own prestige collapsing; and when an entire administration is discredited, its successor will be chosen by the people themselves and not in an obscure parliamentary bargain. The federal structure provides a device, for which there is no equivalent in France (or Britain), for first testing leaders outside the parliamentary system in the capital and then projecting them rapidly into national prominence. Moreover, just because the people of the United States are of diverse origins (which is the origin of most of their mutual suspicions), there is a strong pressure on them to display their loyalty by acceptance, public and private, of the national symbols—the constitution and the flag. There are bitter quarrels over policy in the United States but these do not endanger the political system because the constitution—naturally interpreted in diametrically opposed ways according to the taste and interests of the individual—serves as a unifying myth worshipped alike by moderates and extremists, by Joseph and Eugene McCarthy, by Henry and George Wallace, by Chief Justice Warren and those who want him impeached. This common loyalty may mean quite different things to those who profess it, but at least it has served to concentrate conflict on men or measures, not on the fundamental structure of the political system.

Although the absolute monarchy was overthrown in France in 1789, and manhood suffrage instituted in 1848—well before most other major countries —nevertheless popular rule has never been securely established there and its enemies, weak in numbers, have been well entrenched among the rich and

---

[8] Alain (Emile Chartier), *Eléments d'une doctrine radicale* (Paris, Gallimard, 4th ed., 1933, first published 1925), pp. 123-4.

powerful. They have failed to win support in their own right, for as Bodley wrote seventy years ago the ordinary Frenchmen will always prefer 'the doubtful probity of the Republicans to the certain incapacity of the Royalists'. Consequently, in their search for weapons by which they can protect the political bastions they control and undermine those of their opponents, they have alternated—ever since the days of the great Revolution itself—between the exploitation of scandal and the organisation of conspiracy.[9]

'I never use the word legitimacy', Jean-Louis Tixier-Vignancour once said in court to the shock and delight of his reactionary public, 'because I know it has had no meaning in France since 21 January 1793.' Since the execution of Louis XVI the challenge from the far Right has remained alive, kept hopeful by the consciousness of the Republic's vulnerability and kept virulent by well-stoked fires of envy and hatred. 'There is a nation to the members of which Frenchmen are more revengeful than to Germans, more irresponsible than to Italians, more unjust than to English. It is to the French that Frenchmen display animosity more savage, more insistent and more inequitable than to people of any other race.'[10] But in moments of victory—at the Liberation, or after the 1961 putsch which de Gaulle, not they, had overcome—the Left too has shown itself capable of a bloodthirsty fervour for revenge.

We saw at the Liberation that the restoration of the Republic was inseparable in the minds of many Resisters from the exclusion from parliamentary life of those who had voted full powers to Pétain or committed some other 'crime'. Republicans, monarchists or reactionaries have in common a liking for proscriptions and excommunications. A French regime usually starts by outlawing one section of France.[11]

Ever since the great Revolution, the concept of patriotism itself has been in dispute. (Even earlier, from the days of the Huguenots and the League, Frenchmen were perhaps more willing than most people to accept, even to appeal for foreign support in their internal disputes.) After the triumph of the Revolution the émigrés retired to Coblenz, and in 1814 the Bourbons returned 'in the baggage train of the allies'. The nineteenth-century Left, therefore, always regarded the Right as dubious patriots, and felt their judgement confirmed in 1871 when the conservatives preferred Bismarck's armies to the revolutionary Communards. The old right-wing families in turn felt unable to serve a State under anti-clerical control which was organised by their enemies, and satisfied their own patriotic feelings in the

---

[9] For an example in the Revolutionary period see Blocq-Mascart, *Du Scandale*, pp. 34–8.
[10] J. E. C. Bodley, *France* (London, Macmillan, 1898), I, 215.
[11] R. Aron, 'Elections, partis et élus', *Revue française de science politique* V, 2 (1955), p. 262. On 1961 see below, p. 203.

army which they dominated and in the empire which it won and administered. Thus the anti-militarist, anti-colonialist attitude of the Left—pacifist first, Communist later—seemed to conservatives quite sufficient evidence that it was their opponents who lacked the most elementary sense of patriotic duty.

The soil for a 'stab in the back' legend was especially ripe in post-war France; for here the drama of decolonisation was played out against the backcloth of the great national humiliation of 1940. Patriotic Frenchmen needed to restore their pride in their country by regaining her place in the world and reasserting a sense of unity at home. But were these aims compatible? De Gaulle meant to regain France's place first alongside and then if necessary against her allies, Great Britain and the United States. In summoning patriotic Frenchmen to his standard he was defying the traditional doctrine that it was the first duty of every soldier to obey without question the orders of the legal government. By proclaiming that that government was no longer legitimate de Gaulle had taken up a double-edged weapon later to be used against his own authority. At the other extreme, some of the collaborators hoped to restore French fortunes—and their own—at Germany's side. Their misdeeds revived ancient hatreds and they first caused, then suffered new injuries crying out for revenge. Thus at the Liberation instead of the hoped-for national unity, there quickly followed first a purge, sometimes inspired by the Communist Party, and then a reaction against that Party which left another quarter of the country in the ghetto. First the defeat and then the victory had divided Frenchmen more deeply than ever, reopening old wounds which would take a long time to heal. During the postwar years this deeply divided country suffered first from acute economic difficulties, then from a succession of foreign retreats as her allies took less and less account of French views over Germany, and always from ministerial instability which her internal divisions generated and the difficulties of government maintained. Under these handicaps, and encumbered by their historical heritage of mutual suspicion and hatred, Frenchmen had to confront the bitter disputes over decolonisation.

Legitimacy struggles are traditional in France. Did Marie-Antoinette betray in calling on foreign troops for help? Yes, for those who believe that legitimacy resides in the will of the people. No, for those who accept with her that royal authority had its own legitimacy. The Third Republic was contested for many years: despite the Ralliement, despite the entry of the Socialists to Parliament, it was only the war of 1914 which saw its legitimacy fully accredited in the eyes of Catholics on the one hand, of the working class on the other. And then there was 1940. But never in the past had France known so many simultaneous contestations of legitimacy as under the Fourth Republic...The East–West conflict does not cause the Communists alone to be stigmatised as traitors...There is moral contestation over Indo-China and Algeria: a regime which tolerates executions and tortures, a regime which violates its own principles in opposing the freedom of other peoples loses its legitimacy even if the governments are elected by the majority of the people's representatives...[There is also] national contestation of legitimacy: no government, no majority is entitled to agree to a diminution of the country's power...[12]

This conflict took different forms at different stages of the process. Wars in Indo-China have always been unpopular in France—Jules Ferry was overthrown in 1885 because of a defeat there which later turned out to be imaginary. Though after 1946 the war was supported not only by the Right but at first by many Socialists and throughout by MRP politicians (perhaps because of their sympathy for the Catholics of Tonkin), it never had any substantial backing from public opinion and no government ever dared to suggest sending a single conscript to fight there.[13] The regular army rightly felt itself to be alone in bearing the brunt of that conflict—a sentiment which only reinforced its natural conviction that France lost her wars not at the front, but at the rear: both the corrupt, local rear, and the indifferent, uncomprehending and distant home front where the nation's fibre was being rotted by all that left-wing pacifist teaching in the schools. Much of the army returned from the Indo-China defeat in a bitter mood which was quickly to be reinforced by developments in a far more sensitive sector—North Africa (see chapter 10).

North Africa was not only more important to France's position in the world, its problems had far greater influence on French opinion because of the French colonists there—100,000 in Morocco, 200,000 in Tunisia, a million in Algeria (chapters 8 and 9). Most Englishmen today have forgotten their once bitter feeling about Ireland, but Rhodesia—far smaller and more distant than Ireland or Algeria—is a recent reminder of the strength of feeling for 'kith and kin'. In North Africa, Frenchmen established in greater numbers and with far closer links to the mother country clung to their position with ruthless desperation; the murders of the nationalist trade union leader Ferhat Hached in Tunisia (1952) and the liberal newspaper owner Lemaigre-Dubreuil in Morocco (1955)—in both cases probably committed by terrorist groups within the police force—indicated the length to which some extremists were prepared to go. Yet few of the settlers were wealthy and their family connections were with Frenchmen of all points of view. The war party, especially over Algeria, included a significant though diminishing number of spokesmen of the traditional Left—Radicals, Socialists and Freemasons. This was not only because of the settler influence; it was a psycho-

---

[12] A. Grosser, *La IVᵉ République et sa Politique extérieure* (Paris, Colin, 1961), pp. 187–8.

[13] Except that Mendès-France, at the moment he came to power to make peace, pledged that if he failed he would, before resigning, pass a bill to authorise the despatch of conscripts.

logical response to imperial decline. French nationalists, like their British counterparts after Suez and like right-wing Americans over Vietnam, reacted against their country's inability to impose its will but above all they resented the high-minded criticism to which it was subjected by other nations whose hands did not seem conspicuously cleaner (indeed, those hands sometimes seemed grimy with pay-dirt scooped up after the decolonisers had withdrawn). This malevolent misunderstanding by a hostile world still further—as in Britain in the Boer War—exacerbated the feelings of exasperation aroused by the successful resistance of a militarily far weaker opponent.

Meanwhile decolonisation also provided a series of occasions for intensifying old domestic conflicts by projecting them abroad. Over Indo-China it was not merely attitudes to colonialism or Communism that were at issue; as the Affair of the Generals showed, Socialists and Radicals still entertained deep suspicions of the clericalism of their MRP partners. In its later stages many political leaders came to doubt whether the war was in the interest of France; it diverted her strength from continents nearer home, and by 1953 a Gaullist leader was comparing it to the Mexican expedition that destroyed Napoleon III. To the extreme Right such views were merely dangerous sophistries, covering a secret sympathy with pacifists or Communists. François Mitterrand, at the Leakages trial in 1956, indignantly denounced those who charged him with guilt by association:

My position over the Indo-China war is well known…the men and material lost there were what we lacked when the North African problem arose. That is my whole policy and, I believe, that of M. Mendès-France. The whole meaning and intention of the opposition which you represent was to throw together, to confuse in the eyes of public opinion, the Communist Party…and those who attempted to preserve France's position in Algeria.[14]

Yet though subjectively false, the right-wing suspicions were not necessarily objectively absurd; within a couple of years of this outburst both Mitterrand and Mendès-France had come to favour negotiations with the Algerian FLN, confirming the instinctive certainty of the men of the far Right that left-wingers would never see a colonial war through to the end. They therefore overthrew the Fourth Republic and brought Charles de Gaulle to power (chapter 7). It remained for him to draw the same conclusions over Algeria as earlier leaders had drawn over Indo-China, and to earn the hatred of the extreme Right by putting his prestige at the service of the policy their opponents had failed to carry through (chapters 11 and 12).

These deep suspicions and hatreds provided fertile soil for charges of trafficking or treason. Financial scandals and dealings with the enemy over

[14] Quoted by J. M. Théolleyre, *Le Procès des Fuites* (Paris, Calmann-Levy, 1956), p. 117.

Indo-China, military conspiracy, left-wing civil disobedience and fascist terrorism over Algeria were the alarming domestic consequences of wars in which many Frenchmen contested the legitimacy of the nation's cause, and were in turn denounced by their compatriots for betraying their country. Similarly, it is no coincidence that a quite disproportionate share of the scandalous sensations in British public life in the period preceding Irish independence arose from attempted repression across the water: the Black and Tan outrages were preceded by the Pigott forgeries, the mystery of the Parnell divorce, the Curragh mutiny, the Sheehy-Skeffington murder, the Casement diaries.

There is thus a much closer connection than at first sight appears between the two themes of the articles collected in this volume: on the one hand the most important recent French scandals and their political significance, on the other the repercussions on French politics of the country's colonial wars. The links are two-way: the major military subversion of 1958 arose from, and that of 1961 developed into, clandestine plotting or terrorism; while the Affairs in metropolitan France discussed below were all of them disagreeable by-products of colonial conflict.

'The Generals' Affair carried within it the corrosive virus which was to destroy the Fourth Republic: conspiracies impossible to disentangle, machiavellian intrigues, feuds between dignitaries of the State, politicians vilified by the army, generals under accusation by the central power. The whole thread of 13 May 1958 was woven in 1950.'[15] But the connection between decolonisation and scandal, close though it is at this period, is a temporary phenomenon of the post-war years. Conflict overseas has provided new occasions for old habits to display themselves. Both participants and public continue to perform their roles in a way that the past has made all too familiar.

By whatever end one takes an incident one is faced by mystery. There are leakages of information; there are startling alliances and friendships; obvious questions are not asked; curious coincidences pass unnoticed; there is an unexpected carelessness about detail within the military administration; there is a lack of common sense...the extent of disagreement among...experts is disconcerting; and the ability of the entire cast to tell lies...unexpectedly impressive,

writes a recent commentator on the Dreyfus affair.[16] The case still throws a long shadow. Time and again the reader thinks of the Stavisky crisis, or the Salengro scandal, or the Affair of the Generals, or the leakages during the other Indo-China war, or the piastres scandal, or the Ben Barka case. Innumerable features are foreshadowed: the frantic search for spies as scape-

[15] Elgey, *La République des illusions*, p. 467.
[16] D. Johnson, *France and the Dreyfus Affair* (London, Blandford Press, 1966), p. 4. The rest of this essay is extracted from my review of his book in the *Spectator*, 11 November 1966.

goats for military or political failure; the damaging indiscretions which so often come from the top; the hysterical certainty that the whole world is in a conspiracy against France; the wild and wicked charges against any minister, or official, or judge, or witness whom it is convenient to discredit; the conviction that no one ever dies a natural death; the cowardice of many politicians; the irresponsibility of almost the entire press; the furious feuds between rival security services, unscrupulous, arrogant and incompetent; the skilful exploitation of judicial technicalities and conflicts of competence; the flabby legal procedure allowing endless hearsay evidence, repetition of slanders long ago disproved, irrelevant sensationalism, and the deliberate confusion of new charges with old. *The* Affair anticipates all the others in a more fundamental respect. Besides the faults and follies, the inefficiency and injustice on both sides, there is plain downright villainy from one poisoned political source, always the same. Perpetually frustrated in legitimate political contests, the French extreme Right is well placed to profit from administrative conflict, judicial favour, military prejudice, and public resentment of national humiliation. From Dreyfus's day to ours it has, sometimes with Communist help, exploited slander and scandal frequently, mendaciously and mercilessly as weapons to ruin its political opponents.

2 From Dreyfus to Vichy[a]

The Third Republic was established by a process of elimination. It came into being because, to the great *bourgeois* and peasant vested interest created by the Revolution, it seemed more satisfactory than any of the previous régimes; and these dominant sections preferred it, not because they thought it likely to bring them benefits, but because it appeared unlikely to injure them.

The politics of these established groups were the politics of fear: but they had two causes for alarm and not one. The Right remained for them permanently tarred with the landlord and clerical brush. Their grandfathers had believed that their property might be threatened by a counter-attack of the *ancien régime*; and the descendants preserved a hereditary mistrust of the forces of reaction, which attached them to 'Left' principles and habits of mind. Yet, in the present, the Right was no longer an economic, even if it might still be regarded as a political and ideological, menace. Now the threat to property came from the Socialists, a growing power on the Left. The men of the middle course feared both sources of disturbance; and the domestic history of the Third Republic depended on which danger was uppermost in their minds.

The answer to that question varied both in time and place. In the old-fashioned, economically individualist regions, where small independent businesses predominated, working for local markets and unconcerned with the activities of the state, the little men who ultimately ruled the country could safely indulge their ideological preference for the Left; in the modernized areas of big business, growing trade unions, national markets, a developing economy needing state aid and transport facilities, more immediate interests prevailed. At the beginning of the twentieth century France was a prosperous, self-sufficient land, a great exporter of capital, where politics were, in Robert de Jouvenel's phrase, a matter of taste, not a factor governing men's daily lives. Questions of principle, the naming of streets or the celebration of Good Friday in the navy, could arouse passionate feeling (of which the dispute over education in Britain during the same years gives a faint indication). But as national politics came to be dominated by economic questions, and to make a real difference to the life of the average man, then the

---

[a] From *France: Government and Society*, ed. J. M. Wallace-Hadrill and J. McManners (London, Methuen, 1957). Five words have been omitted from the first sentence.

conflicts of interest proved the more powerful influence. Between the Dreyfus affair and Hitler's war, the middle of the road groups hesitated between their twin aversions. The Radicals who represented them in the new century, like the Opportunists who had done so in the old, preferred to fight elections in alliance with the Left, but to govern with conservative support. Their dearest wish was to do nothing, their favourite slogan 'neither reaction nor revolution'. They were appropriately compared to the radish, 'red outside, white inside, and sitting in the middle of the butter-dish'.

The decisive factor, then, was fear of the dynamic groups in society, which could not be allowed power lest they should set Frenchmen once again at one another's throats. So the Third Republic, which had come into existence because it divided the country least, set out in 1875 on the line of least resistance, guided by the shortest-sighted, most unconstructive elements in France. These groups, the middle *bourgeoisie* and the propertied peasantry, were numerically important, but they took care to buttress their voting power by institutional devices. Of the sixteen Chambers of the Third Republic, thirteen were elected under a system which helped the parties of the centre against the extremists. In the Senate, the countryside and small towns were so over-weighted against the developing and modernized regions, that enemies of the régime on both sides were almost unrepresented. Constitutional conventions served similar ends: the office of President of the Republic had been shorn of effective power, but to make quite sure that no ambitious President would emulate Napoleon III, the parliamentarians were careful to elect only the most colourless candidates to the post. They preferred a weak executive with weak men managing it: and over the years a sort of political natural selection developed, so that leaders were no longer bred. When France needed a strong man in 1917, she turned to one who had been kept out of office for all but three years of his career (and later repaid his services by refusing him the Presidency of the Republic). When the need recurred in 1940, there was no one in politics to answer the call.

The moderate groups could thus manipulate the political system in their favour. In addition they formed the largest single block of opinion in the country. But they could never confidently rely on the support of a clear majority of the voters, and at election times they needed an understanding with one or other of their rivals. To seek support from the Right, except in an emergency and for a short period, would shock their own clients, still ferociously hostile to the reactionaries. At the polls, therefore, the Radical strategy was 'no enemies on the Left'. This course too was dangerous, for these allies had unwelcome social and economic aspirations; but their attention could usually be diverted into the harmless channels of anti-clericalism.

The Third Republic, then, was based on the predominance of a great vested interest and the discredit or exhaustion of the rival social forces. Such a régime could never hope to attract enthusiasm or escape mediocrity. President Grévy, attending an exhibition in the eighties, was told that there were few outstanding items but that the average standard was high. 'A good average,' he replied, 'but that's just as it should be in a democracy.' With this state of affairs many groups, and those the most influential, were reasonably content; but others, and these among the most vigorous and active, always felt themselves excluded from effective citizenship.

These 'internal *émigrés*', spiritually disinherited in the Republic, came of very diverse origins. Some were attached to an older social order, devout Catholics and members of fashionable society. But others belonged to the modern economic world, the industrial workers and, especially after 1930, the managers and technicians. Moreover, at all times the discontented were numerous in the new generation; the ardent idealism of youth could feel little loyalty and no enthusiasm for the prudent, uninspiring, even corrupt régime. Indeed just before the Dreyfus case J. E. C. Bodley went so far as to suggest that most of the best Frenchmen were among the three million who never voted. It did not greatly concern him that the governing class of the country had no contact with fashionable society, for he regarded both as utterly worthless. But it was equally out of touch with the practical men who managed the affairs of France. The British Parliament was dominated by commerce, agriculture and industry, the French Chambers by the professions. Yet, Bodley pointed out, the élite even of the intellectuals held aloof from the sordid trade of politics; the parliamentarians were professional men indeed, but third-rate ones.

It was in just these characteristics of the Third Republic that 'Alain', its chief philosophical defender, found matter for rejoicing. In his view the function of the deputy was precisely to represent the ordinary undistinguished citizen against the eternal conspiracy of the strong, the rich, and the successful —those who have 'arrived' and have consequently been corrupted by the embrace of society. Alain's argument is not to be lightly dismissed; it helps to explain why the roots of the régime in popular affection went so much deeper than might have been expected, and why Bodley's plausible belief that the slightest strain would upset a system wholly unsuited to the French was soon resoundingly disproved in the Dreyfus affair, the syndicalist troubles, and the First World War. But the fear and suspicion of leadership, which characterized Alain's point of view, were weaknesses for which a price had to be paid. Because of the detachment from the Republic of the most powerful groups in society, France drew many of her political representatives from sections standing outside the 'natural' governing class and even, it was claimed, outside the main stream of national tradition. Charles Maurras, the great reactionary pamphleteer, was exaggerating but not romancing when he maintained that under the Republic politics were dominated by the 'four confederated states', the Jews, Protestants, Freemasons, and *métèques*. This situation, felt by many good Frenchmen to be unnatural, imposed a further strain on national unity. To those who could not look upon the Republic as *their* régime, Maurras' distinction between the *pays légal* and the *pays réel* seemed to expose a fundamental fault (in both senses) in French society.

Despite these difficulties the system justified itself triumphantly in 1914. For all the attacks on Republican inefficiency, its military performance contrasted favourably with that of the Second Empire; for all the divisions among Frenchmen, the despised democracy proved capable even in adversity of maintaining national unity for longer than any of the autocratic belligerents. But if in the short run the crisis of the war was surmounted, over the years it undermined the foundations of the régime, accelerating all the forces making for disintegration. For the do-nothing, *immobiliste* outlook of the dominant groups, the aversion from power of the men who held power, was only one of many paradoxes. The population was failing to reproduce itself—except in the benighted regions where the party of enlightenment and progress had proved unable to destroy the influence of clerical reaction. In politics it was impossible to strengthen the executive because this was demanded by the Right, who sought to modernize government only in order to halt the evolution of society. Consequently, in social policy effective progress was blocked by the intransigence of the Left, who rejected on political grounds the institutional changes indispensable to a reforming policy. And in the economic race France was falling behind during, and indeed because of, the democratic régime. Napoleon III had made himself unpopular by imposing free trade to foster industrial development. But leaders of the Third Republic had more respect for the electorate. In 1892 Jules Méline discovered the political advantages of high protection. A French Baldwin, a bogus-bucolic spokesman of industrial interests, Méline (unlike Baldwin) did win votes, especially peasant votes, by his tariffs. Existing farms and firms secured a comfortable life and easy profits. Industry progressed, though less rapidly than in other countries. But in time foreign markets contracted, enterprise came to seem unnecessary and unmannerly, new businesses found it hard to enter the charmed circle. Fiscal and social as well as commercial policy helped to protect small, weak, inefficient units against the threat of competition, to 'close the windows' of the French economy against the menace of fresh air. This commitment to backwardness was accepted not only by a short-sighted peasantry and petty *bourgeoisie*, but equally by the most respectable sections of informed opinion. Georges Duhamel had tried in vain to win election to the *Académie française*: he owed his eventual success in 1930 to his satire on the machine civilization of the United States.

The war inflicted terrible material losses on France, and exacerbated all the conflicts and strains in society. Economically, paying the price for her easy-going policies, she fell farther behind other powers. Internationally, both through the greed and ambition of her dominant groups and through unforgivable abdication of responsibility by America and Britain, France overstrained herself by trying to play a rôle which had been far beyond her strength for more than a century. And under the pressure of social back-wardness, economic depression and international insecurity, the political foundations cracked. When politics came to centre on the real conflicts of the twentieth century instead of the abstract preferences of the eighteenth, the differences among Frenchmen proved too sharp to be resolved by the normal processes of democracy. By 1938 the parliamentary system was half suspended; in the well-known phrase, the crisis of 1940 did not kill the Third Republic, it merely drew attention to the fact that it was dead.

The reactionaries welcomed that crisis as a 'divine surprise'. By this re-mark Maurras was of course greeting not the victory of the hated Germans, but the unexpected chance to sweep away the no less detested Republic. The counter-revolutionaries were to have yet another opportunity to display that bankruptcy of statesmanship which had for a hundred and fifty years been their political hall-mark. Pétain's alleged dictum, 'France will never be great again until the wolves are howling round the doors of her villages', is at least *ben trovato*. For four years the motley parade of enemies of the Republic, some respectable but inept, others disreputable but clever, yet others traitorous and barbaric, displayed in succession their shoddy wares to an increasingly resentful public. The Vichy experiment showed once for all that that favourite scapegoat for France's ills, her governmental system, was a mere symptom of weaknesses deep-rooted in French society.

It was a reopening of old wounds that drained French strength in the thirties and forties. Past conflicts were renewed, often by the former protagonists or their heirs. Admiral Darlan's father, Minister of Justice in Méline's cabinet, had wished to prosecute the first Dreyfusard pamphleteer. Captain Maxime Weygand subscribed to the memorial for Colonel Henry the forger. A du Paty de Clam became commissioner for Jewish affairs under Vichy.[1] Maurras, sentenced for collaboration, exclaimed: 'The revenge of Dreyfus!'

[1] But du Paty was a very lukewarm anti-semite; and Darlan *père* came to doubt Dreyfus' guilt and was dropped from office. (Méline, true to the Baldwinesque principle of letting sleeping dogs lie, had refused to prosecute the pamphleteer, Bernard Lazare.)

The burden of history

The main French parties, Communists excepted, were born in the aftermath of the Affair: Radical party, *Alliance démocratique, Fédération républicaine*, Socialist party all appear in the first five years of the century. Outside parliament the monarchist *Ligue de l'Action française* and the united *Confédération générale du travail* date from the same period; the Christian Democratic *Sillon* movement from which MRP was to spring, and the 'Mascuraud committee' which raised Radical funds, are a little older. Many leaders of the twenties and thirties were ministers, supporters or collaborators of Waldeck-Rousseau: Barthou, Caillaux, Doumer, Doumergue, Herriot, Paul-Boncour, Poincaré, Reynaud, Sarraut, Tardieu. Briand entered the Chamber in 1902; Léon Blum, Charles Maurras, Marc Sangnier awoke to interest in politics through the Affair; Chautemps, Darlan and Flandin were the sons of politicians who began ministerial careers in the nineties.

There is thus a real unity about the period from Dreyfus to Vichy. It was in the nineties that the Republic first won national acceptance with the *Ralliement* of the Church, the Méline tariff, and the Russian treaty.[2] In the 1893 election, despite the resounding scandal of Panama, only 16 per cent of the votes went to reactionaries (compared with 45 per cent eight years before) and only three *départements* (against thirty in 1885) showed a majority against the Republic. In parliament Léon Bourgeois, in 1895, was the first prime minister to depend on the support of the Socialists (and also the first to be ejected by the Senate); and his successor Méline was the first republican to rely on the Right for his majority.

In the country the great political tendencies were themselves changing. The Left came increasingly under Socialist influence and turned away from its historic nationalism towards a passionate anti-militarism. The Right accommodated itself to a new world of manhood suffrage, general education, mass organization and propaganda, where mere social prestige no longer sufficed. A new, noisy, urban, popular movement developed, very different from the old conservatism of the respectable classes. Led by the journalistic firebrands of the *Action française* and the demagogic priests of the Assumptionist order, these forces were violently nationalist, bitterly anti-parliamentary, and closely linked with the new plebeian forms of revivalist Catholicism. It was a sign of the times that in 1900 the turbulent city of Paris elected its first right-wing municipal council.

The Radicals too were changing; abandoning the Left position they occupied in the early years of the Republic for the cautious respectability of the centre, they were ceasing to be a movement of intransigent opposition and becoming a party of government and compromise, which soon established

---

[2] I owe this point to Mr R. S. C. Donald. Each of the three sections of the Right—clerical, *bourgeois*, and nationalist—was affected by these events.

almost a permanent claim to the Ministry of the Interior. In this process they lost their traditional hold on the great cities, especially the capital, but acquired in compensation a new provincial clientèle among the prosperous peasantry and the small-town *bourgeoisie*, the lawyers, doctors and shop-keepers who dominated the politics of the Third Republic. The Freemasons transferred their support—and the only effective political machine in France —from the Opportunists to the Radicals, and the lodges soon became the driving force of thriving Radical local committees. With this more powerful and yet more moderate Radicalism many Opportunist Republicans, conservatives with important business and press interests, found it easy to co-operate. This combination was influential but uninspiring; and in the first decade of the new century intellectual leaders of all shades of opinion— Barrès and Bergson, Maurras and Péguy and Sorel—threw down their various challenges to the dreary régime and the quiet life it had been created to preserve. So clearly did they recognize their common enemy that Maurras himself, the prophet of order, strong government, and nationalism, the bitter opponent of popular movements, the believer in 'politics above all', for some years gave open sympathy and encouragement to the revolutionary, semi-anarchist, anti-militarist, anti-political syndicalists of the CGT.

The peculiar importance of the Dreyfus case was that it brought into bitter conflict the three institutions which, according to Bodley, were the foundation-stones of French social stability. He had denounced the worthless parliamentary and fashionable classes, but he had given high praise to the useful work and honourable devotion of the army, the clergy, and the *Université*, the teaching profession. Hardly had his book appeared when the Dreyfus affair arrayed the first two in a savage struggle against the third. Already, in the eighties, Jules Ferry's educational laws had provoked conflict between Church and *Université*. Yet these professions had something in common, for both were recruited from the people, drawing on *boursiers* either of the State or of the Church; and their mutual hostility had apparently been abated by the *Ralliement*. The army on the contrary was the last strong-hold of the gentleman in the governmental system, the one form of public service which the scions of the old aristocracy felt able to undertake. But until the Dreyfus case it was popular among republicans. This general esteem was abruptly forfeited by the arrogant claim of its leaders to preserve it as a state within the state, independent of the hated republican politicians, and by the contention of its champions, led by Maurras, that social order and social hierarchy should take precedence over justice to the individual. It is now becoming fashionable to maintain that the ruin by forgery and perjury of an innocent man is comparatively venial, provided the motive were an impersonal devotion to a social class or an official department. To France's credit this repulsive view, though widely held and vigorously propagated, did not prevail.

Yet the anti-Dreyfusards were right in maintaining that more than the fate of an obscure though wealthy Jewish captain was at stake. The partisan legends of both sides might be equally false: there was neither a plot against the Republic as the Left alleged, nor a conspiracy to subvert the social order as the Right pretended. But once the battle was joined, great political consequences were bound to follow, since the winning side was almost certain to abuse its victory. It did. Under the Combes ministry which held office from 1902 to 1905, the doctrines of the Left went far to wreck the machinery of government. Camille Pelletan, the Minister of Marine (Alain's ideal minister), reduced the navy to a state of sorry inefficiency. General André, appointed to the War Ministry as one of the few reliable republican generals, overplayed his hand by using the masonic lodges as sources of information about Catholic officers. This scandal of the *fiches* made it impossible to carry through the purge of the army, which though no longer a law unto itself remained a stronghold of the men of the old order, a 'permanent *ralliement*' as it has been called. Through it such men could, like Lyautey, work honourably for France outside her own borders, building a great empire for which voters and politicians showed only indifference or distaste. They could, like Foch, serve her in war; and like Pétain, Weygand, and Franchet d'Esperey, they could unhappily justify the Left's suspicion that few senior officers were trustworthy guardians of democratic government.

The second loser from the Dreyfus struggle was the Church. Though many of its responsible leaders would have preferred an attitude of prudence, the noisy popular priests and press, under Assumptionist leadership, threw themselves into the engagement and contributed to the anti-semitic venom of the reactionary side. Inevitably the whole Church suffered from their defeat. But though the anti-clerical campaigns were a direct consequence of the Affair, another motive played its part. Waldeck-Rousseau's coalition, assembled in June 1899 to defend the Republic, embraced many shades of opinion, from the wealthy *bourgeoisie* who later formed the *Alliance démocratique* to the Jaurès wing of the Socialists. The cabinet itself for the first time included a Socialist, Alexandre Millerand, later a reactionary President of the Republic, the pioneer on the well-travelled road to fame and power which winds its tortuous way from Left to Right. Dangerous firebrands like this, toying with notions of introducing income-tax or facilitating strikes, alarmed the Opportunist wing of the majority; the attack on the religious congregations proved an admirable way of diverting their attention.[3] 'Old

---

[3] The dates are significant. Millerand announced his strike bill at a Socialist meeting on 15 October 1899. As soon as the Chamber met the business republicans attacked Waldeck-Rousseau,

General Hokum leads an unbeatable army'; and the anti-clerical campaign thus inaugurated was to dominate politics for the next five years. No more was heard of the strike bill; the proposed income-tax was quietly abandoned; and the *Alliance démocratique* group rallied to the republican cause and the separation of Church and State. In the intransigently Left Combes government, to which Alain pointed with pride, the Minister of Finance was Maurice Rouvier, the archetype of the shady businessman in politics, who had been kept from office since the Panama scandal.

With the separation of Church and State in 1905, the clerical dispute lost much of its bitterness. The class struggle became the focus of politics; the ideological quarrels of the old society were overlaid by the conflicts of interest of the modern world. In all western Europe, Sir John Clapham has remarked, France had least 'practical socialism' (public ownership, welfare legislation, cooperation, redistributive taxation, etc.). Ill-paid, ill-housed workers followed the revolutionary syndicalists, who repudiated capitalism, democracy, army and nation. When the terrible Radical guerrilla Clemenceau came to power he relied on the Right for support against strikes in the country and Socialists in the Chamber. Aristide Briand, in turn revolutionary agitator, parliamentary broker in Church affairs, and prime minister, broke a railway strike by calling up the workers he had once championed to the army he had traduced. Socialists joined reactionaries in demanding electoral reform, loathed by Radicals. The *bloc des gauches* was splintered.

Germany exploited these rifts in French unity. In 1905 she took advantage of the separation crisis, the Pelletan–André régime and the Russo–Japanese war to force out the Foreign Minister Delcassé, maker of the *entente cordiale*, whose premier Rouvier was bent on appeasing Berlin. Six years later, in a second Moroccan crisis, another business prime minister, Joseph Caillaux, took the same line. But the panic mood of 1905 had gone; and Caillaux's successor was the unyielding Raymond Poincaré, who in 1913 became President of the Republic. Against Briand's conservatism and Poincaré's nationalism Radicals and Socialists drew together again. The 1914 election was won by a Left reunited under Caillaux in support of an income-tax and opposition to longer military service.

The flood of war swept differences away, and for three years Frenchmen stood together in *union sacrée*. When this foundered, Poincaré in 1917 called to power the last of the Jacobins, Clemenceau, who promptly arrested Caillaux and his disreputable ally Jean-Louis Malvy, Minister of the Interior

who in his reply promised to act against the congregations. For a year nothing happened. Then on 7 October 1900 Millerand, under Socialist pressure, reaffirmed his intention to introduce the strike bill; on the 22nd Barthou, leader of the business group, warned the prime minister that his majority was in danger; and on the 28th Waldeck-Rousseau promised to deal with the congregations at once.

since 1914, accused of tenderness to defeatists. Clemenceau brought the country through to a victory which solved none of the major problems that had confronted France on the eve of war. In the next decade Poincaré, Briand and Caillaux still faced Germany abroad and financial troubles at home; and if the war had temporarily eased the former difficulty, it had aggravated the latter.

By 1914 France's easy-going economic policy was beginning to show its weaknesses. Competitive effort was discouraged by high protection, thwarted by Malthusian habits of mind, starved by the policy of the banks. These had chosen (for huge commissions) to place French savings abroad rather than at home; 36 per cent of all French investments were outside the country, especially in Russia and Turkey, and much of this vast stake was lost through the war. Moreover the burdens of government were inequitably distributed. The war increased these burdens enormously, but diminished no whit the stubborn selfishness of the wealthy. Wartime finance was profligate; the whole cost was borne by loans, raised on ever stiffer terms as the conflict dragged on. Not until 1916 was the income-tax at last imposed. And after the victory the business men and rich peasants continued to fight bitterly for as long as they could against new taxes, and then to evade them. Their policy was to make Germany pay, and the vain effort to do so weakened France's international position by offending her allies. In the end the Germans and the French rich both resisted successfully, and it was the *rentier* who bore the cost of the war when, in 1926, Poincaré devalued the franc.

The immediate political effects were surprising. The small saver in France had seen what had happened to the currencies of central Europe, and so far from blaming Poincaré for the loss of four-fifths of his capital, he was grateful for retaining what was left to him. The country moved towards the Right. Already, in the 1919 elections, fear of Bolshevism had given the conservatives their first victory at the polls. They overreached themselves in the occupation of the Ruhr. But the *cartel des gauches*, victorious in 1924, fell to pieces when it tackled the financial problem; Clemenceau dismissed it with contemptuous comment, 'o+o+o = o'. In 1928 Poincaré's prestige produced a repetition of the 1919 miracle and another right-wing Chamber. When the world slump came belatedly to France, successive Ministers of Finance (always safe and orthodox men) pursued a policy of deflation and economy which exasperated salaried classes and wage-earners alike. Disgruntled *rentiers*, resentful workers and petty *bourgeoisie* were all affected by the smouldering discontent; and in 1934 the spark of the Stavisky scandal caused a furious blaze where previous affairs of the kind had died away (or been smothered) without attracting much attention.

The Concorde riots of 6 February 1934 were the first since 1848 to destroy a government. So began the critical phase of the Third Republic. Devaluation, even though it might have been worse, had yet struck a heavy blow at confidence in the domestic future. The rise of the Nazis destroyed the hope of security abroad. The effects were none the less powerful for taking time to show themselves. Fear of ruin and fear of war became the dominant motives in men's minds; and the régime was too fragile a construction to stand the strain. The change was sudden; in the summer of 1933 a shrewd English observer had described France as the most stable country in Europe; barely six months later the convulsions had begun.

The immediate mood in the 6 February riots was not of fear but of rage. Abuses, tolerated in prosperity, aroused fury in a time of economic distress, among the small men who had lost their savings, the ex-servicemen, the lower middle class who pride themselves on not being proletarians, who stand aloof from normal political activity, and who participate only in an occasional violent eruptive movement under a Boulanger, a Déroulède, or even a de Gaulle. Their wrath was directed against the Radicals, back in office since the 1932 elections, corrupt and easy-going as they had been for so long. The party had indeed its 'Young Turks' such as Pierre Cot, Léon Martinaud-Déplat and Pierre Mendès-France, a strangely assorted trio as they seem today.[b] But though their hopes and ambitions were high, their influence as yet was small; and their seniors were incapable of dealing with any form of political demonstration more violent than a parliamentary interpellation. Under the pressure of the rioters the government resigned. But power, so far from being seized by a young and dangerous Fascist movement, was peacefully transferred to a self-satisfied octogenarian ex-President of the Republic, Gaston Doumergue. This, however, did little to diminish the resentment and alarm of the Left at the triumph of the riotous leagues, at the deflationary economic policy of successive cabinets, at the menace of Nazi Germany. For motives which differed widely, Radicals, Socialists and Communists buried their feuds, and combined to win the 1936 election. The Popular Front government introduced a series of overdue reforms. But with its victory came a wave of spontaneous strikes, bloodless, but terrifying to an intensely class-conscious *bourgeoisie*; and the reforms, though in the long run fully justified, were unfortunately timed when Germany was organizing for war.

For French foreign policy had broken down. Conscious of France's inferiority against her dangerous neighbour, Marshal Foch had in 1919 wanted to perpetuate her temporary ascendancy by dismembering the enemy,

[b] Cot became a leading ally of the Communist party; Martinaud-Déplat a pillar of conservative governments; Mendès-France a reforming premier who later joined the anti-Gaullist left-wing socialists.

detaching the Rhineland from the Reich. This safeguard, unpopular with the United States and Britain, had been renounced by Clemenceau in return for a guarantee of support from these two powers, which the prospective allies had almost immediately repudiated. Alone, or even with her Eastern European clients, France was too weak to pursue successfully either a 'hard' or a 'soft' course towards Germany. Poincaré's policy of the strong hand failed in 1924, for neither French nor international opinion would accept it for any length of time. But Briand's attempt to trust the Germans paid no better dividends; reparations were scaled down, allied troops evacuated the Rhineland five years before the treaty required—and the Nazi vote promptly rose to six million. In 1926 Poincaré had dealt with the financial crisis while there was still something to be saved; eight years later his old friend Barthou was assassinated before his attempt to check Germany's diplomatic progress could bring results. From that day forward, except for an intermittent and futile pursuit of the will o' the wisp of Mussolini's goodwill, the Quai d'Orsay abandoned any serious effort to halt the Nazi advance, and sank into increasingly abject dependence on Whitehall.

Domestic disputes and foreign alarms combined to make 1936 the year of schism, when French national unity broke under the strain. The Germans, unopposed, reoccupied the Rhineland in March, and thenceforth the self-styled realists worked more and more openly for an understanding with Hitler. Pierre Laval in the foreground, Caillaux and Malvy in the shadows provided continuity between the new defeatists and their predecessors in the previous war.[4] At the same time internal tensions were brought to a head by the election of seventy Communist deputies and by the great stay-in strikes which greeted the advent of the Popular Front government. Conservative leaders were growing more and more hostile to the parliamentary system. Capitalist magnates like Ernest Mercier, influential right-wing politicians like André Tardieu, prominent figures in the army and police, flirted openly with authoritarian ideas. French politics became a cold civil war. Just before becoming prime minister, Léon Blum was savagely beaten in the street by *Action française* thugs: his Minister of the Interior[c] was driven to suicide by the slanders of the right-wing press;[5] and the *cagoulards*, a group of Fascist dissidents from *Action française*, began their campaign

---

[4] Laval had first entered office as an associate of Caillaux, whose followers now included Emile Roche, who first proposed ceding the Sudetenland to Hitler: Montigny, Laval's chief ally in July 1940: and Baudouin, once a protégé of Rouvier and later Vichy Foreign Minister. Peyrouton, Malvy's son-in-law, became Pétain's Minister of the Interior—and Eisenhower's Governor-General of Algiers.

[5] Fascist papers like *Gringoire* led this abominable campaign; but the dishonour of starting the slanders belongs to the Communists.

[c] Roger Salengro.

of terrorism and murder. With the Spanish war and the Munich crisis, the internal and external conflicts became inseparably bound together. Most domestic conservatives drifted into a defeatist acceptance of a Europe dominated by Germany; many actively preferred Hitler to Blum. But some attitudes to Nazism were not decided by class-war motives. A minority on the Right remained anti-German (though often pro-Italian). Pacifism was strong among Radicals, Socialists and trade unionists. And the most vociferous pro-Nazi agitators were an ex-Socialist, Marcel Déat, and an ex-Communist, Jacques Doriot.

These furious disputes proved too much for a political régime designed expressly to provide a weak government. It was a fair-weather system, constructed by groups which wanted a quiet life, and worked by men whose talents flourished in peaceful circumstances. Specialists in lobby politics like Camille Chautemps, or eloquent orators like Édouard Herriot, rose to the top; men of action like Clemenceau or his former secretary Georges Mandel were frustrated at every turn. The nominal leaders, as Daniel Halévy remarked, thought with Alain that their duty was to defend the interests of the little man against attack—not to govern the country. When the years of crisis came there was no one to rise to the occasion. At home the deputies abdicated, abandoning their powers and authorizing the government to legislate by decree. Abroad, under the sly Georges Bonnet 'whose long nose', as Mandel bitterly said, 'sniffs danger and responsibility from afar [and who] will hide under any flat stone to avoid it', French foreign policy fell into complete subservience towards Britain. In 1939 France declared war only with extreme reluctance and hesitation; characteristically the Chambers, despite the requirements of the constitution, were never called on to vote the decision.[6]

During the months of 'phony war' defeatism was rampant. The Communists, outlawed after the Nazi-Soviet pact, began an underground anti-war campaign among the workers which strengthened the hand of the pro-Germans and pacifists (who were not identical, for many of those least eager to fight Hitler were ardent to attack Stalin). When the invasion came, panic spread rapidly. Most of the politicians behaved badly enough; but the moral collapse of the old governing class was still more complete, and the leaders of the army, the first to despair of the Republic, themselves became the militant chieftains of the defeatist camp. One man alone among those in a position of power might have provided a rallying-point. But Mandel, handicapped by being a Jew, was also the most unpopular and isolated man in political life.

Thus the Third Republic, which had confronted the ordeal of the First

[6] Credits were voted; their purpose was of course known, but was prudishly not specified.

World War with such unexpected success, failed ignominiously in the second. The reasons were material as well as moral. Behind her economic Maginot line France was falling farther and farther behind her rivals. It is true that after 1918 (as after 1945) the pace of her impressive post-war recovery matched that of her neighbours. But in 1928 she had less than half as much industrial machinery per head as the other industrial nations of Europe. And in the decade before Hitler's war her economy, unlike that of others, declined. Between 1929 and 1938 French industrial production fell by a quarter, while Germany's rose by the same proportion and Britain's increased by a sixth. In agriculture it was much the same story. Corn prices in France exceeded the world price by 30 per cent in 1913, by 200 per cent in 1939.

In manpower, again, France suffered terribly in the First World War: of eight million men mobilized no less than three-quarters were killed or wounded. The economic handicap was severe; allowing for the indirect losses such as the shortfall in the birthrate, it has been calculated that by the end of the century war and war preparation will have cost France a third of her potential male labour force. The direct military consequences were serious too. The population was not reproducing itself. In 1870 France could call on as many men of military age as Germany; in 1940, less than half as many. Moreover the leadership of her army had stagnated under the soporific effect of victory, while the Germans had learned from the stimulus of defeat. The Riom trial, intended to save the reputations of the soldiers at the expense of the hated politicians, was to show instead how completely the military chieftains had failed either to foresee the development of modern warfare, or even to use the men and materials available to them in the battle.

Yet whatever weight is given to these factors, the moral collapse remains undeniable. The partisan prophets of the Third Republic, Maurras and Alain, had each played their part in the demoralization of their countrymen. The one found his audience among the wealthy, the well-born, the powerful and *bien-pensant* classes which dominated industry and administration and the armed forces. For forty years he had preached unrelenting hatred, exposed or invented scandal, and persuaded the 'élite' of France that the people were cowardly and degenerate, the political leadership rotten with corruption, the country ripe for a terrible and deserved catastrophe. The other's disciples filled the teaching profession, the enormously influential 'republican clergy'; and with equal persistence he had taught them to mistrust all leaders, to discount talk of foreign danger as a mere device to cover sinister designs at home, to mock at appeals for sacrifice or discipline, and to identify civic virtue with comfortable and anarchic individualism. So the masses distrusted those who might have led, and the classes hated and despised those who might have followed. Maurras with his exclusive nationalist passion, Alain with his fanatical democratic zeal, each striving to undermine the foundations on which the rival idol rested, helped to bring the whole temple crashing to the ground.

Yet the downfall of the Third Republic cannot be blamed only on the weakness of the régime, the violence of ideological conflict, or the fear and hatred of the workers which gripped a middle class deprived of its sense of security. In addition, Frenchmen of all opinions knew well enough that their country could no longer hope to police Europe alone, and the years between the wars showed them that they could expect no Anglo-Saxon help until too late. When Germany revived, stronger and more aggressive than ever, the struggle to resist came to seem increasingly hopeless. It is significant that the German propaganda campaign of 1940 was directed at French patriotism rather than at French individual selfishness. Its theme was not 'Why throw your life away for a hopeless cause?', but 'Why sacrifice the future of the nation by another blood-letting in the interests of the foreigner?' Such ideas influenced many of the defeatists and pacifist leaders, who resigned themselves with regret to France's decline, and sought only the comfortable dependent status of a satellite power which no longer attempts to determine her own fate or influence that of others. The Republic had chosen to travel on the line of least resistance; Vichy was the terminus.

So the Third Republic committed suicide in due constitutional form, and by a seven-to-one majority the National Assembly voted to confer on Marshal Pétain powers not only to govern without parliamentary control, but to legislate and draw up the new constitutional settlement as well. During the four years of authoritarian rule which followed, France once again proved herself, as Bodley had called her, 'the land of political surprises where lost causes come to life again'. One after another the alternatives to the Republic were tried and discarded.

In the early months the old-fashioned reactionaries held power, dominant in the Marshal's entourage and numerous in the cabinet. Most of them had belonged to or sympathized with *Action française*, many had been active in the 6 February riots or victims of the Popular Front, and their aim was to replace the detested democratic system with a traditionalist, authoritarian, Catholic régime. Marshal Pétain's *Ordre nouveau* was nothing but Marshal MacMahon's *Ordre moral*, taken out of storage rather than brought up to date. These men had no love for either Britain or Germany; their external policy was *attentiste*, and after their Pyrrhic victory in overthrowing Laval in December 1940, most of them were soon driven from power by Nazi pressure.

Next came the leaders of the financial, industrial and academic worlds.

31

Men of this type had once formed the core of the Orleanist party, had rallied to the conservative republic when it seemed better able to protect their privileges, and were as prompt to desert it in adversity. The Darlan cabinet was full of distinguished professors and energetic business men. Thirdly (though all these groups overlapped) there were the technicians, resentful of politicians who interfered with the smooth running of their services, or convinced that a democratic state was too unstable a base for positive or constructive activity. During the thirties the admirals, the *conseillers d'état*, the *inspecteurs des finances*, had grown more and more exasperated with the Republic. So general was the disaffection that the Vichy régime has been called 'the French state stripped of its democratic façade'. Concerned for efficient administration, usually contemptuous of archaic reaction, but indifferent or hostile towards political liberty, such men (including some of those from private business) were heirs of the Bonapartist tradition.

All these groups collaborated with the Germans, while often trying to moderate their demands by the passive obstruction at which Frenchmen excel. By 1944 all had failed, and the newest enemies of democracy came into their own: Darnand with his ruthless militia, Déat and Doriot and the Paris Fascists who, under German protection, had bitterly denounced the traditionalists of Vichy, and loudly demanded a popular, national-socialist system. Manœuvring with his customary skill among the factions, Laval employed his disreputable talents to bargain—though on ever less favourable terms—on his country's and his own behalf.

The men of Vichy fulfilled none of their promises. Government, dependent on the whims of an easily influenced octogenarian, grew less firm than ever. Ministers changed as rapidly. Policies became even less coherent. The factional struggle for power went on with unabated fury. Class antagonisms were not resolved but aggravated by Vichy's blatant favouritism for the rich. Centralization and bureaucracy were not relaxed but carried further. The new masters had charged that justice was tainted under the rule of their adversaries; under their own it was poisoned. The new moral order had corruption, delation and cruelty for its fruits. And the very factions which had once proclaimed themselves the only true Frenchmen, which had implied that their opponents were outside the pale of the nation, now committed themselves to collaboration with the enemy. Seventy years had been needed to discredit the Third Republic. Its authoritarian critics condemned themselves in four.

In resistance to the Germans and to the Frenchmen who increasingly became their tools, many of the 'internal *émigrés*' found a full part to play. In some right-wing and even royalist circles, especially in the army, the resistance early gained a foothold. The Catholic democrats, growing in numbers and activity under the inspiration of the *Sillon* for half a century, now 'found themselves' as an organized movement. When in June 1941 French national interests came to coincide with those of the Soviet Union, the heroic conduct of the Communist rank and file wiped out among the less politically minded resisters the memory of past and the suspicion of future betrayals by the party bosses. And, like any revolutionary movement, the resistance was largely an affair of youth. So men hoped that from the trials of war, occupation and liberation a genuinely new democracy would arise. In 1945 only one voter in twenty-five favoured the restoration of the Third Republic. Only one in eight voted for the old Right, even under its resistance leadership. The former republican figureheads had forfeited their claims to power by their defeatism before the war, and the anti-republican 'élite' by collaboration during it. It was time for new men. For a brief moment it seemed that the Republic had at last won over the best of those who had stood aloof: that devout Catholics, militant workers, and youthful idealists could take their place as full citizens, helping to build the Fourth Republic, *la République dure et pure*.

PART II

LEGACY OF EMPIRE:
INTRIGUE IN PARIS

3   The Generals affair[a]

'France, delivered from the corruptions of the Empire, has entered into the period of the austere virtues.' So proclaimed Jules Ferry after Sedan. He was wrong; under the Republic as under previous régimes, scandal has remained the most conspicuous of French political institutions.

Part of the reason is to be found in the ferocity of French politics. Control of a huge centralized administrative machine was contested, with sectarian bitterness, between clericals and freemasons. The stakes were higher than in Britain, and the tricks were lower; no holds were barred by men who disputed, not specific policies, but the foundations of the State itself. In the Dreyfus case the Army, a stronghold of the Right, fought with forgery and perjury to maintain its autonomy; the triumphant Republicans in turn overreached themselves by attempting a purge in which they used the masonic organization to spy on officers who went to Mass. Where no scandal exists, it is readily invented; fifteen years ago, a leading and popular minister was driven to suicide by Fascist slanders on his war record.[b]

Moreover, political morality is low where authority is diffused. Responsibility is not enforced by a coherent opposition upon a government with undisputed power: instead it is dissipated among several hundred professional politicians, each sufficiently influential to attract temptation, but sufficiently obscure to have little fear of the consequences. A chain of intermediaries of diminishing honesty links the politician—often without his knowledge—with the crook; its origin is frequently in the minister's *cabinet*, the group of half a dozen personal or political friends whom each minister brings into office with him to form a buffer against both his official advisers, and the outer world.[1]

Where political authority is so weak, the permanent services become powerful; where the political struggle goes so deep, their reliability is essential. No part of the government machine is quite immune from political

---

[1] The *cabinet* is in many ways a useful, perhaps an indispensable device; and many ministers, notably Laval, have been well served by *chefs de cabinet* far more honest than themselves. But the system helps to spread influence without responsibility; the fall of M. Félix Gouin (the Prime Minister whose entourage took too active an interest in the import of Algerian wine) shows the dangers to which it may lead.

[a] From *The Cambridge Journal* IV, no. 8 (May 1951); originally entitled 'L'Affaire des Généraux'.
[b] Roger Salengro: above, pp. 5, 28.

influence. Frenchmen thus suspect (usually wrongly) the worst of their public men; that they will both behave improperly, and cover each others' improprieties; that in Professor Brogan's words: 'the State is not a referee but a player—and probably a dirty player.' Suspicion falls especially upon the security services, which are both secret and semi-political. Partly removed after the Dreyfus case from military control—a deprivation never forgiven by the army—security came in theory into the sphere of the Ministry of the Interior, a Home Office up to its neck in politics. But this responsibility was always blurred in practice;[2] and war and occupation came to shake the whole structure of French administration. The post-war civil service was recruited from various, often mutually hostile sources; officials who had served on under Vichy, men who had joined de Gaulle in London or Algiers, men whose resistance records were rewarded by a post in government service. New feuds and hatreds, political and personal, had sprung up; it was often hard to tell whether a man had worked for his own hand or for a cause, or whether a René Hardy was a hero or a traitor.[c] Much was possible in these hectic years which even in France could never have occurred in normal times; and in this context the affair of the generals must be seen.

II

On September 18th, 1949, there was a fight on an *autobus* at the Gare de Lyon between a French soldier and two Indo-Chinese Communist students, just back from the World Youth Congress in Budapest. The students were arrested, and one of them was found to be carrying two documents. The first of these was a copy of a report by General Revers, chief of the general staff, advocating that a soldier should forthwith be appointed High Commissioner in Indo-China; the second was a highly eulogistic biography, or autobiography, of Revers's friend General Mast, the head of the *Institut des hautes études de défense nationale*, and a Far Eastern expert. The police inquiries led them to a certain Roger Peyré, manager of the small import and export business of Rossi et Cie, in the rue de Prony; he was arrested, taken to the DST (the counter-espionage department of the Ministry of the Interior),[3] and interrogated for 32 hours. He admitted receiving the report from Mast, with Revers's consent, and passing it on to two Indo-Chinese whom he believed to be pro-French; he added that one of them, M. Van Co,

[2] Part of the trouble in the Stavisky case was the conflict between the Sûreté Nationale and the Paris Prefecture of Police.

[3] Direction de la Surveillance du Territoire; a department of the Sûreté Nationale, it deals with counter-espionage within French territory, while the SDECE (see p. 40) is responsible elsewhere.

[c] On Hardy see G. Wright, 'The Dreyfus Echo: Justice and Politics in the Fourth Republic', *Yale Review*, Spring 1959 (which also deals with The Affair of the Generals).

the Paris agent of General Xuan,[4] had given him $2\frac{1}{2}$ million francs, of which he had distributed a million each to the two generals and the rest to a prominent Socialist ex-minister.[d] At dawn on the 22nd, the ministers of the Interior and of Defence called on the Prime Minister to tell him the news; that evening, the two latter ministers decided that the country could not afford a scandal involving the chief of the general staff at a time when delicate negotiations in Washington were expected. To hush up the affair, the Minister of Defence laid down that no military secret was involved, since only the political and not the military parts of Revers's report had leaked. This decision meant that no prosecution would lie: the arrested men were released and their papers were handed back. The generals, who denied taking money but could not deny their friendship with Peyré, agreed quietly to retire from the army; and the affair seemed to be over. In fact it had just begun.

III

M. Ramadier, the Socialist Minister of Defence, and M. Queuille, the Radical premier, were experienced politicians of a type familiar in France, and differing from one another in little except party allegiance.[5] M. Moch, the Minister of the Interior, was a Socialist of a very different kind, the ablest and most determined, and perhaps the most unpopular of the country's post-war leaders. But there were other ministers who had a claim to be consulted in the affair, and notably M. Lecourt, the Minister of Justice, and M. Coste-Floret, the Minister of Overseas France, both members of MRP. Coste-Floret was responsible for the policy in Indo-China which had come under heavy fire in the Revers report; he was an excitable southern law professor, trained in the tough politics of Algiers,[6] and in the suppression of the inquiry he smelt an intrigue. On the 27th September he sent to the Prime Minister a startling report which claimed to reveal a complex plot. General Mast was to be appointed to Indo-China, to the political profit of Van Co and to the financial profit of Peyré and his friends; General Revers had 'leaked' his own report to assist Mast's campaign; and the Socialist Party was to be enlisted by the prospect of trading and financial concessions, granted by Mast, to replenish the depleted party funds. The agent here was

[4] The former Prime Minister of Indo-China.

[5] Queuille had served in a score of pre-war cabinets, in 12 of them at the Ministry of Agriculture. Ramadier had been president of the Parliamentary group of freemasons, and had been disciplined by his party more than thirty times. In the thankless post of Minister of Food, just after liberation, he was christened by his enemies Ramadan, 'l'homme du jeûne perpétuel', and (because of his conspicuous beard) 'le père Noël à la hotte vide'.

[6] When the Communists were dropped from the Government in May 1947, Coste-Floret as Minister of War wished to declare a state of siege.

[d] André Le Troquer, later President of the National Assembly—ruined in 1958 by a scandal of a different kind. And see below, pp. 157-8.

to be M. Bouzanquet, who was both a partner in Rossi et Cie and a secretary of the Socialist trade union federation, *Force Ouvrière*; but neither the Socialist leaders nor Bouzanquet himself were aware of the plot.[7]

No action was taken, for the Government was breaking up; but two days later, on the 29th, a news-letter to which a member of M. Coste-Floret's *cabinet* contributed[8] published a report that Revers was responsible for the leak, and had been paid. Giving this attack as his reason, Revers decided not to retire after all; but he brought no legal action, and it was suspected that he was really taking advantage of the fall of the Government, and of the support of his friend Colonel Fourcaud, the deputy head of another secret service, the SDECE.[9]

This organization dated from the early days of the Free French movement in London, when it was called the BCRA, and headed by de Gaulle's powerful adviser 'Colonel Passy'.[e] When de Gaulle resigned in 1946, the organization was brought under the Prime Minister's office, given the task of dealing with counter-espionage outside the country, and removed from the hands of Passy[10] to those of a Socialist deputy, M. Henri Ribière. Ribière's authority, however, seemed very much less effective than that of his remarkable deputy. Colonel Fourcaud was Russian-born, had fought the Bolsheviks before 1920 and had contacts with the Fascist *cagoulards* before the war; during it, he was several times parachuted into occupied France. He was described as a *condottiere*, as a cloak and dagger character, and as a man who conspired morning, noon and night.[f] Fourcaud did not hide his passionate resentment against Ramadier and especially Moch, who had in his view covered up a case of spying, and victimized General Revers, in order to conceal their own sordid intrigues.[11] But since the Americans had confidence in Revers, Fourcaud decided that he must be rescued at all costs: Peyré must withdraw his charges, and the scandal must be extended, to shift the blame from the general to the men who had dismissed him. Peyré had worked for the SDECE before, but when the affair began, Captain

[7] Coste-Floret never explained how a man or a party could be induced to act by a bribe of which they were not informed; and later, under examination, he declared that the whole plan was merely a 'dream' in the mind of Van Co. But however absurd, the story clearly influenced the attitude of Colonel Fourcaud.

[8] But both he and his editor denied that he was the source.

[9] Section de Documentation Extérieure et de Contre-Espionnage.

[10] Passy (whose real name was Dewavrin) had placed considerable funds in Britain and America, for political purposes which remain conjectural.

[11] Early in the morning of October 29th, Fourcaud called on M. Wybot, the head of the DST, and told him that the two ministers ought to be impeached and shot for treason; if the generals were guilty, they too should be court-martialled and shot, but he believed that Revers, at any rate, was innocent. To Captain Girardot, however, the colonel said that he was not sure about Revers, but that in any event he must be 'whitewashed'.

[e] Three words omitted from this sentence.

[f] Cf. below, p. 48n.

Girardot—the officer in contact with him—was ordered not to see him again. Fourcaud countermanded this order. Girardot was to see Peyré, and warn him that his life was in danger; but if he would make a new statement exculpating Revers, and providing evidence about the activities of his Socialist friends, he was to receive money and help to get out of the country.[12] On the night of October 13th, Girardot called on Peyré, accompanied by the latter's lawyer, M. Rochas;[13] at 4 o'clock next morning, Peyré tossed up. 'You've won', he said to Girardot as the coin fell; and he proceeded to dictate a long new statement in which nothing was said about Revers receiving money or being privy to the leak of the report. On November 30th, Peyré and his family left France for South America, where they remain; on the same day Colonel Fourcaud met in Paris a friend who was editor of the Gaullist paper at St Etienne; next day, the paper published an article giving the Fourcaud version of the story. On December 7th, Revers was replaced as chief of the general staff; on the 26th, *Time* published a violent attack on him for negligence over military secrets, which were said to be leaking via France to Russia, and the cat was out of the bag. The Prime Minister, M. Bidault, made a statement in the Assembly on January 17th, 1950, and a parliamentary committee of inquiry was set up.

On the 24th, *Carrefour*, a sensationalist Gaullist weekly, published the complete text of Peyré's statement to Captain Girardot, of which only four men had copies—Peyré and Girardot themselves, General Revers and Colonel Fourcaud. The unfortunate M. Ribière, who claimed that Girardot's activities had been concealed from him,[14] ordered an inquiry. Girardot was brought to the DST and interrogated for 21 hours by the heads of the department in person:[15] two other officers who had heard part of his instruc-

---

[12] This account follows that given by Girardot to the committee of inquiry, which has been accepted partly because the committee were convinced that he was an honest and non-political witness, partly because of confirmatory evidence, and partly because of Colonel Fourcaud's attitude. The latter denied his subordinate's account, but would not accuse him of lying: he pointed out that Girardot had first told his story to the DST, when he was exhausted after a long interrogation (it is interesting that someone of Fourcaud's experience should give this reason for not taking it seriously). He could not explain why Girardot should have repeated it to the committee. And while denying the whole he admitted many of the principal points, even that Girardot might 'subjectively' have thought that his task was to clear Revers at any cost.

Girardot's version was confirmed by Colonel Morand (see pp. 46, 48) and, except for the part about the Socialist friends, by M. Rochas (see note 13); but that part was supported by statements by Peyré to several friends before his departure, that he was being questioned on this subject by Girardot, knew nothing about it, and was therefore not likely to get the support he had been promised. Fourcaud's witnesses were two SDECE colonels, who had heard only part of the conversation, and were his close friends. One said he 'had not heard' the alleged orders, the other denied them—thereby, it appears, contradicting a previous deposition.

[13] Rochas was a close friend of Girardot. He had just resigned from the Paris bar to join that of Meaux, and let himself be persuaded that during the two-day interval he was not bound by professional etiquette.   [14] Fourcaud denied this.

[15] M. Wybot, head of the DST, and his superior, M. Bertaux, the head of the Sûreté Nationale itself.

tions from Fourcaud were also brought from their beds to be interrogated: and on January 30th, by telephone, Fourcaud 'declared war' on the DST.[16] Girardot applied to be heard by the committee of inquiry; his superiors tried to obstruct the request and, having failed, ordered him to say as little as possible; but feeling that he was being made the scapegoat for the whole affair, he told the committee everything he knew—perhaps the only important witness to do so.

IV

Though the committee of inquiry were primarily concerned with investigating the leak of Revers's report, there were several other topics involved: the political activities of Peyré; the financial activities of Van Co in political circles; Peyré's unhindered departure from France; and the various attempts to use the affair for political ends. On the question of the report, they soon decided that it had passed through the hands of General Revers, General Mast, and Peyré, to Van Co, who had sent it on to General Xuan. But Peyré had also given it to another Indo-Chinese, Vinh Xa, who although a cousin of Bao Dai was of secret Communist sympathies, and had conveyed a copy of it to the Indo-Chinese Communists, by whom it was broadcast. Contesting this explanation, General Revers developed a remarkable theory. The leak might have occurred in the Ministry of Overseas France, where the report had been microfilmed for reasons which were not convincingly explained;[17] Van Co's secretary took one copy to Indo-China for General Xuan, but handed a second to the Communists; and the Ministry of Overseas France was blaming Revers, the man who had denounced their policy, to divert attention from its own negligence in letting the secretary go. The fight at the Gare de Lyon was staged for this purpose by the DST, which was full of officers from de Gaulle's BCRA who hated Revers for staying in France during the war:[18] indeed they had for years been plotting to ruin him by involving him in scandal, and had recently tried to poison him. As if this were not sufficient, M. Teitgen (an MRP minister) had inspired the article in *Time*, and the executive committee of MRP had decided that Revers must be removed: M. Coste-Floret had said so in a train.[19]

[16] But he invited Wybot and a colleague to meet him at a café near the Etoile, in order to explain that there was nothing personal about this war.

[17] The Ministry of Overseas France had its own security service, the BTLC. Its chief, Major Maleplate, told the committee that when he first heard the suggestion that the microfilm might have been the source of the leak, 'I was so shocked that I decided to go on leave'.

[18] Revers had supported Vichy until 1942, and was a member of Darlan's *cabinet*.

[19] No time or place were given for Coste-Floret's remark, and the DST denied all Revers's charges; if they were true it was odd that the SDECE, which was the BCRA itself under a new name, should have been supporting the general. But he may have been right about the fight at the station: even Moch admitted that the official story was thin. And when M. Chabanais of the DST

This bold counter-attack was not successful, though the general scored some points. His theory was not only inconsistent, and denied by all those accused, it was also unplausible; the Ministry of Overseas France had every interest in keeping secret so damaging a report, while the campaign for a change of policy had much to gain from publicity. But Revers's relations with Peyré were in themselves enough to condemn him. Peyré had been before the war a local secretary of Doriot's Fascist party, the PPF: he had continued a member, as he claimed, to inform the resistance movement, and had betrayed the PPF to the police in 1944. He had been convicted for fraud before the war and for collaboration after it, but the latter conviction was quashed because Revers and Bouzanquet testified to his resistance activities—of which both men admitted to the committee of inquiry that they knew nothing. Yet Revers had made of this man a close friend and confidant, had obtained the Legion of Honour for him and tried hard to get him promotion in it. Letters were produced in which the general asked Peyré to let him know what the Cabinet had discussed at its last meeting, to find out when he could conveniently have an interview with the Prime Minister (Ramadier), to oppose the grant of extra powers to General de Lattre de Tassigny, or to obtain a fifth star for Revers himself.[20] The chief of the general staff had no doubt that Peyré was more powerful than himself. General Mast's relations with Peyré were more recent but were also intimate.[21] The committee condemned both generals severely, and they were dismissed from the army.

It was never established whether Peyré had really paid them any money: and no foundation was found for the wilder charges of wholesale corruption of politicians by Van Co. Colonel Fourcaud did indeed put in a list of 97 members of parliament which he had obtained from Peyré;[22] the Com-

was asked by the committee whether the affair had not been a remarkable piece of luck, he replied 'It was a miracle'. The Communist commissioner asked 'whether, in your service, you believe in miracles?' and witness answered 'Oui, et l'on aide, quand on le peut, à les faire apparaître'. He then reassured the astonished committee that no one could possibly have staged the incident, and certainly the DST had not done so.

[20] Another letter called for a 'barrage' against a particular appointment as *directeur adjoint du personnel* in the Ministry of War, and urged the candidature of the military governor of Paris, 'bon républicain dont, pour cette raison, le MRP veut se défaire en l'envoyant adjoint au général commandant la 3e région à Rennes'. During the next year M. Schuman was Prime Minister and M. Teitgen, also of MRP, Minister of Defence; but Revers's candidate was appointed a year later, under the Queuille Government. Ramadier, the Minister of Defence responsible, was severely attacked for political appointments in the army by M. Monteil of MRP, who in 1950 sat on the committee of inquiry into the affair of the generals.

[21] It appeared, though Mast denied it, that Peyré had *carte blanche* to invite politicians to dine with the general. When the chairman of the committee remarked to Madame Mast that: 'la maison du général Mast paraît avoir été très ouverte', Madame replied: 'Pas tant que cela; vous n'y êtes jamais venu.'

[22] Even Right-wing deputies commented that Fourcaud's behaviour was peculiar. Released from arrest by the personal order of the Prime Minister, his friend M. Bidault, Fourcaud came before

munists covered the walls with bills reproducing the list, headed *Les Sales Mains*, and the old Panama cry of 'A bas les chéquards' was raised again.[g] But the list proved to have been compiled haphazard to serve as a basis for possible invitations to Van Co's receptions, and a few months later the Communists were saying that it was a deliberate attempt, arranged of course by Moch,[23] to cover the real *chéquards* by implicating innocent men.

V

The Government had promised to the committee the fullest assistance, but their performance fell so far short of this that the absence of evidence began to seem in itself almost a ground for suspicion. The committee were assured that they had received a complete dossier: but a series of items were found to have been omitted. Some were supplied later, including a record of the burning of several other documents (claimed to be only spare copies of those handed in); but one page of Peyré's interrogation was not to be found.[24] Again, the DST had committed many admitted and grave irregularities during those 48 frantic hours in September; they were excused as being the result of haste, but the committee were not quite satisfied that they were accidental. The most serious was the illegal restoration of Peyré's and Van Co's papers (the former filling four suitcases) on their release. Moch claimed that no damage had been done, and all the cheques could easily be retrieved within three days; but the Ministry of Justice would give no assistance, and when members of the committee went to the bank themselves, the cheques had been removed the day before for judicial investigation.[25] The committee asked for the prosecution of Bouzanquet for giving false evidence about Peyré's resistance record: the Minister of Justice (a Radical) refused. The

the committee three days later and handed in an item of the dossier on which he was supposed to be examined, commenting that it was worthless, but knowing perfectly well that it was bound to cause the maximum of political exploitation and scandal.

[23] Since the list was handed in by Fourcaud, Moch's mortal enemy, this is a little hard to believe.

[24] There was also no trace of a page of Van Co's accounts containing the words 'versements Paul' (i.e. Peyré), the initials 'R', 'M' and 'LT' and the sums 1 million, 1 million and ½ million. The officer who interrogated Peyré suggested to the committee that these were in pencil and might not appear on the photocopy in the committee's hands. But at the next day's hearing he declared that he had never seen this paper, and that the idea that he had seen it had been put into his head by the newspapers: he was then suddenly taken ill. His colleague, the next witness, declared that he had experimented with photocopying pencil marks, which showed up perfectly; but he was positive that this page had never existed.

An Indo-Chinese witness later declared that every self-respecting Annamite kept at least four different sets of books.

[25] The Ministry of Justice was then asked to show them confidentially to the committee's rapporteur. The letter was never answered.

[g] In the Panama scandal of 1890, a hundred deputies were said to have been bribed to vote a law benefiting the ill-managed canal company.

Ministry of Finance would give no information about the extensive and notorious traffic in Indo-Chinese piastres.[h] Peyré had escaped prosecution, and had been able to take his whole family abroad; the Government's efforts to extradite him were suspected to be as feeble as they were ineffective. It was not wholly surprising that many Frenchmen suspected that the key to the mystery was missing in the spring of 1950 because it had been thoroughly hidden in the autumn of 1949.

Shortly after leaving France, Peyré had written to a friend saying that in doing so he had followed the wishes of 'R' and of Albert. The latter was Bouzanquet: the correspondent thought that 'R' was Ribière, who had dined with Bouzanquet early in November. But Ribière denied knowing Peyré or receiving any request for help from him or from members of the government. Another likely 'R' was Captain Girardot, who had a room in the offices of Rossi et Cie and was known there as Rabier. He admitted having promised Peyré assistance to escape, but denied having given it; the promises were broken, he said, presumably because Colonel Fourcaud did not wish to lose his main source of information. The committee eventually concluded that 'R' was almost certainly General Revers; but that whoever 'R' might be, the failure of the police to keep any check on Peyré was suspicious. In a final effort to solve the mystery, the committee investigated the account of a customer in the Restaurant-Bar de l'Etape who had told a table-companion that a few weeks ago Peyré was sitting in that very place, when in came a policeman who handed him a number of passports and told him 'in military language' to get out of the country forthwith. The teller denied having told the story, but his hearer brought a witness to support him: in this fruitless chase after hearsay evidence the search for Peyré's protectors petered out.

The sources of Peyré's influence proved equally elusive: the rapporteur complained that on that subject the committee seemed to meet a 'wall of silence'. General Revers did indeed hint that Peyré's contacts were in several ministries held by Socialists, but the one name he gave turned out to be that of the very man who had stopped Peyré's advancement in the Legion of Honour. From Revers's evidence it was clear that Peyré had excellent sources of information but far from clear that he could exercise effective pressure; over three years Revers had asked him to act in a number of matters, in none of which had he obtained results. Yet the silence of witnesses may have had other reasons. For when Jacques Peyré was being pressed hard on the point, he put in evidence a letter written to his brother in South America by M. Castellani—a Gaullist member of the committee of inquiry

[h] In which Peyré and his associates were involved: see J. Despuech, *Le Trafic des piastres* (Paris, Deux Rives, 1953), pp. 85–97. On the French secret service in Saigon see *ibid.* pp. 115–16.

itself.[26] The committee and the RPF were shortly reduced in number by one, and Roger Peyré had perhaps demonstrated that he still had a card or two up his sleeve. A Gaullist weekly, seconded by demands for 'inquiry' by the Communists, carried on a campaign suggesting that the real source of Peyré's power was a contact with the Presidency of the Republic itself. These charges broke down completely when the editor concerned was examined, but they led to one of the oddest incidents of the inquiry, the '*affaire* Morand'.

Colonel Morand was a former member of the SDECE, who was summoned to give evidence before the committee. But M. Chamant, a Right-wing member of it, arranged instead that Morand should come to his house in the suburbs and there give evidence to three members of the committee only—the Gaullist chairman, a Radical who was an old friend of Morand's, and Chamant himself. Morand wrote to another friend in the Elysée saying that he was subjected to heavy pressure to implicate the President's son and members of his staff, but had not done so: and the letter found its way to a Socialist member of the committee, who bitterly attacked Chamant and his colleagues. They explained that Morand would not come to Paris because he said he was in danger,[27] and that his evidence was too sensational to publish and too fantastic to be worth passing on to their colleagues. Morand was summoned to attend the committee, but did not arrive. He wrote to say that he had been out of Paris when the summons arrived, and had left no address: when he eventually appeared, he admitted having received the summons in Paris, and only leaving thirty-six hours later. His evidence was as unsatisfactory as his conduct: he denied having any knowledge which would connect Peyré with the Elysée, denied giving such information to Chamant and the others, and when asked about 'pressure' replied that he had 'subi des pressions qui n'en étaient pas'—adding unnecessarily 'Il y a des nuances!'. His one definite statement was that he had heard part of Colonel Fourcaud's instructions to Captain Girardot (a fact which neither of them had mentioned) and that he confirmed Girardot's version. The three deputies who had heard Morand resigned from the committee soon after-

---

[26] Jacques Peyré also remarked casually to the chairman, 'Si je parle ce sera terrible.'

Castellani's letter, written in January, ran: 'Mon cher ami—Vous aviez disparu de Paris, mais pour cause! Vous faites le tour du monde.—Merci pour vos bons vœux. Acceptez les nôtres en retour, bien sincères et bien cordiaux. Le gouvernement Bidault tombera fin janvier. Je crois que nous allions à grands pas vers de nouvelles élections. Bien amicalement vôtre. J. Castellani. Envoyez quelques timbres pour les enfants d'Amérique du Sud.'

The suggestion was made that Castellani had acted on the committee as a representative of the 'Fourcaud version', and an analysis of the questions he asked tends to confirm this impression.

[27] It later appeared that he had been dismissed from the SDECE because his expense accounts were extraordinarily high, and had agreed to stay out of Paris for a year; if he attended the committee, he feared that he would meet Ribière, his late chief, in the lobbies of the Assembly.

wards (for other reasons) and refused a confrontation with the witness, M. Michelet, the chairman, remarking cryptically that he would have plenty to say when the time came.

VI

The committee's life was thus thoroughly unhappy. Its initial attempt to keep its proceedings secret was frustrated by the Communist member, who passed selected items on to *L'Humanité*. The committee was thereby driven into accepting day-by-day publicity, which enabled witnesses to prepare their stories in advance, and made its work almost impossible. Suspicions that every member was grinding his own political axe were confirmed by incidents like the Morand affair, and made more damaging by the obstructiveness of the Government. At the end of April two interim reports were adopted, one condemning the generals, the other exonerating Ramadier on the ground that, in quashing the prosecution, he had in the national interest committed what would normally have been a dereliction of duty. Against the wish of the committee the Assembly decided to debate this report forthwith, and five Right-wing members resigned: they were replaced by Socialists and members of MRP. The committee spent two final months investigating mare's nests,[28] and finally produced a report criticizing the irregular proceedings of the DST, demanding reorganization of the secret services, and asking for further inquiry into Peyré's departure, and into the traffic in piastres. This report was debated in November: the Communists demanded the impeachment of Moch, their most dangerous opponent, and in a secret vote, without discussion, carried their motion by 235 to 207—fifty short of the absolute majority required by the Constitution. It seems that about forty of the MRP, led by M. Coste-Floret's brother, and perhaps mostly influenced by party motives rather than by a belief in Moch's guilt, had given the Communists their triumph; the break-up of the Government was barely averted. A week later, General de Lattre was appointed High Commissioner in Indo-China; after nearly 18 months' delay and under the pressure of military disaster, the policy of Revers's report was at last adopted.

Politically the affair has done a good deal of harm to the centre coalition, partly by discrediting prominent political figures, especially Socialists, but even more by sowing suspicion between allies: the Socialist–MRP combination has been weakened if not destroyed. Gaullist indiscretions have not

[28] The chief of these was the story that Peyré belonged to a *Sainte-Vehme*, a Nazi secret society headed by Marcel Déat. There was partial corroboration, but little to connect Peyré with the affair; and when after eight sittings the witness agreed to produce his evidence, it turned out to be a letter posted in Tours by an informant whom he did not know: the witness himself was said by the police to be in close contact with the Communist Party, and in particular with the Communist member of the committee of inquiry.

allowed the RPF to reap the full benefit from their promising slogan, 'l'affaire des généraux, c'est l'affaire du régime'. The Communists have gained by throwing mud all round, and more especially by exposing the seamy side of 'la sale guerre': wars in Indo-China have been loathed in France since the days of Jules Ferry, 'le Tonkinois'. Most of all, political cynicism has received a further reinforcement: and the non-voters were already the largest party in France.

One problem remains: for whom was Peyré working? Was he, as he claimed, a patriotic Frenchman, risking his life and his reputation in the service of his country? Or was he a spy, a concealed and characterless Alger Hiss? And if so, who were his masters? He had a Fascist past, and had served the Germans during the war, perhaps for ulterior motives and perhaps not. On the other hand, he was well-informed about the French Communist Party, and had excellent contacts with Viet Minh: and after all it was the Communists who gained in the end by the leaking of Revers's report. But, again, his brother and his friends had been in the OSS in Tunisia, he had himself claimed to know Mr. Forrestal, and three well-informed witnesses (General Revers, Colonel Morand and Captain Girardot) confirmed that he had American contacts, particularly with the entourage of a distinguished general who had recently become head of a well-known university.[i] Lastly was he, as the committee of inquiry thought, not a spy at all, but a French Sydney Stanley,[j] a boaster and bluffer who had no real influence on governmental action, and only attempted one political *coup* in his life—the campaign to send General Mast to Indo-China—with the simple motive of financial profit for himself? We are not very likely ever to discover the answer.

[i] Dwight D. Eisenhower. The OSS was the U.S. wartime secret service.

[j] Central figure of the Lynskey Tribunal hearings in 1947; condemned by it for peddling his alleged influence. See S. W. Baron, *The Contact Man* (London, Secker and Warburg, 1966), and John Gross's chapter in *The Age of Austerity*, ed. M. Sissons and P. French (Harmondsworth, Penguin Books, 1964).

f (See p. 40.) Years later, after the 1961 attempt on de Gaulle's life, Colonel Fourcaud—now 'retired'—testified in court: that he had known of such a plot over a month beforehand; that he had suspected it was a put-up job organised by the authorities; and that he had not reported it to them. *Le Monde*, 7 September 1962, p. 6. A later attempt (also suspected in some quarters to be bogus) used one of the methods discussed by Fourcaud at this trial.

4 The Leakages affair[a]

I. CAST OF CHARACTERS

Andre BARANÈS: journalist on *Libération*; found not guilty of improperly giving defence secrets to his editor, M. d'Astier. Police spy? Patriot? Communist agent?

Alfred DELARUE ('M. Charles'): collaborator, sentenced to 25 years; escaped from prison and became M. Dides' assistant.

Jean DIDES: Chief Inspector in charge of anti-Communist activities at the Prefecture; dismissed 1954; Poujadist deputy 1956.

Roger LABRUSSE: head of civil defence section in secretariat of National Defence Committee; given six years for passing defence secrets to Baranès.

Gilles MARTINET: assistant editor of *France-Observateur*; accused of publishing confidential information.

Jean MONS: secretary of National Defence Committee; dismissed 1954; acquitted of negligence.

Roger STÉPHANE: journalist on *France-Observateur*; accused of publishing confidential information.

Jean-Louis TIXIER-VIGNANCOUR: head of Vichy radio, 1940–2; counsel for Baranès, 1954; deputy, allied to Poujadists, 1956.

René TURPIN: Mons' personal assistant; given four years for passing defence secrets to Labrusse.

Jean VALLOIS: Inspector at Prefecture; in charge of shadowing Baranès.

Roger WYBOT: head of the counter-espionage section in the Ministry of the Interior (Direction de la surveillance du territoire, DST).

Jean BAYLOT: Paris Prefect of Police, dismissed July 1954.

Georges BIDAULT: MRP; Foreign Minister under M. Laniel, till June 1954.

Emmanuel D'ASTIER DE LA VIGERIE: *Progressiste* (fellow-travelling) deputy; editor of *Libération*.

André DUBOIS: Paris Prefect of Police from July 1954; now Resident in Morocco.

Edgar FAURE: Radical; Finance Minister under MM. Laniel and Mendès-France; Prime Minister 1955.

Christian FOUCHET: 'Gaullist'; Minister for Tunisian and Moroccan Affairs under M. Mendès-France.

Léon MARTINAUD-DÉPLAT: Right-wing Radical; Minister of the Interior under M. Laniel.

Pierre MENDÈS-FRANCE: Radical: Prime Minister June 1954–February 1955.

[a] From *Occidente* 12.5 (November–December 1956); originally entitled *The Case of the Leakages in France*. Many printers' errors have been corrected.

François MITTERRAND: UDSR; Minister of Colonies under M. Laniel, June–
September 1953; of Interior under M. Mendès-France; of Justice under
M. Mollet, 1956.
André PELABON: M. Mendès-France's *directeur de cabinet*.

II. THE PLOT

In the political undergrowth of most countries there flourish some unpleasant
weeds. Men engaged in a struggle for power rarely reject the weapons placed
in their hands by the faults, follies or frailties of their rivals. Italy has her
Montesi affair, America her Hiss case, Britain her Burgess and Maclean
incident and her Lynskey tribunal. Yet France remains the classic land of
political scandal.

There are several reasons. The keenest and least scrupulous scandal-
mongers are usually men of the extreme Right. The true reactionary regards
a left-of-centre government as an unnatural aberration, conceived in folly
and imposed by fraud, which it is his duty as well as his pleasure to destroy
as best he may. In France, where his hatred is directed not against a party
but against democracy itself, he is unrestrained by any concern for the
health of a detested regime. To protect itself against such virulent enemies
the Republic has been compelled by prudence (and also impelled by long
habit) to employ a politically minded police force—or rather several police
forces, divided by bitter professional rivalry and so irresistibly tempted to
play politics. Since all administrations were suspect, they have been kept
feeble by a jealously watchful Parliament. Thus political authority was not
wielded by a few men in the public eye, but split in fragments among many
whose names were unknown and whose conduct could not be scrutinised.
In this favourable soil the weeds of scandal sprouted.

Animosities were intensified by the war and the occupation. The former
collaborators, defeated at the liberation, remained unrepentant and bent on
revenge. They counted on exploiting two assets: fear of Communism, and
resentment at France's decline as a great power. The colonial wars of the
Fourth Republic have been opposed by much of the non-Communist Left;
thus they gave the extreme Right an opportunity to confound all their foes
in a common charge of anti-patriotism.

By the spring of 1954 the Indo-China war was loathed in France. Failure
at the front was accompanied by odious profiteering in the rear. Ideological
critics of the war were now reinforced by realists who feared that it was
undermining French strength in Europe. The battle at Dien Bien Phu
brought passions to a head. At a military ceremony at the Arc de Triomphe,
the Prime Minister and Minister of Defence were assaulted by demonstrators
of the extreme Right; the police seemed unable (or unwilling) to control the

riot.[1] The Foreign Minister, M. Bidault, was believed to have appealed to America to aid France with atomic weapons; apprehensive people feared that world war might break out in a matter of hours. In the National Assembly M. Mendès-France led a vigorous attack on the Laniel government, overthrew it on 10 June, and to the general surprise was elected Prime Minister.

He formed a cabinet which for once was not a mere reproduction of its predecessor. Only two of his senior Ministers—M. Faure at Finance and M. Mitterrand at the Interior—had served under M. Laniel; both had disapproved of his North African policy, and M. Mitterrand had resigned over it early in September 1953. Nearly all the other Ministers were newcomers, and the Cabinet was correspondingly detested by the many displaced Excellencies. It was charged with neutralism—somewhat hesitantly at first, but with vigour after M. Mendès-France refused to link his fate to that of the European Defence Community. Thus it was against a background of cut-throat political warfare that the scandal of the defence leakages developed.

General Navarre (like many a beaten soldier before him) later claimed that treason was everywhere; the Indo-China Command assumed that anything told to Paris would become known to the Viet-minh. On 24 July 1953 he reported on the strategic situation; six days later the substance of his report was published by M. Roger Stéphane in the neutralist weekly *France-Observateur*. On 26 May 1954 General Ely reported on the same subject to the National Defence Committee, a mixed body of Ministers, officers and officials; the tenor of his remarks appeared in many newspapers, notably *L'Express*, a weekly supporting M. Mendès-France. Copies were seized by the police, the office was raided, and a junior Minister in the Laniel government (M. Jacquet), who admitted having once been in touch with the paper, resigned office. In the same week M. Stéphane published in *France-Observateur* accounts of the Defence Committee meetings of 14 and 26 May; and on 8 July the assistant editor, M. Gilles Martinet, gave details of the proposed dispatch of conscripts, discussed at the Committee on 28 June. Besides these publicly known leakages there were graver ones, of which only official circles were aware. A copy of General Ely's report was found on the body of a dead Viet-minh officer; it had apparently been in enemy hands at the time it was delivered to the Defence Committee. And very detailed transcripts of the proceedings of the Committee on 14–15 May, 28 June and 10 September 1954 somehow came into the possession of André Baranès,

[1] Those present included the Prefect of Police, M. Baylot, whose men had under him confirmed their ugly reputation for violence; on Bastille Day 1953, seven North African Communists had been killed in a clash with the police, and a student demonstration had been beaten up still more recently. No one missed the startling contrast with their ineffectiveness on this occasion.

a Communist journalist on the fellow-travelling daily *Libération*, who was also a paid informer for the Prefecture of Police.[2]

Baranès' transcripts were based mainly on the notes taken by the secretary of the Committee, M. Jean Mons. M. Mons' personal assistant, M. René Turpin, and another senior member of the secretariat, M. Roger Labrusse, were fellow-travellers.[3] Hating the war in Indo-China and shocked by certain decisions of the Committee they served, these officials tried to counteract those decisions by revealing them to opposition politicians, especially M. d'Astier de la Vigerie, the fellow-travelling aristocrat who edits *Libération*. After a long investigation four of these men were brought to trial in March 1956 before a military court; M. Mons for negligence, MM. Baranès, Turpin and Labrusse for unauthorised possession or communication of secret documents (though not with intent to serve a foreign power). The *parquet militaire* (Judge Advocate's department) would have liked to proceed against others also. But the Minister of Defence, General Koenig, decided against prosecuting *L'Express* on the ground that the matter there published had not concerned national defence, and against asking the Assembly to raise M. d'Astier's parliamentary immunity because the evidence was too thin; for these decisions he was later attacked with vigour by the extreme Right. MM. Stéphane and Martinet were however prosecuted for articles published many (in one case twenty) months before; but by a judicial decision which disgusted the *parquet militaire*, their cases were sent to a civil court.

Several explanations for the affair were offered. The *parquet* held that all the leakages were part of one political operation, by which fellow-travelling and neutralist officials passed information to sympathetic journalists and politicians in an endeavour to stop the Indo-China war. The Left charged that the ideological misconduct of Turpin and Labrusse had been exploited for another political operation—a sordid reactionary intrigue against themselves. The DST, the counter-espionage section of the Ministry of the Interior, accused M. Mons himself of being a Communist agent; this for them was the real case, obscured by political wrangling on both sides. The Right were out for still bigger game, and claimed that the accused officials were mere scapegoats for guilty Ministers. Baranès' counsel, Maître Tixier-Vignancour (sometime head of the Vichy radio and in 1956 a parliamentary ally of the Poujadists) argued that his client's perilous and patriotic activities had been wantonly sabotaged by politicians anxious to conceal the truth, and avowedly used the military court to tar the whole Left—*Mendésistes*

[2] Baranès had previously been employed for the same purpose by the DST, which had got rid of him (see pp. 64–5). The Prefecture had cut his pay from 200,000 francs a month to 80,000; *Libération* paid him 59,000.

[3] Labrusse sat with MM. Martinet and d'Astier on the *Union Progressiste* executive.

as well as fellow-travellers, *Esprit* and *L'Express* as well as *France-Observateur* —with the black brush of treason.

Each thesis had its answer to the vital questions. For whom was Baranès working? He faked a manuscript, which dealt only with the Defence Committee proceedings, by inserting it in a bogus report of a meeting of the Communist *Bureau Politique*: at Communist or reactionary instigation? The DST thought him a Communist double agent, supplying their own hated rivals the Prefecture of Police with information calculated to mislead French Intelligence and confuse the political situation. For the Communists themselves he was a police *agent-provocateur*; for M. d'Astier, a venal scoundrel out only for money; for the *Mendésistes*, any of these three; for the extreme Right, a patriot hero.

How were the 'political operations' of Left and Right linked to the case? MM. Stéphane and Martinet denied receiving information from any of the defendants; and though the *parquet* and the Right claimed that their cases were an essential part of the affair, the Left held that the prosecutions were irrelevant to it and should never have been launched, while the DST regarded them as legitimate in themselves, but tiresome obstacles to a serious inquiry. The right-wing conspiracy was variously interpreted. M. Mitterrand saw it (at least at first) as the heart of the affair, M. Mendès-France as an ugly excrescence on a grave case of espionage. But both believed the plot was directed against their government, whereas M. d'Astier thought it had been mounted to discredit the neutralists and *Progressistes* and only subsequently turned against M. Mendès-France. For the Communists, needless to say, the Americans were at the bottom of it all.[4] The DST disbelieved in the right-wing 'political operation' and cared little about the left-wing one; for them the true guilty men were M. d'Astier (here the Right and the *parquet* agreed with them) and M. Mons (about whom they stood alone).

Who was informing, and why? According to the *parquet* and the Left, only junior members of the Defence Secretariat, purely for anti-war ideological motives. In the DST view, however, they were probably spies like their chief. The Right too smelt treason in high places, but located it among their political enemies, and insisted—seconded naturally by all the defendants whatever their politics—that the Secretariat could not be the sole source of the leakages. Labrusse and Turpin admitted passing on scraps of political material, but denied giving Baranès the extensive military details contained in his manuscripts. Baranès claimed he had them from the Communists; if for once he told the truth, the Party had another informant.

Here was the core of the affair. But it became encrusted with a mass of

---

[4] Also for the *New Statesman*, whose Paris dispatch of 31 March 1956 was based on an untrue headline in *L'Humanité*.

dubiously relevant material. Attention was constantly diverted from the main question as there was spread before the public gaze the unsavoury picture revealed by previous scandals. The Prefecture was at odds with the *Sûreté*. The administration made improper attempts to interfere with the judiciary. The rival government services, which should have assisted the inquiry, confused or sabotaged it. And the able and unscrupulous representatives of the extreme Right were avowedly alert for every opportunity to damage their political opponents—and with them the Republic.

III. THE SEQUEL

On 2 July 1954 M. Christian Fouchet, who had just taken office as Minister for Tunisian and Moroccan Affairs in the new Mendès-France Cabinet, had a visit from one of his former *compagnons* in the RPF, Chief Inspector Dides of the Paris Prefecture of Police (who in 1956 was to be elected with Conservative backing as Poujadist deputy for a Paris suburban constituency). M. Dides handed to the Minister a report which he claimed to have received from a highly placed Communist (namely Baranès) who was risking his life to serve his country. This report purported to describe a meeting of the *Bureau Politique* of the Communist Party, at which M. Duclos had given a full account of the National Defence Committee of 28 June—which he claimed to have had from a Minister. M. Fouchet examined the account; it was authentic. But why, he asked, had M. Dides reported to him instead of to his superiors, the Prefect of Police and the Minister of the Interior? M. Dides, as he was revealingly to tell the military court two years later, felt that this 'was not the response he was entitled to expect'. For he had been brooding over the scandal of the first world war, when Clemenceau had had a left-wing Minister of the Interior banished for leniency towards enemy agents,[b] and had arrived at a sensational conclusion: that the traitor was none other than the new Minister of the Interior himself. According to M. Fouchet, he said so; according to M. Dides, he merely 'expressed reserves' about M. Mitterrand: did he not write for that dangerous paper *L'Express*, and meet the Viet-minh agent Van Chi? M. Dides saw no reason to mention that Van Chi (who later denied being a Viet-minh agent) had acquaintances on the Right as well as on the Left; nor that an exactly similar leak from the Defence Committee had occurred six weeks earlier, before M. Mitterrand took office.

M. Fouchet again surprised his informant by saying that he would report the matter to the Prime Minister. M. Mendès-France promptly summoned M. Mons, from whom he learnt of the May leakage—of which the outgoing Ministers had not thought fit to inform their successors, and had left no

[b] Jean Louis Malvy: above, pp. 25–6.

significant documentary record.[5c] The Prime Minister sought and received confirmation from M. Baylot, the Prefect of Police; his account included the report of the Defence Committee proceedings but not the charge against a Minister. The Premier asked his personal assistant M. Pelabon, who had Intelligence experience, to investigate in the strictest secrecy; and departed for the Geneva conference.[d]

On 10 July M. Baylot was dismissed. This came as no surprise, for even before his failure to prevent the Arc de Triomphe riot, his administration had been much criticised, and it was thought he retained his post only through his close association with M. Martinaud-Déplat (M. Laniel's Minister of the Interior and a bitter enemy of M. Mendès-France). M. Dides also had just been removed from his supervision of anti-Communist activities to an innocuous position at the port of Paris. But he was not a man to be diverted by so trivial an administrative detail. He addressed a sealed copy of his report to the President of the Republic, using as his messenger another of his political friends, a Conservative deputy named Vigier, whom he had convinced of M. Mitterrand's guilt. M. Vigier 'thought himself entitled' to look at the report before passing it on—and to invite four leading journalists to inspect his documentary proof of treason in the Cabinet. They did not credit his story. Yet, in his own words, M. Mitterrand's alleged treachery was soon 'la fable de Paris'—busily spread at home and abroad by several distinguished opposition leaders, of whom only one (M. René Mayer) saw fit to mention it to the government.

The Committee was to meet again on 10 September. M. Pelabon hoped at this meeting to trap the informer, and careful precautions were taken. On his instructions the DST examined every corner of the meeting-room and took up the carpet in a vain search for a concealed microphone. During the meeting the Prime Minister himself observed his colleagues; only the secretary, M. Mons, was taking full notes. For two days beforehand DST detectives shadowed both M. Dides and Baranès, who had now been identified

---

[5] Neither the Prime Minister nor the Minister of Defence was informed by his predecessor. The outgoing Minister of the Interior, M. Martinaud-Déplat, said he had mentioned the matter casually to M. Mitterand when the latter took over: M. Mitterrand had no recollection of this. On 31 May M. Martinaud-Déplat had had from Baranès a report showing that the Communists knew Defence Committee secrets: this vital document he burned. M. Dides had another copy, which he gave in October to the examining magistrate; M. Baylot claimed he had not shown this to M. Mitterrand because he was not asked to—proof, said M. Mitterrand, that he had never been told it existed. M. Baylot did say he had told his successor M. Dubois about an inquiry (the only one recorded in the files) into the lower-grade Secretariat staff: but that he had said no more because M. Pelabon had urged him to keep silence.

[c] But M. Pleven, the former Minister of Defence, gave full information, when asked, to M. Mendès-France: Théolleyre, *Le Procès des Fuites* p. 141 (cf. pp. 46, 136).
[d] The conference which ended the (first) war in Indo-China.

as his informant. Those assigned to the former found that he was warned of their activities by his friends among the police; those watching Baranès soon discovered that they were not alone—for he was also being followed by their colleagues from 'la maison en face'. The rival police forces had no love for one another; and after a complaint from the new Prefect of Police, M. Dubois, the DST withdrew its men.

The sequel was unforeseen. On 10 September M. Dubois gave instructions that from 5 p.m. (the very hour the Committee was to meet) Baranès need no longer be watched all the time; he later explained in court that full-time shadowing had become useless as Baranès had detected it (not perhaps difficult in the circumstances).[6] For two days the suspect had been closely watched by two sets of police; now for the crucial week he was observed only intermittently by one—sometimes not until the afternoon. The court was told that the working hours of detectives, and 'technical reasons', explained this odd procedure. It was still more astonished to learn that vital reports had been kept from the Prefect and abstracted from the files—only to reappear mysteriously eighteen months later.

Despite all precautions, the 10th September meeting also 'leaked'. On the 17th Dides received another report from Baranès; as usual he did not inform his superiors. M. Dubois summoned him, warned him against inter-service rivalries, and asked him to pass on what information he had; he replied 'Comptez sur moi'—but said not a word of Baranès' report. It was the last straw.

M. Mitterrand was now in personal charge of the affair; he had been recalled from holiday just before the Committee met, and given the known facts. Being aware of the rumours against himself, he concluded that an anti-government plot was afoot. The Prime Minister was telephoning repeatedly from London urging his colleague to act quickly, for he found himself so suspect in the eyes of France's allies that he could achieve nothing. MM. Mitterrand and Pelabon resolved to give M. Dides a final test. At their request, M. Fouchet agreed to summon him at 8.30 a.m. on 18 September. This time the Inspector gave only a bare verbal summary of his precious document. On leaving M. Fouchet's Ministry he was arrested by the DST,[7] and found to be carrying two carbon copies of Baranès' report on the Committee of 10 September; the top copy has never been traced.[8]

---

[6] But he himself said he *had* been followed all the week. By whom? By the SDECE, proclaimed his counsel. This was described by M. Dubois as 'a *really* secret secret service', directly controlled by the Prime Minister; its official chief said it had never followed Baranès.

[7] M. Pelabon had wanted M. Dides arrested earlier, but MM. Dubois and Wybot had opposed this. M. Dubois was not told of the new decision. He could not remember, in court, whether the arrest of M. Baylot had also been proposed.

[8] The DST had a theory (but would give no evidence) that he had handed this copy to Mr. Lallier, security officer at the American Embassy, whom he had met on both 10 and 17 September. A month

On interrogation he denied all knowledge of Baranès. He was released in the evening; meanwhile his subordinates had destroyed all records of his activities.

Two other developments occurred on this eventful day. First, the police searched Baranès' apartment. A colleague, Delarue, had telephoned to warn him and tell him to burn his papers. But two manuscripts in his handwriting were found, which recorded the Defence Committee proceedings of 28 June and 10 September, but made no mention of the Communist Party.[9] Secondly, M. Mons visited the DST to explain how his secretariat was organised. Next day he told M. Wybot that he had kept his notes on the last two Committee meetings, instead of destroying them as usual (and as he had told M. Mendès-France on 2 July). When he handed in these notes, it became obvious that Baranès' manuscripts were based on them. The DST turned its attention to the members of the Secretariat, and by the night of 30 September they held the confessions of two culprits—but failed, despite efforts to which several witnesses testified, to implicate M. Mons. Turpin had passed information to Labrusse, and Labrusse to Baranès; but whom had Baranès told?

It was a question easier asked than answered, for Baranès had disappeared. M. Dides at once announced that his precious informer had been murdered by the Communists—and, moreover, that when Communist headquarters were raided in 1952, the DST chief's name had been found among the members of the 'Communist policemen's friendly society'. M. Wybot's name had indeed been found among the Communist records—as a 'dangerous anti-Communist'. He successfully sued M. Dides for libel.

Nor was Baranès dead. He had sought refuge first with the Conservative daily *Figaro*, then with M. André Hugues, a fence-straddling Radical deputy (who stoutly maintained that he had sheltered the fugitive out of sheer humanitarianism), finally in a monastery in Nièvre. There he was traced by the DST, arrested, and brought back to Paris. He said just what the DST wanted to hear: that he was a '100% Communist' who had been feeding to Dides the information that the Party wished the authorities to have. But before the examining magistrate he changed his tune, and now described himself as a patriot working for the government within the Communist ranks; by giving the Party the innocuous scraps of information he obtained from Labrusse, he had discovered that they already possessed

later Mr. Dulles told M. Mendès-France that he had been sent documents from Paris intended to discredit the French Government, but had disbelieved them. Some military information contained in Baranès' reports also appeared in the *New York Times*, though nowhere in the French press. M. Dides himself said the top copy had been destroyed because his secretary spilt a bottle of ink over it.

9 Why did he not destroy these revealing documents first of all? It was among the most puzzling points in the whole case.

full details about the Defence Committee; but his efforts to discover the true culprit had been frustrated by his arrest. Later he changed again, and said all his material came from Labrusse, and that earlier he had been trying to delay the inquiry so that he should not come to trial while M. Mendès-France was in office.

IV. THE DEBATE

Early in December the National Assembly debated the affair. The attack was led by M. Legendre, a right-wing member best known as spokesman for the rapacious sugarbeet-growers' lobby, who had been carefully primed by M. Dides and Mᵉ Tixier-Vignancour, Baranès' counsel. In the tone of a public prosecutor before a revolutionary tribunal, he charged that M. Mitterrand had resigned from the Laniel Cabinet in September 1953, not as publicly stated owing to differences over North Africa, but at the request of the President of the Republic because he had been responsible for the July 1953 leakage to *France-Observateur*. The Mendès-France government was a nest of concealed neutralists, working to change France's system of alliances; instead of fighting Communist espionage they had protected the guilty, persecuted the Communists' enemies, and broken up M. Dides' organisation, the one effective counter-espionage unit in France.

M. Mitterrand's reply was devastating. M. Dides' political friends had been traducing France to her allies and diverting attention from the real source of the leakages. The previous administration had failed to discover the culprits; but M. Dides' arrest had led directly to their exposure, and so to the restoration of confidence abroad. The so-called Dides organisation consisted only of the utterly unreliable Baranès and the convicted collaborator Delarue. And what member of the Laniel Cabinet would associate himself with the accusation about 1953?

Everyone knew where it had originated; and after a painful silence M. Bidault rose. He accepted M. Mitterrand's reasons for his resignation; but on the July 1953 leakage the evidence he had given to the examining magistrate must remain confidential (though it was known to every lobby gossip). Yet for once an accusation did not remain indefinitely in suspense. The charge had arisen from a police report that M. Mitterrand's car had stood before M. Stéphane's house all one night before the journalist wrote his article. This report went to President Auriol, who told M. Bidault that he had it from the Minister of the Interior, M. Martinaud-Déplat. But the vehicle was not M. Mitterrand's; there had been an unfortunate error of one digit in the number. There were withdrawals, and apologies, and denials of responsibility; M. Martinaud-Déplat claimed that M. Auriol must have made a mistake as to his informant, for he had never seen such a report.

Yet this object-lesson did not in the least check the political exploitation of the affair; the reactionary pack merely turned to another scent.

The judicial examination was in the hands of a military magistrate who was later joined (and in effect superseded, despite his protests) by a civil colleague, M. Duval. They decided to prosecute MM. Stéphane and Martinet for articles now many months old; but these cases were transferred to a civil court. In April 1955 M. Wybot wrote to his Minister denouncing M. Duval for incompetence and partiality, shown in his confusion of cases which (according to M. Wybot) were quite distinct, and in his release of Baranès while Turpin and Labrusse remained in prison. The independence of the judiciary, M. Wybot rashly remarked, must be somewhat attenuated in matters of espionage. Executive efforts to interfere with the course of justice are a matter of constant complaint in France; this one, unlike many, had no consequences. But when it was revealed to the military court a year later, the presiding judge took the gravest exception to M. Wybot's action, and referred it to the constitutional guardian of judicial independence, the Supreme Council of the Magistrature.

The atmosphere of the military court was peculiar. It could sit only at unusual times, as the room was lent by a civil court, whose President would from time to time look angrily round the door until his military confrères took the hint. Witnesses, counsel and even judges sometimes mistook the time of meeting and failed to appear. The tribunal comprised three civil magistrates and six officers, several of whom had fought in Indo-China or Korea. Its President, M. Niveau de Villedary, was a choleric personage whose face often became as scarlet as his robes, and who sometimes had to suspend the sitting and take smelling-salts to clear his head. He had recently presided at the acquittal on collaboration charges of the owner-editor of the abominable Fascist journal *Gringoire*, whose contributors had been tried just after the war and given heavy sentences.[e]

The President made it plain that he was not interested in politics: his rulings made it equally plain that French judicial interpretations of what is 'political' have changed little since, sixteen years ago, every magistrate in the land save one took the oath to Pétain. Thus M. Baylot might not be asked whether M. Dides' burned records were his own property or that of the Prefecture ('of no interest now'); nor why M. Dides was unaware that the *Progressiste* Labrusse was working on defence secrets when M. Baylot did know ('of no interest'); nor M. Dides, why he could produce no financial accounts ('a commentary not a question'); nor M. Dubois, how Baranès' vital report of 31 May, missing from the Prefecture's files, came to be produced by M. Dides in October, after his dismissal ('not within

[e] This was the journal whose slanders had hounded Salengro to suicide in 1936: above, pp. 6, 28.

witness's competence'—though he had been Prefect of Police at the time). Counsel was rebuked for irrelevance for asking M. Dides how he had got an American visa for Delarue, who had been sentenced for collaboration (witness merely denounced the injustice of the conviction—an attack on the judiciary which the President for once let pass); and censured for asking the hypothetical question, would M. Dubois have informed his successor if such an inquiry had been in progress when he left the Prefecture (answer 'Certainly').

On the other hand an ultra-Conservative ex-Minister could attack M. Mendès-France's handling of the Indo-China peace talks and hint that he had been in collusion with Molotov. And questions like these were asked constantly: Was not a girl on M. Mendès-France's staff a niece of M. d'Astier? (No.) But had he not attended her wedding, indeed been a witness? (No.) Had not M. Stéphane belonged to M. Mendès-France's secretariat? (Never.) Were not unsold copies of *France-Observateur* sent by Van Chi to Viet-minh and distributed to French prisoners of war? (Already investigated and disproved.) How came the name of Mitterand (with one 'r') in Van Chi's notebook of telephone numbers? M. Mitterrand, when asked this, repeated that he had met Van Chi only once: (there is in fact a well-known fellow-traveller named Jacques Mitterand, no relation to the Minister). 'Curious', said counsel, looking at his dossier, 'it's your Christian name.' The President gently observed (with no rebuke) that the notebook gave no Christian name.

Such a check to Baranès' counsel was rare indeed. But others in court found it easy to arouse the President's wrath. Pressmen were a special object of his displeasure: he accused them of bias, regretted that he could not keep them out, and excluded one of them for interfering with the rights of the defence: the reporter had smiled when counsel referred to 'Baranès' honour'. How the other barristers fared may be judged from this extract from the cross-examination of M. Mendès-France by Me Tixier-Vignancour:

Counsel: The Navarre plan, published by *L'Observateur*,...could have come only from a Minister.

Witness: I am not here to defend the Ministers of July 1953, with whom I was in disagreement.

Counsel: Some of them were your Ministers too.

Witness: ...I make no reproaches against my predecessors, but I claim that my Government did its duty. To whom did you allude in saying 'it could have come only from a Minister'? (Counsel did not reply.)

Maître Hayot, counsel for Turpin: Maître Tixier-Vignancour could have meant only M. Edgar Faure or M. Mitterrand.

Witness, nodding: I have answered Me Tixier-Vignancour. He retorts: you had 1953 Ministers in your Government. He can only be referring to M. Edgar

Faure or M. Mitterrand. I desire to express my indignation at Me Tixier-Vignancour's abominable attempts to spread suspicion...[10]

The President: (to Maître Tixier-Vignancour): Has Me Hayot correctly interpreted you?

Maître Tixier-Vignancour: I repeat what I said...M. Mendès-France claimed he was not here to defend the Ministers of July 1953. I replied: some were in your Government, and Me Hayot said that I was accusing MM. Faure and Mitterrand. I defy you to prove that you heard such an accusation.

Witness: No—only an insinuation.

The President (to Me Tixier-Vignancour): The insinuation was only in Me Hayot's interpretation of your words.

Me Hayot: I protest. I have been thirty years at the bar. I wish to explain.

The President: You are interrupting me. Be quiet. You are insolent.

Me Hayot: ...I shall protest to the Bar Council and to the Head of the Bar.

The President: Your attitude is intolerable. It is insolent. I call upon prosecuting counsel to initiate disciplinary proceedings against Me Hayot.

Me Baudet, counsel for M. Mons and representative of the Bar Council: I am in a peculiar position here: I say little on behalf of my client and much for my colleagues...It seems that the interventions of the spokesman of one of the two 'clans' irritate the Court, while those of the spokesman of the other clan appear to be thought justified. Monsieur le Président, I see Me Hayot looking grieved and sad. Could you indicate to him that you intend to protect the rights of the defence? And I venture to hope that you will withdraw the floor from prosecuting counsel—as you sometimes do from counsel for the defence.

V. THE INQUIRY

Late in April the inquiry took a new turn. M. Mitterrand drew the court's attention to the 'invisible hand' which effaced all trace of the culprit as soon as it appeared. The document of 31 May was suppressed by M. Martinaud-Déplat, those of June and September were kept from the Minister by M. Dides, the meeting of Baranès and Labrusse on 13 September was notified to the Prefecture but not to the Prefect. The examining magistrate asked for the reports of the detectives shadowing Baranès; three times he was told there was nothing after 10 September. Yet the disappearance of these documents was referred to just before the Assembly debate by the extreme Right journal *Nouveaux Jours*, and during it by M. Legendre—who claimed in court to have learned of their existence from the editor of

---

[10] *Witness added:* 'You (Me Tixier-Vignancour) would share my contempt if you had any *sens national*.' This remark provoked indignation in the audience and on the bench, suggesting no one could doubt the patriotism of this able lawyer—whose first parliamentary election was annulled for fraud; who in 1940 favoured a German-type, anti-semitic single party in France; and who as head of the Vichy radio scandalised even the violently reactionary *Action française* by giving so much time on the air to the French Nazi leader Marcel Déat (de Gérin-Ricard and Truc, *Histoire de l'Action française*, Paris 1949, pp. 239–40).

Nouveaux Jours and to have deduced their contents by 'logical reasoning'. The editor, whose evidence was self-contradictory, denied informing M. Legendre.

After the debate M. Mitterrand had ordered an inquiry; nothing could be found. Yet Me Tixier-Vignancour could name in court the officers who had shadowed Baranès (when this knowledge became an embarrassment he claimed to have drawn the names from a hat!). On the very day the court summoned the Prefecture officials for questioning, the missing reports turned up in the archives, in the middle of the press-cutting file on the case. By bad luck for the Right, this file had been examined only a week before by a new inspector, who mildly thought it 'unlikely' that he had missed these twelve large sheets clipped together. However, the reports proved as disappointing as the witnesses. The officer in charge had been on leave and knew nothing; his replacement suffered from chronic amnesia. It was on the young inspector directly responsible for the shadowing, M. Vallois, that suspicion came to centre.

It was M. Vallois who, when the Prefect asked for information, told his superior 'nothing to report'; he who was responsible for the Prefect's replies to the examining magistrate (the last of which added for good measure that the DST had again taken over responsibility after 10 September—'an assumption', he told the court); he who claimed that Baranès had not been properly watched on 13 September. But in court one day M. Mitterrand announced that he had asked for an administrative inquiry into the erratic movement of documents in and out of the Prefecture; and that same evening at 6 p.m. there was found (in a pile of old reports awaiting destruction) the complete plan of Baranès' shadowing, which showed that he *had* been followed all day on 13 September, and that his lunch with Labrusse had instantly been reported by radio to the Prefecture—though the Prefect was never told. The inquiry further showed that on the morning of 18 September a full report on Labrusse's work, politics, and relations with Baranès was under a paper-weight on the desk of M. Vallois, who had asked for it. Two days later it was found buried in his out-tray (later it again disappeared and reappeared). M. Vallois swore that he never saw it, that for two weeks he quite forgot to ask where it was, and that until he heard Labrusse's arrest announced on the radio on 1 October, he had believed the latter to be (as the detectives' reports described him) an innocent official in the Ministry of Education.[11] The administrative inquiry concluded that these famous

---

[11] He pointed out however that when he *did* eventually report the Baranès–Labrusse meeting, on 1 October, this report never reached the examining magistrate; nor did the photographed correspondence between Baranès and M. André Hugues, the Radical deputy who later sheltered him in his flight.

reports had been kept not in the files but in M. Vallois' safe. When he was sent in great haste to Morocco he left behind his key, but not the combination; in March 1956 the Prefecture telephoned Rabat, asking him to ring back, and even the most bitter opponents agreed this must have been to get the combination so that the reports could be restored to, and 'found' in the archives.

Suspicion of poor M. Vallois was therefore general; only the President tried to defend him. But for whom was he working? For no one, he himself insisted; for MM. Pelabon and Mendès-France, claimed Me Tixier-Vignancour; for M. Wybot (anxious to discredit the rival Dides organisation), suggested the Prefecture official who conducted the administrative inquiry; for the Communists, hinted M. Wybot (helped by Me Tixier-Vignancour's allegation that Vallois had once been a Young Communist); for M. Baylot, chorused the entire Left. The Prefect of Police had promoted M. Vallois just before his own downfall; and in the critical week of September he had been seeing M. Dides, his ex-subordinate, whose organisation he had created. When asked the direct question, M. Mitterrand said he had his doubts about M. Baylot—and was silenced by the President for making charges without proof. Yet though the Minister of Justice was thus rebuked for answering a question, M. Dides could charge that Minister with perjury, and M. Baylot could accuse Me Hayot of being a secret Communist, without rebuke from the court.

Me Tixier-Vignancour disliked the new turn in the inquiry, which he had so rashly set going. His protest failed to stop it, but he found a useful diversion in the tapping of M. Dides' telephone. It was by this convenient (but illegal) means that the DST had known of M. Dides' rendezvous with M. Fouchet, after which they had arrested him. They firmly denied learning anything about Labrusse in this way, but the Minister of the Interior would not allow the records to be produced—a new concealment of the truth against which the President again protested. This was the final detour in the long meanderings of the case.

The prosecutor summed up very mildly, asking for the acquittal of Mons and Baranès, and nominal sentences on Turpin and Labrusse. The first was 'a captain who had lost his ship', rather than a criminal. The second had in Colonel Gardon's view served the Communists better than the Prefecture, but perhaps unintentionally. He could not be condemned for giving documents to M. d'Astier—whom the government would not prosecute because the evidence was thin—nor for giving them to his superior M. Dides, for this was no offence. Turpin and Labrusse were indeed guilty of the June and September leakages, though they might be given the benefit of the doubt on the May ones; but their twenty months in prison were, the colonel implied, quite sufficient punishment since their motives were neither venal nor treasonable.

The court took a more severe view. They duly acquitted M. Mons, and also Baranès: the latter was found to have obtained secret information, but not to have committed an offence since he acted on the orders of M. Dides; and he was found not guilty of giving it to M. d'Astier (though it was not clear whether the court thought he had not done so at all, or whether they believed he had acted legitimately—i.e. under orders which made him an *agent-provocateur*). But Turpin was given four years imprisonment, and Labrusse six (the maximum being ten); and they were jointly to pay the whole costs of the trial. These were enormous, since witnesses were repeatedly brought from Morocco to explain the strange conduct of the police—for which the responsibility of the luckless accused seemed singularly remote.

VI. CONCLUSIONS

What conclusions can be drawn?

1. *The case for the Left.* This is strong on accessory points—the importance of M. Dides' organisation, the reliability of Baranès, and the behaviour of the Right—but weaker on the leakages themselves.

M. Mitterrand claimed that the Dides organisation consisted only of Baranès and Delarue: M. Dides, that he had fifteen informers and ten inspectors under him. Yet, as M. Mitterrand pointed out, the others seem to have been somewhat inactive; in May, June and September alike only Baranès produced any 'evidence'. The records had thoughtfully been burned, and the tribunal discouraged questions about the matter. Asked whether M. Dides' fantastic charge that M. Wybot was a Communist was based on information supplied by the organisation, M. Baylot evaded the question. M. Dides himself confessed that though he knew Labrusse as a fellow-traveller, he had no idea that he was working on defence secrets; Labrusse's counsel commented 'Drôle de réseau'.

M. Dides freely admitted that Baranès' information was erratic; others were more critical. Baranès had once been employed by the DST itself. M. Bertaux, then head of the Sûreté, claimed that his material was either verifiable but familiar, or interesting but impossible to check. M. Bertaux's successor, M. Hirsch, found that Baranès could not give the information he wanted, on the current Communist anti-American agitation. But since he handed in a good deal of material on affairs abroad, M. Hirsch decided to consult the Quai d'Orsay before dismissing him. They reported that it was worthless. M. Hirsch then told Baranès henceforth not to submit reports but to answer questionnaires; he did not explain, but Baranès realised, that these would be drawn up partly to test the informer's reliability. This lack of confidence decided Baranès to work no more for the DST. In M. Dides he found a more sympathetic paymaster.

Seven of Baranès' reports were found, apart from the Defence Committee documents. These were submitted for inquiry to a section of the *Sûreté Nationale* independent of the DST, and of which the chief had served under M. Martinaud-Déplat; he reported to M. Mitterrand's successor. These documents too were found worthless. Asked to account for this, M. Dides replied that he was not interested in 'le roman ou l'habillage', and that his records (so unfortunately burned) had contained hundreds of invaluable reports by Baranès. He was asked why Baranès always reported meetings of the *Bureau Politique* on the wrong days; he did not deny this, and admitted that he had never verified his informer's reports—that would have been very difficult, he said. He agreed too that in four years of informing, Baranès produced no military material until in May 1954 M. d'Astier's secretary gave him an introduction to Labrusse. The secretary revealed that there was a special safety-catch on the door of M. d'Astier's office, to which Baranès claimed to have access; yet he had never mentioned this device and was unable to describe how it opened.[12]

The political exploitation of the case was patent. In July 1953 M. Mitterrand had been wrongly accused of a leakage by (according to President Auriol) M. Martinaud-Déplat. In June 1954 the same politician suppressed evidence of the 14 May leakage, and records of the inquiry into it were removed from his Ministry, leaving suspicion free to fester against the incoming government. In July the evidence of the leakage of 28 June was faked by M. Dides' employee Baranès so as to suggest treason by the new Ministers. They could have been cleared by investigation of Labrusse: the latter's views and employment were both known to M. Baylot, who kept silence. An inquiry into Baranès might have led to Labrusse: M. Baylot kept his informer's name from the Prime Minister. When in September the DST put a watch on Baranès, the Prefecture insisted on taking it over—but concealed the discovery of Baranès' contact with Labrusse: M. Baylot's appointee M. Vallois was probably responsible for this, and certainly for withholding documents proving that contact from the examining magistrate.

But these arguments did nothing to show the source of the leakages. Those of July 1953 and of 26 May 1954 enabled left-wing journals to use confidential information: left-wing sympathisers were plainly responsible, whether Ministers or officials. But what of the far more detailed Baranès documents? Leftist opinion came increasingly to hold that these had never gone to the Communists at all, but were released by the Right to Baranès to be forged

[12] But he did indicate correctly that it would not open from inside.

in a way which would discredit M. Mendès-France. But by whom? There were leakages under both the Laniel and the Mendès-France cabinets: and this fact exculpates the outgoing, as well as the incoming Ministers.

2. *The case for the Parquet.* This was that all the 1954 leakages were from Turpin and Labrusse to their *Progressiste* friends MM. Martinet, Stéphane and d'Astier. Since it convinced so fair-minded a prosecutor as Colonel Gardon, it should be given great weight. But there are difficulties about it. It was denied by everyone involved (though Baranès later went back on his denial). The Baranès manuscripts were far too detailed for anyone—still less two men successively—to pass on from memory; it was never shown that either Turpin or Labrusse had the opportunity to take complete notes; it appears that in both May and September Baranès reported to M. Dides *before* seeing Labrusse; and he alleged that the Communists already had far more information than Labrusse gave him.

Most of his Defence Committee reports were plainly derived from the Mons notes to which it seemed likely he had some other access. But some items were not. Could these have come from the official minutes, based on the notes and (until June 1954) circulated to Ministers? Or from the preparatory documents (also circulated until that time)? Or from M. Mons' brief comments to some of his staff on the meetings themselves? The point was hotly disputed, both in public and in camera. The accused officials naturally wished to suggest other possible sources; the Right clamoured to hang the guilt on a Minister.

3. *The case for the extreme Right.* In its popular form this was pure propaganda, which bore no relation to truth or even plausibility. Thus the Poujadist journal *Fraternité Française* on 7 April charged that the 'Mendès–Mitterrand group' had given secrets to their *Progressiste* friends to destroy the Laniel government, and had 'prefabricated' both the September leakage and the attack on M. Mons, in order to provide scapegoats and a diversion. This asks us to believe that secret information was given away, in May by politicians out of power who had no access to it, in June by means unexplained, and in September by officials (*ex hypothesi* innocent) who sacrificed themselves to protect their Ministers!

Maître Tixier-Vignancour was on stronger ground in contrasting the treatment of the May 1954 leakages by the two cabinets. He claimed that M. Laniel had prosecuted *L'Express*, punished a colonel who had given it information, dismissed two *Agence France-Presse* officials who had reproduced its articles in a press survey, and dismissed M. Jacquet: while M. Mendès-France had quashed the prosecution, freed the colonel, dismissed the AFP chief for not reinstating his subordinates, and offered M. Jacquet an embassy. The Right at first treated M. Mitterrand as a much maligned man: but when he refused to dissociate himself from M. Mendès-France, they again turned on him, and M. Dides even declared that the 'invisible hand' denounced by M. Mitterrand was really his own.[13] Me Tixier-Vignancour contended that the new Ministers had known all about Labrusse and the source of the leakages, but had protected their allies of yesterday, and tried to use the affair against M. Martinaud-Déplat, the chief anti-*Mendésiste* in the Radical Party. The reticent M. Vallois was assumed to be the agent of M. Pelabon and the Prime Minister. But this theory is disproved by the fact that the documents concealed by M. Vallois were accessible to the extreme Right; and by the absurdity of assuming that M. Mendès-France would protect an official whose discovery could alone clear his own cabinet of domestic and foreign suspicion.

Me Tixier-Vignancour seized every opportunity to throw suspicion on republican politicans. He claimed that a Minister must have informed *France-Observateur* both in July 1953 (when its article was published before M. Mons' report was complete) and in May 1954 (when inter-ministerial committees, not attended by M. Mons, had preceded the Defence Committee meeting, which was still in progress when the article was set up). But the insinuations of the Right, like the suspicions of the Left, meet the same difficulty: there were leakages under two governments.

Only one Minister, M. Edgar Faure, served in the Defence Committee in both cabinets, and only three other persons attended the three meetings from which leakages had occurred: the Cabinet Secretary M. Ségalat (whose brief notes bore no relation to those of Baranès); the Committee Secretary M. Mons; and the President of the Republic. M. Faure was indeed accused by Baranès, both to the DST, and to his protectors MM. Baylot and Dides— though the latter preferred to cast M. Mitterrand as villain of the piece. But he could not have been the source of Baranès' reports: he had not taken extensive notes. And all 'guilty Ministers' theories are open to other fatal objections. None of M. Mendès-France's Ministers would have informed the Right: to discredit the cabinet in this way would ruin all its members. If one of them were informing the Communists, why should the latter insert Baranès as an unnecessary and therefore dangerous extra contact? Above all, why did Defence Committee leakages cease abruptly with the arrest of the four defendants in September 1954?

---

[13] M. Mitterrand charged M. Dides with cowardice for not making these accusations when he was present; M. Dides challenged the Minister to a duel; the latter replied that he did not fight guttersnipes. Duelling is illegal in France.

4. *The case for the DST.* M. Wybot was no ordinary witness: he was head of French counter-espionage. But his case was flimsy. M. Mons had failed after two warnings to secure his papers; he had concealed the existence of his notes from M. Mendès-France in July, and said they were burned in September (only admitting their survival next day when he realised his aide Colonel Ruellan knew about them); and the famous recorded conversation showed he was guilty. This had not been admitted in evidence, but M. Wybot had it circulated to persons of influence, so M. Mons' counsel themselves put it before the court. M. Mons claimed that in it he had been defending his subordinates and his Secretariat. He had not believed that the leakages could originate there, for until 23 September he had not known how very full they were. He had himself initiated every security improvement at the Secretariat. He never told M. Wybot he had burned his notes: nothing stopped him from doing so, but he had kept and revealed them.

His strongest point was that on 2 July he had told M. Mendès-France of the May leakages which so many others had concealed: this decisive aid to the investigation certainly clears him of any deliberate treason or plot. His weakest was his failure to produce his notes on the same occasion, which set the inquiry back two months, during which slander and scandal had free play. He said he could not speak without authority from the President of the Republic. But when he did seek this authority (eleven weeks later, and only *after* telling the DST that the notes survived), the President at once told him to give them, not to the police, but to M. Mendès-France.

Can his conduct in July, with its strange mixture of frankness and reticence, be accounted for? M. Wybot's charge of Communism is no explanation; it found no credence outside the DST; and it was belied by M. Mons' whole career. He began as an anti-Communist trade unionist like his friend M. Baylot; resisted Communist penetration in Paris at the liberation; was denounced by the Communists when Resident at Tunis; and had a record at the Defence Secretariat incompatible with Communist sympathies. His character witnesses ranged from government Socialists like ex-President Auriol and M. Ramadier to Right-wing leaders like M. Bidault and Marshal Juin. M. Mendès-France however, while rejecting the charge of Communism, condemned M. Mons' 'incomprehensible' silence in July.

Yet the explanation may be simple: that M. Mons, while not plotting against the new Ministry, shared his Right-wing friends' suspicions of it. Speculation may go further. The Prefect of Police was a close friend and a fervent anti-Communist; he also held a high security post and was at that moment verifying (as he claimed) or concocting (as the Left charged) Baranès' reports of Defence Committee meetings. When M. Baylot lost his official post, he asked for a job in the Secretariat for his son-in-law, who—

on M. Mons' insistence and despite protests from the Ministry of the Interior—was appointed on 10 September, the very day of the next Committee. M. Wybot, who had held his position under many governments, might wish not to endanger it by openly championing one political faction. His early interrogations apparently suggested M. Mons was involved in an anti-government plot; but later he brought his charges of Communism (which he also levelled against Baranès who was probably, and M. Vallois who was almost certainly far closer to the anti-Mendès Right than to the Communist Party). The most dramatic moment of the whole case came when Labrusse appealed to M. Mons: 'You know the truth. Whom are you protecting?' 'No one' was the reply; and M. Mons specifically denied giving information to M. Baylot. There was no scrap of direct evidence to contradict him.

VII. IMPLICATIONS

The case throws light on the behaviour of police, judges and politicians in France.

Discretion was a neglected virtue in the administration. Left-wing civil servants tried to torpedo a government which they found too warlike; right-wing police officers retaliated against one which they thought unduly pacific. Turpin and Labrusse fed information to one set of politicians, Dides to another. When M. Wybot criticised M. Duval, this report to his Minister came into the hands of Maître Tixier-Vignancour. The DST chief himself circulated his case against M. Mons to selected personalities (not including defence counsel). M. Mendès-France learned all about a secret session of the court. Police reports to the Prefecture never reached their destination, but became known to reactionary politicians. These practices were the consequence of political intrigue and inter-service rivalry, both ferociously pursued. Such feuds ruin orderly administration. Yet there are compensations for the damage.

In France, where many citizens await an opportunity to upset the regime, the problem of subversion is both graver and wider than in Britain or America; it involves whole parties and leagues, not merely sects and individual agents. For the security police to concern themselves with politics is a duty, not a misdemeanour. They ought of course to keep out of the ordinary party conflict; but the temptations are great and the line is hard to draw, especially when that conflict is organised and supervised by their own Prefect and Minister. Thus the French police service develops mixed motives as well as wide powers and arbitrary habits; and it may be just as well that it is divided against itself, so that each force can expose and counteract the abuses perpetrated by its rival. Had the DST alone been concerned, M. Mons' position would have been unenviable; had there been no one to oppose the

69

Prefecture, MM. Mendès-France and Mitterrand would have found themselves defenceless.

If the police service was riddled with politics, the judges were proud of their independence of the administration. The first examining magistrate demanded (though he did not get) information about M. Boris and two other members of the Prime Minister's secretariat.[14][f] The second annoyed the DST by linking the Stéphane and Martinet cases to the others. The President of the court complained to the High Council of the Judiciary about M. Wybot's attack on M. Duval, rebuked the DST chief for circulating his denunciation of M. Mons, criticised the Prefect of Police for not giving the information about M. Boris, condemned the government for not asking the Assembly to raise M. d'Astier's parliamentary immunity, and generally distributed his censures lavishly over the administration. Not all French judges at home, and very few overseas, have shown such determined independence, or such scepticism about the police (few indeed have had as much cause). That such qualities constitute a safeguard for liberty has often been shown. Yet in some respects the conduct of these magistrates was not reassuring. They asserted their authority vigorously against delinquents of the Left, while treating those of the extreme Right with 'comprehension', and allowing Maître Tixier-Vignancour to use the court for his outrageous political smear campaign. The notorious laxity of French rules of evidence made this easy, and no doubt M. Niveau de Villedary tried conscientiously to hold the scales even; but his sense of balance left much to be desired.

Few dangers menace a democratic regime more insidiously than hostile judges. In Weimar Germany murderers of democratic politicians, or leaders of revolt like Hitler, were acquitted or given derisory sentences, while a pacifist journalist who revealed illegal rearmament was condemned for treason. French justice is, of course, in nothing like so bad a state; and moreover its errors can be discussed much more freely than in this country. *L'Express* could publish articles severely condemning the course the trial was being allowed to take; for French magistrates cannot invoke the thunders of contempt of court in the arbitrary manner of their English brethren. This vulnerability to criticism has its dangers, yet perhaps it too is just as well; for sometimes judges and public seem to need reminding that there are enemies of freedom outside the administration as well as within it.

These external enemies are to be found on both political extremes; and

---

[14] He wrote informally to a Prefecture official, informing neither the Prefect nor the Minister of the Interior. The latter, thinking the request unusual and the procedure improper, asked the magistrate for his reasons; he neither replied nor issued—as he might have done—a formal legal demand.

[f] Georges Boris (1888–1960) worked closely with Léon Blum before the war, with General de Gaulle's Minister of the Interior in London, and with Mendès-France in 1944–5 and again during the latter's premiership.

in France as elsewhere the far Right feeds on the menace of Communism. In a land where a quarter of the voters are Communist, how can they be excluded from government service? yet how can they safely be admitted to it? No more than other democracies has France solved the problem; no less than others has she suffered from its unscrupulous exploitation in party politics. In the 'pigeon plot' of 1952, M. Martinaud-Déplat, then Minister of Justice, his friend the late M. Brune at the Interior, and M. Baylot at the Prefecture, brought conspiracy charges against leading and rank-and-file Communists, which were not sustained by the judiciary.[15] Before the military court in 1956 M. Baylot referred somewhat complacently to the charge of McCarthyism which had been levelled against him, while M. Martinaud-Déplat pointed with pride to his once famous denunciation of fellow-travellers, sex-perverts, intellectuals, and other undesirable citizens.

In 1954 the leakages case gave a second opportunity. The Indo-China war was dragging on, more and more hated in the country, rotting public life with scandal and corruption, paralysing France in military and international affairs; yet as M. Stéphane said in court, Ministers and officials who explained in private the impossibility of victory would proclaim its imminence in public next day. On the Left, ideologists doubted whether the French cause was wholly just; elsewhere, practical men wondered if the game were worth the candle (it was not denied that the whole Defence Secretariat staff had thought it folly to fight on). A conscientious journalist might well feel it both his patriotic and his professional duty to reveal the truth about *la sale guerre*. But to the fire-eaters of the extreme Right this seemed a stab in the back of the French Army (though as a matter of fact the back belonged mostly to Vietnamese and Foreign Legionaries). The emotional power of such legends is only too familiar from the German experience; and in the bitterness of defeat the leakages provided a ready-made set of scapegoats. In addition, they permitted a political attack—but this time not on the Communists but against all the opponents of the Indo-China war. That attack miscarried; and by 1956 louder shouts had drowned the voices of the Legendres, Baylots, and Martinaud-Déplats. They had been superseded by men more violent in abuse, more vulgar in vocabulary, and even less inhibited in choice of targets. These were the propagandists of the *Mouvement Poujade*.

[15] M. Duval was examining magistrate. Several Communist leaders were charged with conspiracy. M. Duclos was arrested (illegally) and found to have two pigeons in his car: the authorities said they were carrier pigeons, while he claimed they were his dinner. A military communications expert, a natural history professor, and the President of the Pigeon Fanciers Federation solemnly examined the celebrated birds and decided they were eating pigeons. M. Duclos was released; the minor demonstrators were (after three years) acquitted or given derisory sentences; the Assembly would not waive the immunity of the accused leaders.

For the militant Right, the last three years had already witnessed betrayals without parallel; treason in Paris explained all the defeats; and now negotiations in Algeria, a 'portion of France' with a million European inhabitants, threatened their country with economic disaster, national dishonour, and the disappearance of French influence in the world. This outlook (akin to but far stronger than Conservative feelings over Ulster half a century ago) found its most vigorous expression in Poujadism, which recruited many former Indo-China soldiers disillusioned with the tamed and shop-soiled Gaullists. When M. Mollet visited Algiers as Prime Minister in February 1956, he was met by violent rioting; the organiser was an *ancien d'Indochine* who had been a leader of the Arc de Triomphe demonstration two years before, and was now a Poujadist deputy. And among the three members attached to the Poujadists, their potential link with the parliamentary Conservatives, are both *M. le commissaire* Dides and Maître Tixier-Vignancour.

The crypto-Poujadist exploitation of the leakages case now had a practical aim, besides mere revenge. In 1954 M. Mendès-France had ended the Far Eastern war and opened negotiations in Tunisia. In 1955 M. Faure had tried to compromise in Morocco; and though he was frustrated by flagrant indiscipline in the Cabinet, the majority and the local administration, the only result was far more drastic concession in far more humiliating circumstances a few weeks later. Now Algeria was the scene of a savage war; and the groups, journals and men who had advocated negotiation in Indo-China before it was too late, were renewing their agitation. These writers, journalists and intellectuals were paralysing the country's will to fight with their criticism of authority, their denunciation of repression, their chatter about liberty, and equality, and fraternity. As for M. Mendès-France, his reputation alone would encourage resistance as long as he remained a political force. So both must be destroyed.

But in a straightforward debate on these themes the Right would have been at a disadvantage; their intransigence had too plainly caused disaster in a past too recent to be forgotten. The leakages case enabled them to turn the argument from general considerations of justice and policy to personal and emotional problems of loyalty and conduct. Instead of having to explain away ugly methods of repression, criticisms in the rest of the world, the ruin of their policy elsewhere, the Right could mount the personal slander campaign which reactionaries always find so congenial. Men of the Left had tried to alert public opinion; generals gladly seized on these indiscretions to explain their own defeat; and joyfully the Right hastened to traduce the motives and character of their enemies, stigmatising *France-Observateur* as 'the *Journal Officiel* of treason', identifying counsel for Turpin and Labrusse with the Communist who betrayed a lorry-load of arms to the Algerian rebels,[16] exploiting both the fear of hidden Communism and the deep-rooted French suspicion of all politicians for their campaign of smear and insinuation. If M. Mendès-France and the intellectual Left could be linked with Communism, accused of betraying secrets and being in touch with the enemy, attacked for stabbing the army in the back, they could be discredited with public opinion. Negotiation in Algeria would be prevented by destroying those who might have conducted it.[g]

The reactionaries had nothing to lose by this debasement of the political coinage. If the prestige of French democracy suffered, so much the better.[17] The strong hand in North Africa, long overdue for local reasons, might also have welcome repercussions at home; for repression soon becomes attractive to those who practise it.[18] Reason, justice and charity do not flourish in an atmosphere of police raids, seizure of journals, war hysteria, and treason trials. The outsider, contemplating France's recent colonial record, might well find candidates for impeachment among the men who had led the country to disaster. But it is the men who tried to save what was left from the wreck that the reactionary extremists clamour to send to the High Court. Thus to force the Left on to the defensive was the political purpose of the *affaire des fuites*.[h]

[16] Me Tixier-Vignancour shouted to them in court, 'He's one of your crowd'. The President would not let them reply.

[17] *Me Tixier-Vignancour:* No need to go into that; the regime is low enough already.
M. Mitterrand: You are seeing to that.
Me Tixier-Vignancour: Oh, enthusiastically! And I shall continue until the regime disappears! [*Le Monde*, 26 April 1956.]

[18] M. Bourdet, editor of *France-Observateur* and a distinguished Resister, was arrested for demoralising the army by his articles on Algeria—and *taken to prison in handcuffs* (though the Prime Minister ordered his release). M. Marrou, a distinguished and non-political Catholic professor at the Sorbonne, wrote in *Le Monde* a protest against some of the abuses of repression in North Africa; the police after waiting a week searched his home and *seized all the letters he had received on the subject.*

[g] The case was exploited by psychological warfare officers serving in Algeria to turn conscripts against the regime: for a (sympathetic) fictional account see J. Lartéguy, *The Centurions* (below, chap. 10), p. 272. The connection with the events of May 1958 (chap. 7) is obvious.

[h] Some Communists may have connived with the extreme Right. A prominent ex-Communist, who knew Baranès very well, identifies him as one of the Party's security cadres; implies that his Party chief must have known of his police contacts and used him as a double agent; and maintains that the documents were forged and passed to Dides so that they would deny Mendès-France right-wing votes and so either defeat him or force him into dependence on the Party's support. Pierre Hervé, *Dieu et César sont-ils communistes?* (Paris, La Table Ronde, 1956), pp. 48–51. The DST also believed that the documents were forged by Baranès at the Party's orders to spread suspicion among politicians and between France and her allies: see their photocopied report in C. Angeli and P. Gillet, *La Police et la politique 1944–1954* (Paris, Grasset, 1967), at p. 331.

5　The Mitterrand affair[a]

Scandals and mysteries in public life are not confined to France. But they grow more thick and lush in French soil than anywhere else. About every other year a major 'affair' seems to spring up, and now the Fifth Republic has one of its own, the Mitterrand affair.

In the past, scandals have generally been of two types. In the first, Republican governments have discovered (or purported to discover) plots to overthrow the political system by violence. In the second type, right-wing enemies of the Republic have tried to discredit democratic politicians in the hope that the mud would stick to the Republic itself. The latest affair could fit into either category, depending on whose story you accept.

The two central figures are M. François Mitterrand, an ex-minister and outspoken critic of the Algerian war, and M. Robert Pesquet, a former Poujadist deputy. Eleven days ago M. Mitterrand claimed that his car had been followed and shot up, and that he had barely escaped with his life. A week later M. Pesquet revealed that he had been in the pursuing car, but claimed that the attack was a fake, arranged at M. Mitterrand's own request.

There are several theories about these melodramatic events. One is that Mitterrand did organise a bogus attack on himself to lend colour to stories of a plot against the Republic: a scandal of the first type. The next theory is that he fell into a trap laid by Pesquet to discredit him: a scandal of the second type. Yet another theory is that Pesquet himself proposed the fake attack, claiming he had orders to kill Mitterrand which he dared not openly disobey.

I don't pretend to know what really happened. But two points stand out *whatever* the truth of the matter. First, M. Mitterrand withheld from the examining magistrate not only M. Pesquet's name but even the fact that he knew an attack was coming. This was very unwise, for it gave his career and reputation into M. Pesquet's hands. And if he had really instigated the whole affair himself, then it showed not just unwisdom but unbelievable stupidity. His many enemies have never accused him of that.

Secondly, whichever story is true, the plotter evidently thought that an attempt to murder a political leader in the middle of Paris made a likely-sounding plot. And unhappily this belief was all too plausible. For French 'counter-terrorists' have carried out many attacks in recent years, first in

[a] Broadcast in 'At Home and Abroad', 27 October 1959.

North Africa, later in Western Europe, without ever being punished. A liberal-minded French newspaper owner in Morocco was shot dead in 1955; the chief suspect is out on bail. An attempt to kill the commander-in-chief in Algiers cost the life of his ADC; the chief criminal, though known, has not been convicted. A month ago the Belgian frontier police arrested another former Poujadist deputy, said to be a friend of M. Pesquet, for smuggling bombs in his car. And the very day before the Mitterrand affair a leading Gaullist announced that 'killer commandos' had crossed the Spanish border with a list of victims in their pockets.

For the Algerian war has poisoned the political climate. By 1958 responsible men had come to think that revolution was their public duty. They believed that the future of France depended on holding Algeria, and that all talk of negotiation was defeatist and indeed downright treasonable. So they incited soldiers and police to defy the legal government, and profited politically from the underworld activities of the extremists. And now the chickens are coming home to roost. Successful conspiracy breeds new conspiracies. Loyal Gaullists complain that last week the General's opponents were planning demonstrations in Algiers, manœuvres in Parliament and pressure from the army in order to force him to change his ministers and his policy. Does the Mitterrand affair somehow fit into this story? Perhaps the Algiers extremists planned to take advantage of the confusion for a little private enterprise of their own. We may never find out, for if it is true to type the inquiry will become even more confused as it proceeds.

Whatever the truth, the present climate of Paris politics is plainly unhealthy. Yet Ireland once poisoned the political life of Britain as Algeria is poisoning that of France. Our army successfully defied the legal government, and our public men were threatened by forgers and perjurers and even assassins. In Britain these effects did not last. Perhaps the consequences of the Algerian war will prove equally temporary in France. But I'm afraid it would be too much to hope that the Mitterrand affair will be the last scandal from Paris.

APPENDIX TO CHAPTER 5 (ADDED 1969)

Pesquet was able to prove—by a registered letter posted before the attack which accurately predicted the supposed victim's behaviour—that Mitterrand had known what was going to happen before the incident, and had concealed the knowledge from the magistrate when he filed charges. Mitterrand was therefore himself accused of contempt of court, and suffered political ostracism for a time; but the case has never come to trial.

Disturbances, of which the 'killer commandos' and the Mitterrand incident were a part, may have been intended to coincide with riots in Algiers which the military would not prevent, and with a parliamentary assault on the Government organised to replace Debré with a prime minister more sympathetic to the settlers' cause, Georges Bidault (see above, chapter 4). If there was such a plot, it failed through bad co-ordination: the settlers were not yet ready to set up their barricades (they did so three months later), nor the soldiers to mutiny (they did so 18 months later) and the parliamentary attack collapsed—only nine deputies resigned from the Gaullist parliamentary party and four of them promptly asked (in vain) to be readmitted. (Among the four was Delbecque, and among the other five were Arrighi, Biaggi and Thomazo: see below, chapter 7.)

In August 1963 the State Security Court condemned Pesquet *in absentia* to 20 years imprisonment for having led an extreme-right OAS terrorist group in Normandy, and he went into exile in Spain. He wrote to *Le Monde* in a letter published—in part—on 24 November 1965: 'It is strange in the first place that for six years the papers concerning the bogus attack in the Rue de L'Observatoire have stayed mysteriously locked in a drawer while neither the Government, usually so eager to strike, nor Maître Tixier-Vignancour my "defence" counsel have thought of getting them out...Then it is even stranger that neither the Government, despite its toughness, nor Maître Tixier-Vignancour, who is a candidate for the presidency, have felt the necessity to make the slightest allusion to the "attack" in the Rue de L'Observatoire, or to recall to M. François Mitterrand, another candidate (and one of the most dangerous in the presidential campaign), that he is still charged with contempt of court...I was persuaded in an ingenious way that what was necessary to defeat the Gaullist policy of scuttle was to use a great political scandal leading to a great political trial to accuse the regime by publishing a number of dossiers that Maître Tixier-Vignancour claimed to have in his possession, particularly that of the Bazooka, allegedly proving the guilt of Michel Debré in the assassination some time ago of Commandant Rodier, Salan's aide.

'I had then told Judge Simon that the organiser of the attack was Maître Tixier-Vignancour, helped by M. Jean-Marie Le Pen. I was nothing in this business but a disciplined executant and nothing was done without the strict supervision of this lawyer in every detail.

'Wishing to allot to everybody in complete equity his share of the responsibility, I have told Judge Simon that if M. François Mitterrand was an active and deliberate [*conscient*] participant in the bogus attack, he agreed to take part in this comedy with the aim of defeating a genuine plot against his life [*contre sa personne*] in which he firmly believed. I have told Judge Simon that in 1963 when I was in exile in Spain I was visited at San Sebastian by the French police and it was proposed to me inter alia to return to France in exchange for my total silence about the background [*dessous*] of the "Mitterrand Affair".'

A day earlier Mitterrand had commented on the affair, pointing out that in six years he had been given no judicial opportunity to defend himself and suggesting that the incident was a plot against him by the unofficial political police forces he had opposed when he was Minister of Justice in 1956 (*Le Monde*, 24 November 1965). Tixier claimed that he could not discuss Pesquet's letter because he knew of the affair only as a lawyer and was bound by professional secrecy, but he suggested that the timing of the letter—six years after the affair and ten days before the first ballot in the presidential election—made it an obvious foul blow in the election campaign. Le Pen alleged that Pesquet himself had belonged to an unofficial police force which was no doubt responsible for the affair. He said that he and Tixier (then friends, though they were soon to quarrel furiously over control of the extreme Right movement in France) had been delighted by the affair and had sought to exploit it politically against Mitterrand who had played no part at all in organising it. *Le Monde* noted that both Mitterrand and Pesquet had referred to the Bazooka Plot, another mysterious scandal which had never come to trial, and wondered editorially 'if the one case has obstructed the other for more than six years'. (All from *Le Monde*, 29 November 1965.) Because of other passages in his letter attacking the magistrates concerned with the original case, Pesquet was himself prosecuted early in 1966 for contempt of court.

6 The Ben Barka affair

I. CAST OF CHARACTERS

Inspector ALCAYDE: police officer responsible for Moroccans in France.
Madame ARNOUL: friend who sheltered Georges Figon on the run.
Jo ATTIA: well-known gangster leader, friend of Figon and Boucheseiche.
Jacques AUBERT: *directeur de cabinet* of Roger Frey, Minister of the Interior.
Colonel BEAUMONT: director of research at the SDECE.
Abdelkader BEN BARKA: brother of Mehdi.
Mehdi BEN BARKA: exiled leader of the Moroccan opposition party, UNFP; the quarry.
Philippe BERNIER: left-wing journalist friend of Ben Barka; invited him to Paris. Acquitted.
Maître BIAGGI: right-wing lawyer for Lopez.
Georges BOUCHESEICHE: gangster and brothel-owner. Convicted in absentia; life sentence.
Commissaire BOUVIER: head of the Criminal Brigade at the Prefecture of Police.
François BRIGNEAU: right-wing journalist, editor of *Minute*.
Commissaire CAILLE: a senior police official at the Prefecture of Police.
'CASAMAYOR': Judge Fuster, the *Monde*'s judicial columnist.
Nadercine CHALLAL: Algerian author of article on the case.
Larbi CHTOUKI: pseudonym of high Moroccan police officer. Convicted in absentia; life sentence.
Pierre CLOSTERMANN: Gaullist politician, friend of King Hassan.
'COHEN': name of ticket-holder on flight to Morocco—Ben Barka's ticket?
Jacques DEROGY: *L'Express* journalist who interviewed Lemarchand.
M. DESHAURMES: subordinate of Le Roy at SDECE; dismissed.
Colonel Ahmed DLIMI: head of the Moroccan police. Acquitted.
Pierre DUBAIL: gangster. Convicted in absentia; life sentence.
Thami EL AZZEMOURI: Moroccan student, friend of Ben Barka who accompanied him to the rendezvous.
EL HOUSSEINI: Moroccan police doctor.
El Ghali EL MAHI: former manager of Oufkir's household; 'commercial student' in Paris, drawing police pay. Acquitted.
Edgar FAURE: ex-premier, became Gaullist minister in 1966; friend of Ben Barka.
Max FERNET: Director of the Police Judiciaire at the Prefecture of Police.
Georges FIGON: gangster with intellectual pretensions. Found shot; verdict—suicide.
Colonel FINVILLE: professional name of Marcel Le Roy.
Jacques FOCCART: secretary-general for African and Malagasy affairs at the Elysée since 1958; de Gaulle's secret service chief.
Georges FRANJU: director of the film Ben Barka was to advise on.

Roger FREY: Minister of the Interior.

Gerald GOHIER: journalist on *Minute* (and police informer?).

General GUIBAUD: appointed head of SDECE when the scandal broke.

HASSAN II: King of Morocco.

Maître HAYOT: Lopez's chief counsel; withdrew.

General JACQUIER: head of SDECE since 1962; retired prematurely.

Maître Pierre LEMARCHAND: Figon's friend and lawyer; Gaullist deputy; recruited 'barbouzes' to fight OAS in Algeria in 1962.

Commandant LENOIR: SDECE officer; suspended.

Julien LE NY: gangster. Convicted in absentia; life sentence.

Marcel LE ROY: head of SDECE Service 7. Acquitted of 'failing to help a person in danger'.

LIWER: currency crook, friend of Jo Attia.

Antoine LOPEZ: traffic officer at Orly; secret service agent; 8 years sentence for 'illegally detaining' Ben Barka.

Commissaire MARCHAND: duty police officer who first took the case.

Jean MARVIER: free-lance journalist, friend of Figon.

Colonel MORVAN: a senior SDECE officer.

Prince MOULAY ALI: King Hassan's brother and Ambassador to Paris.

General Mohamed OUFKIR: Moroccan Minister of the Interior. Convicted in absentia; life sentence.

Jean PALISSE: gangster. Convicted in absentia; life sentence.

Maurice PAPON: Prefect of Police.

Judge PEREZ: magistrate who tried the case.

Georges POMPIDOU: Prime Minister.

André SIMBILLE: Prefecture police official, Fernet's assistant director.

Louis SOUCHON: police officer, head of narcotics squad at the Prefecture of Police; delivered Ben Barka to Boucheseiche; 6 years sentence for 'illegally detaining' Ben Barka.

M. TAHIRI: the UNFP's Paris representative and Ben Barka's host.

Maître TIXIER-VIGNANCOUR: right-wing lawyer, counsel for Lopez.

M. TOUBAS: the public prosecutor.

Jean VIGNAUD: crook; friend of Figon; police informer?

Roger VOITOT: police officer at Prefecture, Souchon's assistant. Acquitted.

Judge ZOLLINGER: the examining magistrate in the case.

II. THE PLOT

Mehdi Ben Barka, an exiled leader of the left-wing Moroccan opposition and organiser of the forthcoming Tricontinental Revolutionary Congress in Havana, left his Geneva home for the last time on the morning of Friday 29 October 1965. He landed at Orly airport, left his bag in a friend's apartment in the rue Jean Mermoz, arranged to go to the theatre with another friend that night, had coffee on the Champs Elysées, and left by taxi for St Germain des Près where he had a lunch appointment to discuss making a film about decolonisation. Waiting for him in that classic left-wing rendez-vous, the fashionable Brasserie Lipp,[1] were three Frenchmen: a film director, Georges Franju; an impecunious left-wing journalist, Philippe Bernier; and an ex-convict with literary pretensions and contacts, Georges Figon. Waiting for him outside were six others: one secret service agent, two police officers, and three gangsters.

Just before Lipp's, Ben Barka was intercepted by the two policemen, Louis Souchon and Roger Voitot, who were in plain clothes. Although he held an Algerian diplomatic passport, when they showed their official cards he made no objection to accompanying them across the road and entering their official car. In the front seat with Souchon, who drove, was Antoine Lopez—traffic official at Orly Airport, close friend of General Oufkir the Moroccan Minister of the Interior, and informer for both the Paris narcotics squad and the French counter-espionage service, the SDECE; he was wearing dark glasses and a false moustache. Ben Barka (who knew Lopez) sat in the back seat between Voitot the policeman and Julien Le Ny, a 'retired' gangster specialising in the corruption of public officials. They headed south, Lopez choosing a route which enabled the car with the other two gangsters, Jean Palisse and Pierre Dubail, to arrive first at their destination. This was the suburban home at Fontenay-le-Vicomte of Georges Boucheseiche, a childhood friend of Lopez who had a hotel in Morocco, where he was planning to set up a chain of brothels; he was also a former Gestapo agent, a police informer, and a 'retired' gang leader who had specialised in the disposal of bodies. He greeted the party in shirtsleeves and red braces, and invited Ben Barka into the house. No one knows for certain what became of the unfortunate man after that.

That afternoon and evening Lopez and Boucheseiche teleponed repeatedly from Orly to Morocco, trying to reach Oufkir or his right-hand man, Commandant Ahmed Dlimi the head of the Moroccan police. Unable to find the Minister who had personally directed the repression and 'interrogation' of Ben Barka's political friends in 1963, they left a message: 'Your guest has arrived.' When finally reached at Meknes, Oufkir said he must get in touch with 'the boss', then rang back from Fez to say he would arrive at 3 a.m. Lopez and Boucheseiche met the plane, but he was not on it. At 9 a.m. Saturday he phoned again to announce his new flight; at 2 p.m. Dlimi flew into Orly from Algiers; at 5 p.m. Oufkir himself arrived. (Later he was to say he had landed at midnight; when this was shown to be false he said he had spent the intervening hours 'on the town'.) He was met, not only by Lopez, but by two compatriots: El Ghali El Mahi, former manager of his household, who drew pay from the Moroccan police but was

---

[1] When Mitterrand was attacked (chap. 5) he was driving home from Lipp's.

living in Paris as a 'commercial student', and 'Larbi Chtouki', apparently the pseudonym of a senior Moroccan police official. Oufkir gave them Boucheseiche's telephone number and his own bag, which they took to the hotel room they had reserved for him but which he never used; meanwhile Lopez drove the General to Boucheseiche's villa at Fontenay and left him there—leaving also, at Oufkir's surprising request, the keys of his own house at Ormoy, seven kilometres away. According to the story later told publicly (but then denied) by Georges Figon, Oufkir proceeded to torture the helpless Ben Barka with a dagger he found in the house; when Boucheseiche protested, the prisoner was transported to Lopez's villa and there tied, hardly able to breathe, to the furnace in the cellar. By now Lopez had driven off with his family to Bellegarde in Loiret where they were spending the long All Saints weekend. But by his own account he was disturbed by the radio news bulletin on Ben Barka's disappearance and returned home, arriving at 10.30 p.m. to find Oufkir, Dlimi, a Moroccan police doctor named El Housseini and several of the gangsters in his house. In his original account he said that Oufkir was in a jovial mood, but later he changed his story (as he did on many points) and maintained that the General was furious.

Soon after Lopez's return, everyone left except El Houssaini, with whom he played cards. Towards midnight, Lopez said, Dlimi phoned from Orly; he collected Oufkir and Dlimi there, and brought them back to his home where he was at once sent off to bed. But peering through his window at 2 a.m. he saw a car draw up with diplomatic licence-plates from which two men emerged; all he heard of their conversation with Oufkir were the Arab words for 'plane' and 'cargo'. (An enterprising group of *Paris-Match* reporters later drove out after midnight to Orly with a trunk strapped to the roof of their car, and easily conveyed it to the loading bay of an Air France plane without interference from police or customs officials.) At 5 a.m on Sunday October 31, when Orly was still quite silent, Oufkir again wakened the traffic manager to drive him to the airport and help him look up timetables, and at 8 a.m he flew off to Geneva. Later he said he had gone there to visit his two mentally retarded children (by his former wife) who were in a nursing-home at Gstaad. But he was seen in Geneva, not in Gstaad, where the police knew nothing of his visit; and it was in Geneva that Ben Barka had lived and kept his money and papers. Dlimi, Chtouki and El Housseini flew to Casablanca by the 9.40 plane that morning, and next day Boucheseiche followed on the same flight.

No sooner had the heads of Moroccan security left France than they hastened to return, Dlimi on Monday November 1st, Oufkir on Tuesday 2nd. As King Hassan of Morocco was shortly to make an official visit to Paris, their reappearance was not surprising; and on the 3rd the French were giving a reception for four Moroccan governors who had just completed a course in Paris, preceded by a dinner given by the Moroccan Ambassador Prince Moulay Ali, the King's brother. By that time the French authorities suspected that Oufkir might be implicated in Ben Barka's disappearance. Roger Frey, the French Minister of the Interior, who was not attending the dinner, asked one of his principal officials to sound out the Moroccan Minister. Leaving the reception, one senior Frenchman murmured to another, 'He's in it'. Meanwhile, at the other end of the social scale, Palisse and Le Ny were insisting to El Mahi that they had to see the General at once. Instead El Mahi satisfied their curiosity with 10,000 francs—about £750—obtained from Dlimi, which between 3 and 4 next morning he handed to Palisse in the street; for this transaction El Mahi later provided several different explanations, the last (with documentary support belatedly sent from Morocco) involving a complicated transaction about his rent. At the Ambassador's dinner, Oufkir suddenly displayed an urgent desire to fly back to Morocco at once, and the senior French diplomat present obligingly booked seats for him and Dlimi in the name of the Quai d'Orsay. They arrived at the airport without baggage and insisted to the air hostess that they must at any cost catch the first plane. This haste was no doubt due to the dinner-time call in which the French Ambassador, phoning from Rabat to the Quai officials, had asked that Oufkir return quickly because the French community might be endangered by the public outcry at Ben Barka's disappearance. But it was a timely departure, for Lopez was arrested later that day.

With the unhampered exit of the Moroccans, one Ben Barka affair ends and another begins. The first was the Moroccan conspiracy against the opposition leader. The second concerns the conduct of the French authorities before, during and immediately after the kidnapping. And the third relates to their later activities, particularly when in January some crucial facts began to emerge. This third affair pivots on the mysterious death by shooting of the key witness, Georges Figon.

The French inquiry succeeded in establishing in considerable detail how the Moroccan plot developed. It was known to his friends—and to SDECE—that there had been several previous attempts on Ben Barka's life, and in 1964 he had told one of them, 'I can't come to Paris—it's stuffed with Moroccan policemen and I'd risk getting kidnapped at Orly itself'. But the successful conspiracy seems to have begun in the spring of 1965, when the impecunious Bernier was approached by Chtouki and offered 40 million old francs (about £30,000) to deliver to the Moroccans his good friend Ben Barka—who would then, Bernier was assured, be made a minister. Bernier claims that he refused, and never set eyes on Chtouki again; it is not disputed that he warned both Ben Barka and Colonel Sadok, the Algerian opposition leader for whom Ben Barka was to have been exchanged. Chtouki left one of his meetings with Bernier to go to a rendezvous with General Oufkir at the Hotel Crillon; according to Bernier, Oufkir, who certainly arrived in Paris that day (21 April 1965), was to discuss plans for dealing with Ben Barka with some unnamed Frenchmen. General Guibaud, by then head of SDECE, was asked in court who they were, but answered that he could not reply because national security required secrecy. The presiding judge assured him that this obligation had been waived for events connected with the Ben Barka case, but the General held his peace. The police said that their inquiries failed to establish that the meeting ever took place.

On 25 April Ben Barka met Prince Moulay Ali in Frankfurt; his terms for returning to Morocco were unacceptable to the King. On 30 April an internal SDECE memorandum—revealed only in court in October 1966—recorded that Oufkir on the King's instructions was trying to contact Ben Barka and urge his return home. This SDECE information—carefully checked, and not based on Lopez's reports—was passed neither to the police nor to the ministerial head of the service, the Prime Minister. At some time in the same month, and perhaps again in May, Chtouki and El Mahi lunched in a restaurant in the rue Oberkampf with three SDECE men: Lopez, his immediate superior Commandant Marcel Le Roy (who used the *nom de guerre* Colonel Finville), and Commandant Lenoir who worked directly to Colonel Morvan, *directeur de cabinet* of the head of the service, General Jacquier. The Frenchmen said they never mentioned Ben Barka. But the restaurant proprietor thought they had done so, either then or at another lunch in May.

As a result of the SDECE note of 30 April, Lopez was sent to Morocco on 8 May to sound his old friend General Oufkir—one of eight visits in six months, which he claimed were all quite independent of the case. (SDECE's Moroccan section supplied him with a 21-point questionnaire but the Ministry would not allow the court to see either the questions or the answers—which would perhaps have revealed that the French secret service, unlike the French President, was opposed to Ben Barka's return.) Oufkir told him that the Moroccan authorities were eager to 'recuperate' Ben Barka and willing if necessary to use 'unorthodox means'. At about the same time, perhaps because of Bernier's refusal, the Moroccans approached Boucheseiche (who would need Oufkir's goodwill to establish his projected chain of brothels). Le Ny suggested to Boucheseiche that they work through Figon, with his intellectual friends, to enlist Bernier as a contact with Ben Barka, who was thought likely to be less wary of a European than of a Moroccan contact. Figon obtained an introduction to Bernier and offered to finance the initial expenses (he borrowed the money from Chtouki) for a film on decolonisation, to be called *Basta*, which Bernier had planned, with Franju as director and Ben Barka as political adviser; it was to be shown at the Tricontinental Congress. Bernier was delighted at this chance to make money and left-wing propaganda simultaneously. On 2 September he and Figon travelled together to Cairo to see Ben Barka. At the last minute he found his passport had expired; at Figon's request, Lopez obligingly took him along to the Prefecture where it was renewed by a helpful police officer—Roger Voitot. Figon later said he was supposed to assassinate Ben Barka on this trip, using a time-bomb with a four-minute fuse hidden in his briefcase; but, fearing the Moroccans had fixed the fuse to blow up victim and murderer together, he threw the briefcase—an article Bernier claimed he never saw— into the Nile instead.

On this trip as on the next one, Bernier was later to find himself in a situation difficult to explain. His ticket and Figon's were both paid for by money given to Lopez by Chtouki, who himself flew to Cairo on a later plane that day; Bernier, who said he never saw Chtouki after May, denied he knew the source of the money. Lopez did his best to make Bernier's situation worse, alleging that he must have seen Chtouki at Orly, and had stayed at the same hotel as Chtouki in Cairo; but after some months he retracted the first statement and an investigation, on which Bernier insisted, disproved the second. Ben Barka accepted the film proposal, and again met Bernier and Figon in Geneva on 20 September; the day before, Chtouki flew to Geneva and Lopez to Morocco. Again Bernier was carefully framed. Figon had arranged to pick up Franju and catch the 8 a.m. plane, but Bernier had a Paris appointment and went instead at 11 a.m., buying his own tourist class ticket at Orly. Yet investigators found a reservation for the 8 a.m. plane in his name and Franju's made out on the 18th, and noting as his phone number one which belonged to Boucheseiche whom Bernier claimed not to know. Figon, who did not want Ben Barka to see Franju yet, did not pick up Franju who stayed at home; Figon himself switched to the 11 a.m. flight, which Lopez held for him when he was late. Paid for by Chtouki, he travelled first-class, and introduced Lopez to another first-class passenger whom he named as Maître Pierre Lemarchand. Lopez said the introduction was in the form, 'You see, Lopez, that I'm protected', but gave varying versions of the reply; Lemarchand's companion (sister-in-law of his client in Geneva) denied that 'protection' was mentioned at all.

Up to this point Lopez had kept his organisation informed. On 17 May he reported to Le Roy that Oufkir was prepared to use 'unorthodox means' to 'recuperate' Ben Barka. On 22 September he reported that the 'unusual team' recruited by the Moroccans had visited Ben Barka, whose recovery was for them a 'permanent objective', at Cairo and at Geneva. Le Roy, who worked in the Research or information-gathering branch of SDECE, thought both reports worth passing on to the other two branches, Exploitation and Counter-Espionage. And there they stopped. Once again, neither the Prime Minister nor the police were told. All the senior police officers who gave evidence—the director of the Sûreté Nationale, the director of Renseignements Généraux at the Prefecture, and the Prefect of Police—agreed that if they had had this information they would have taken measures to protect Ben Barka. But the head of Counter-Espionage (responsible for SDECE's contacts with the police) was never asked to explain why the reports were not passed on. Le Roy's chief, Colonel Beaumont, later told the court that Le Roy had sent them forward not because they seemed alarming but because they gave new information which might be useful: the identity of a foreign agent, Chtouki, and the pseudonym under which Ben Barka often travelled. (The head of Renseignements Généraux said the police had known the pseudonym for two years. Their source? SDECE.)

Still determined to meet Franju, Ben Barka arranged a new rendezvous for early October, but there was a muddle over dates in which Figon again seems to have played his part. As a result Figon flew to Geneva with the film contract on 6 October without either Bernier or Franju; instead his travelling companion (according to Lopez) was Chtouki. Lopez himself went two days later, accompanied by Georges Boucheseiche; it is said that Le Ny was also there. Ben Barka's friends later suggested that only his departure for Djakarta saved him on this occasion.

At this point the plot thickens—and the information thins out. On 8 October Lopez reported his trip to Geneva, saying reassuringly that he had learned Ben Barka was to return to Morocco next month. He did not mention Boucheseiche, whose presence was revealed only a year later after investigations by Le Roy's counsel; 'that trip has rather gone out of my mind', was Lopez's explanation. He also belatedly identified the Lemarchand of the 20 September flight as a lawyer, Gaullist deputy for Yonne, close friend of M. Frey, and former head of the 'barbouzes' (the unofficial force recruited to fight the OAS extremists in Algiers in 1961–2); Le Roy said this information was never conveyed to him, but only to a colleague who 'forgot it'. On the 10th, Figon, apparently alarmed that the Moroccans meant to drop him without paying, gave Lopez a blackmailing letter—which was to be passed on to the Moroccans but clearly threatened Lopez and the SDECE as well. Figon warned that unless he promptly received 20,000 francs, the first instalment of 100,000, he would 'spill the beans to the press'. On the 12th Lopez provided a substantial report informing his superior of Figon's blackmail letter, and warning that the Moroccans' intention was not merely to contact Ben Barka but to 'kidnap and perhaps eliminate him'. Le Roy now instructed Lopez to break with Figon, for (he said) he would not allow contacts with criminals. Thus he admittedly knew Figon's background, and indeed he was later to claim that all Figon's information was merely worthless gossip from a 'liar and thug'. On this ground, and whether or not under orders, he passed on none of Lopez's new information to his superior officers until November 12, well after the kidnapping. Thus the first two reports admittedly went beyond Le Roy to an unknown level at which they stopped. At the moment when they began to become more sinister, it is officially maintained that one intelligence officer, acting alone, both withheld his information from his own superiors, and (by telling Lopez to break with Figon) cut himself off from receiving any more.

The Moroccans did not pay up, and on 12 October Figon told the whole story to François Brigneau, the editor of the least reliable and most successful of Parisian scandal-sheets, the right-wing anti-Gaullist *Minute*. Brigneau later said he had not believed the story, but he kept in close touch with Figon, who at this point seems to have turned to publicity or blackmail as consolation prizes for losing the kidnapping money. There were indeed later reports that through Lopez the Moroccans were organising a new scheme, excluding Figon, to approach Ben Barka with a bogus offer to sell arms. On the 19th, 25th and 26th Lopez telephoned to Dlimi in Morocco. On the 20th, Chtouki flew from Geneva to Paris. On the 21st Le Roy gave Deshaurmes, one of his subordinates, a list with four Moroccan names; according to Le Roy in court, they were the four governors on their course, but Deshaurmes was almost sure they were Oufkir, Dlimi, Chtouki and El Mahi. Unfortunately the list was not left in Lopez's file; according to General Guibaud, Le Roy removed it on November 2 with another document (contents unspecified despite counsel's urgent demand). Deshaurmes said Le Roy asked him to draft a note for the appropriate geographical section, then changed his mind less than an hour later and said, 'Those Moroccans are certainly not coming to talk to Ben Barka but to plug him [le flinguer], don't do anything yet, I'll see. This changes everything.' Le Roy however claimed that the internal inquiry within SDECE found that all the four witnesses present recalled the phrase 'le flinguer' as coming from Deshaurmes, not from himself. The presiding judge wanted to call as witnesses the SDECE officers present at this scene, and General Guibaud was willing if the Minister consented— but the Minister refused, insisting they must stay anonymous. Deshaurmes lost his job for 'incompetence'.

On the 25th Figon and the gangsters met at one of their favourite haunts, a private bar called the Résidence Niel; also present were Lopez, El Mahi— and two of the Moroccan governors. Boucheseiche, from Morocco, flew back to Paris. The denouement was fast approaching, and it was precipitated by the victim himself. On 26 October Ben Barka called Bernier from Geneva to say he would be coming to Paris on the 29th, and to propose a rendezvous with the elusive Franju. They agreed to meet for lunch, and Figon, seeing a last chance to lay hands on the cash, passed on the good news to Lopez— who now, Figon said, had to be blackmailed into participation by the old threat of publicity. Lopez's own story was that he saw and spoke to Chtouki at Orly on the 28th; Chtouki urged him to help and in his presence telephoned to a 'correspondent in the Ministry of the Interior', who approved; this unknown person said he had recently been introduced to Lopez, who at once assumed it was the Minister's good friend, Maître Lemarchand.

Lopez promptly set about recruiting the police officers whom Chtouki considered essential to the success of the scheme, given Ben Barka's natural wariness. He chose his old friends and close professional allies, Inspector Louis Souchon of the *Brigade Mondaine* and his young assistant Roger Voitot. Lopez, who since 1962 had been authorised by the prime minister's office to work with them in the narcotics squad, was ideally placed at Orly to help them fight the drug traffic; he had even gone further and, at Souchon's insistence, bought a hotel—in partnership with Mme Boucheseiche—for use as a 'mousetrap'. Now he was asking a return favour in the name of the SDECE to which they both knew he belonged. But what a favour! Souchon, a fifty-year-old officer with an impeccable record both before and since he joined the force, was to jeopardise his reputation, his pension and his liberty by illegally using his official position to induce a prominent foreign political leader to go to a clandestine rendezvous outside Paris. Lopez had to persuade Souchon that this was a likely way for the King of Morocco or his emissary to arrange a secret meeting with his exiled opponent.

Souchon said he had been hard to convince, even after Lopez had given him a two-hour midnight lecture on Moroccan politics to explain the importance of the operation—adding as a clincher, 'Foccart's in the know' (*au parfum*). (Jacques Foccart, under the innocent title of presidential secretary for African and Malagasy affairs, was alleged to be de Gaulle's co-ordinator of secret service activities—and the one and only Gaullist to retain his post ever since the General returned to power.[2]) But Souchon still wanted reassurance, so Lopez promised him that he would get a 'green light' from the Ministry of the Interior. According to Souchon he was phoned next morning by a man with a young deep voice who announced himself as M. Aubert—the Minister's Directeur de Cabinet—and who confirmed the assignment. But M. Aubert's voice, as everyone heard when he gave evidence in court, is a barely audible whisper.

[2] In 1969 Poher dismissed Foccart, but Pompidou reappointed him.

III. THE INVESTIGATION

Two hours later, Souchon and Voitot were outside Lipp's waiting for Ben Barka to arrive. But when he came he was not alone; his companion, Thami El Azzemouri, was a Moroccan student who was to advise him on the film. Too scared by his leader's apparent arrest to give the alarm at once, El Azzemouri went into hiding; his wife warned the Moroccan student leaders in Paris, who contacted M. Tahiri, the party's Paris representative and Ben Barka's prospective host at the theatre. Tahiri told the missing man's brother, Abdelkader Ben Barka, who alerted his French friends and especially Edgar Faure (a former prime minister who in 1955 had presided over Morocco's advance towards independence, and in 1966 was to become a Gaullist minister). Faure telephoned the *cabinet* of the Minister of the Interior on the morning of Saturday 30th, and that afternoon Inspector Alcayde of the Renseignements Généraux, who before 1962 had been responsible for Ben Barka's protection in Paris, was instructed to tell Abdelkader that no French authorities were detaining his brother, and to advise him to start a legal action. Unfortunately Abdelkader's information, obtained at third hand from the terrified El Azzemouri, was inaccurate on a crucial point; learning (wrongly as it turned out) that his brother had been intercepted at the Drugstore (next door to Lipp's) he assumed—as did the journal *Le Monde*—that this was the familiar Drugstore on the Champs Elysées (the one at St Germain des Près had opened only a couple of days before). There were other delays, partly because Ben Barka's friends were suspicious of the police (perhaps understandably given the circumstances of his disappearance) and acted less quickly than they might have. The official inquiries thus got off to a start which was both false and belated, and the authorities were subsequently to make this a major point in their own defence.

However misled the official investigators may have been, there were men both in the secret service and in the Prefecture who were better informed. But the extent to which SDECE's left hand knew what its right hand was doing was, as always, controversial. Lopez claimed the information he gave Le Roy was complete, Le Roy said it was the minimum to serve for Lopez's later defence but not enough to explain what was happening. Their differences centred on four phone calls. Lopez said he had left one message for Le Roy at the office on the Thursday afternoon, the day before the kidnapping; another with Mme Le Roy at 9 a.m. (after Le Roy normally left home) on the Friday morning to say the rendezvous was for that day; a third at the office hours later to say where Ben Barka was; and finally he had reached Le Roy and told him the whole story in a long call on Sunday morning. The Thursday call was never traced by the internal SDECE inquiry (which showed no tenderness for Le Roy, by then the official scapegoat); Mme Le Roy said Lopez left her no message on the Friday morning but she told him her husband was at Orly (and so easy to reach); Le Roy denied ever receiving the Friday lunchtime message, and said that on Sunday morning Lopez gave only a partial and incomplete account.

Lopez said the lunchtime message ran: 'Don Pedro to Thomas: the rendezvous has taken place at Fontenay, near my home'. Le Roy cast doubt on whether the call was ever made: Lopez had not mentioned it when he first gave evidence to the police, and until February 1966 no one in the office admitted to receiving it. But M. Carcassonne (alias Leduc), a Gaullist business man and former intelligence officer present at the club from which Lopez said he phoned, testified that he had called somebody from there; and the SDECE inquiry eventually unearthed a belated recollection. M. Boitel, an officer who had denied taking such a message over and over again, suddenly had it recalled to his mind by reading in *France-Soir* a reference to Fontenay-le-Vicomte (a name which had naturally appeared in many press reports in the preceding weeks). M. Boitel's superiors and colleagues testified to his unblemished reputation, but he suffered—unfortunate handicap for an intelligence officer—from lapses of memory owing to a war wound. Though he could not be sure whether he had delivered the message orally or in writing, he now became positive that he had passed it on. Le Roy found three other colleagues, including the one who was with him when he briefly visited the office that afternoon, to deny that any message was there either then or next morning. One of the three had meanwhile been suspended from SDECE, allegedly for reasons unconnected with the case.

It is not contested that at 11.36 a.m. on Sunday, October 31st, Lopez phoned Le Roy from his weekend at Bellegarde. (The call lasted 17 minutes; evidently the post office kept much better records than the secret service.) But though this time the existence of the call was not in dispute, its content was; Le Roy admitted that Lopez had mentioned the presence of Oufkir and Dlimi at his house and the references to 'plane' and 'cargo', yet affirmed there was nothing to connect them with Ben Barka. But he did not deny Lopez's account of how the conversation began: Lopez—'Have you heard the radio?' Le Roy—'It sounds Oufkirish'. And whatever he learned from the call, Le Roy failed to pass it on to his superiors—three of whom were in Paris that Sunday despite the All Saints holiday. He did indeed claim that he tried to telephone his immediate boss the Director of Research, Colonel Beaumont, but that the woman who answered said he was not there; Beaumont replied that he had left word of his whereabouts for every minute of the long weekend—and that there was no woman to answer the phone. At all events it was not until normal business resumed on Tuesday 2 November that Beaumont heard from Le Roy of Lopez's report. By 11 a.m. General Jacquier was being harried by senior ministers about the kidnapping of a prominent foreign politician in the middle of Paris, four full days before. Jacquier told Le Roy to go straight to the Prefecture and to the Ministry of the Interior and offer every assistance to the police; instead, Le Roy went off to a longstanding lunch appointment with M. Carcassonne and Commissaire Caille, head of the second (political) section of the Renseignements-Généraux division in the Prefecture of Police. Here he was most disagreeably surprised to find that Caille seemed to know all about the kidnapping and to believe that the SDECE was deeply involved in it; in particular Caille told him that Lopez had been present at the crucial moment outside Lipp's.

M. Jean Caille had been an exceptionally loyal and energetic officer in fighting the OAS extremists of the Right when, as de Gaulle moved towards accepting Algerian independence, they transferred their terrorist activities from Algiers to Paris. This episode had earned Caille the total confidence of his Minister and the bitter hatred of the fascists. It also brought him into close touch with Maître Lemarchand, who seems to have organised the struggle against the same enemies in Algeria by less legal and official means. (Lemarchand lost a libel case on this matter in January 1967). Lemarchand had been Figon's schoolfellow and was now his lawyer; through him in April 1965 Figon had tried to obtain a false passport. Here then was a Gaullist deputy, especially hated by the right-wing enemies of the regime, who was closely linked to an equally hated police officer, to the Minister of the Interior, and to one of Ben Barka's kidnappers. Whether or not Lemarchand was himself involved in the case, both the extreme Right and the criminals hoped to implicate him: the former for revenge and to damage the government, the latter to persuade the authorities to hush the whole business up. Figon in the press and Lopez in the inquiry certainly tried persistently to involve him, and some of their stories were altogether false. Thus Lopez at first claimed he had gone to the kidnapping disguised in order not to be recognised by Lemarchand who was present—but Lemarchand was able to prove he had spent the whole of that Friday in Yonne, his provincial constituency. El Mahi said Lemarchand was with the gang at the Résidence Niel on 25 October; Figon told a similar story but did not survive to give evidence, and El Mahi retracted when confronted with Lemarchand, saying he had made the statement at the instigation of Lopez. Lemarchand proved his Geneva trip on 20 September was unconnected with the case; the carefully arranged meeting with Lopez and Figon, and the compromising phrases said to have been used, are very reminiscent of the elaborate attempts to frame Bernier on the same and other occasions. But Lemarchand—himself not a particularly reliable witness—was at least, as the acquaintance of both Figon and Caille, one of the earliest and most important channels of information to the authorities.

Besides Lemarchand, Caille had another source: a mysterious informer who reported to him on the Monday that Figon had been boasting in bars about his part in a kidnapping, and on Tuesday morning that Lopez was involved. Le Roy also claimed that at their lunch on the Tuesday Caille had referred to Ben Barka having been injured by a dagger; Figon was later to say so too, and a respected Swiss journalist published the same story on 18 November, claiming 'a prominent French public figure' as his source; but Lemarchand denied that Figon ever said it to him or he to Caille, and Caille denied mentioning it to Le Roy. Nor would Caille identify his other informant. When M. Zollinger asked to see him in January, the unfortunate officer suddenly succumbed to a very bad cold which showed no sign of ever disappearing; when at last Zollinger went to his bedside, Caille pleaded professional privilege, and refused to name his informant. Just before he was due to appear in court, Roger Frey speaking in Parliament disclaimed any knowledge of his intentions or any desire to give him instructions, but vigorously defended a policeman's right to protect his sources. Caille would not divulge the name, and was upheld by the presiding judge; two journalists who had contacts with Figon were called as witnesses and confirmed that Figon had indeed been boasting in bars. In any case, by Monday 1 November Caille was looking for Figon. He found from the police files, he said, that Lemarchand was Figon's lawyer—and continued to maintain this even though the only file produced named Figon's previous counsel, Me Hug.

At Caille's request, Lemarchand telephoned to Figon who called on him at 11 a.m. on Tuesday 2 November and told his story; later he was to assert that Caille was also present (as he had predicted in advance to a woman friend, Mme Arnoul, whose evidence generally impressed the court). Both the lawyer and the policeman denied this strenuously. Lemarchand was not, however, the most truthful of witnesses. For over two months he steadfastly denied having met Figon since their encounter at Orly on 20 September. When he admitted to the 2 November meeting, and was accused before the Bar Council of unprofessional conduct, he maintained that he had done his duty both to his client and as a citizen, arranging a deal by which Figon told all he knew about Ben Barka's whereabouts in return for a promise of immunity. This explanation, made the more credible by Figon's carefree behaviour in the next few weeks on the run, was naturally denied by the police—and was repudiated in court by Lemarchand himself. Asked why he had affirmed it to the Bar Council, he replied 'Why, to get acquitted'. But he had also told the same story to a couple of journalists, separately, and had not issued a denial when it appeared in print.

Intrigue in Paris

By 2 November, then, when Oufkir and Dlimi coolly returned to France from the safety of Morocco, a good deal of information was—and more should have been—in the hands of the French authorities. With the King of Morocco about to pay an official visit to Paris, the French police might normally have taken more than usual interest in the comings and goings of his rebellious subjects. Thus, in the first place, Ben Barka's impending arrival from Geneva should have been known to them in advance; they had for two years known the pseudonym under which he travelled, and immigration control was at the Swiss end. Indeed though the Prefect of Police denied that his services knew, the Minister told Parliament that the immigration authorities did. (They come under the Prefecture's old rival, the Sûreté Nationale in the Ministry of the Interior.) In the second place, the French wiretapping services do not deserve their reputation for sleepless activity if Lopez's 'telephone festival' from Orly to the Moroccan ministries on the evening of October 29 failed to attract their attention. Thirdly, the comings and goings of General Oufkir would normally have been observed by the police, if only to avoid the risk of having a well-hated Minister of a friendly country assassinated on French soil like the King of Yugoslavia a generation before; indeed, Oufkir himself, remarking that as a Minister of the Interior he knew what was what, said they must have known all his movements.[3] However, his disembarkation card somehow took three whole days to reach the Ministry; and in any case by the official story it was unthinkable for police protection to be provided for a friendly Minister—while Ben Barka had himself asked in 1962 for his own protection to be discontinued.

The first clues for the regular police came on Monday 1 November when Caille passed on the news of Figon's boasts. On the same day Bernier, after telephoning many of his intellectual, legal and political friends over the weekend, vainly attempting to alert the local police at the Champs Elysées on Sunday, and contacting M. Aubert, went of his own volition to see the duty detective temporarily in charge of the case, Commissaire Marchand. He reported Chtouki's approach to him, and specified Figon's role and a phone number; police identified the house, visited it, found no Figon, and— nineteen days later—searched it. Bernier warned that Ben Barka in Oufkir's hands would not survive for long; the duty officer preferred not to consider so disagreeable a suggestion, and omitted this exchange from his account as 'exactly the sort of thing one doesn't want to put on record from a witness'. Next day Marchand handed over the case to M. Bouvier, head of the Criminal Brigade. Bernier told Bouvier (whether he had also told Marchand

[3] When Georges Bidault, then leader of the extreme right-wing opposition, was interviewed on BBC television early in 1963, the French authorities were convinced he could not have entered Britain without the government's knowledge.

was disputed) that Figon might be weekending either with Lemarchand, or at Fontenay where the movement of Moroccan cars had allegedly been observed by Moroccan students. The detectives told both Bernier and Franju to keep Figon's name to themselves for the time. The frontiers were not closed as they had recently been when Madame Dassault (wife of a millionaire Gaullist deputy) was kidnapped. The description of the suspects was circulated at 1 p.m. on November 4—three days after Boucheseiche had left France and a few hours after the rest of the gang, with El Mahi's 10,000 francs, had presumably done so too.

The regular police were picking up fragments of information, but had no particular competence for evaluating it (Marchand admitted that he had no idea who General Oufkir was). No such extenuating circumstance can be pleaded for SDECE, or at least for some of its officers. By late September Le Roy's superiors admittedly knew that the Moroccan government had recruited an 'unusual team' to 'recuperate' Ben Barka by 'unorthodox means' if necessary—but admittedly did not pass this supposedly unimportant information on to their own chief, General Jacquier, his ministerial superior, M. Pompidou, or the police. By mid-October Le Roy himself was failing to inform his superiors—allegedly because he regarded Figon as a worthless source, but perhaps because they preferred not to know too much. He did not tell them that the Moroccans meant by the 'recuperation' of Ben Barka that he might be kidnapped or eliminated, that their instruments were French gangsters who were blackmailing the Moroccans for money, or that a Gaullist deputy close to the Minister of the Interior was somehow connected with the affair. A week before the kidnapping Le Roy (according to Deshaurmes) knew the names of the Moroccans involved, but they did not remain in the files. On the morning itself he left for Orly shortly before Ben Barka's plane was due, supposedly to welcome General Jacquier, whose arrival was not expected until nearly three hours later and whose reception took very little time to organise—according both to Jacquier and to Lopez who usually made the arrangements, but was of course occupied with another 'reception' that morning.

Even if Le Roy received (as he claimed) no message from Lopez on the 28th or 29th, it is hard, as Judge Perez remarked, to account for his behaviour on Sunday 31st. He had himself reported to his superiors on Oufkir's desire to 'recuperate' Ben Barka, and had learned—but not reported—that that might mean kidnapping. He knew from the radio that Ben Barka had disappeared. He knew from Lopez's call that Oufkir and Dlimi were in Paris. His first comment on the disappearance was 'It sounds Oufkirish'. Yet he did nothing effective—or nothing at all—to inform his superiors, claiming later that Lopez's call had referred only to Oufkir and not to Ben Barka, and that he felt Oufkir's presence at Paris made it quite unthinkable that the General could be involved. Indeed so strong was Le Roy's relief at this reassuring piece of news that an hour and a half after speaking to Lopez he told an inquirer from the Prefecture that no 'officier traitant' of SDECE had contacted Ben Barka on the 29th—technically correct as Lopez's title was different (it was…'*honorable correspondant d'infrastructure*') but unforgivably misleading, as his superiors insisted. Yet even at this stage Le Roy was not the only SDECE officer to withhold information. We know that the note of 30 April about Oufkir, and Le Roy's own earlier reports of information from Lopez, had not reached the top of SDECE let alone anyone outside the organisation. And on Saturday 30 October—before Oufkir's first visit to Paris—an earlier call from the Prefecture, asking whether the SDECE had any information on Ben Barka's kidnapping, was passed on by the duty officer to the proper service (geographical section IIIA) and General Jacquier was notified. But the Ben Barka file was not produced (or asked for). On Saturday as on Sunday SDECE's answer to the Prefecture was No.

On the morning of Tuesday 2 November, the first working day after the holiday. Le Roy gave Colonel Beaumont a written note of Lopez's Sunday morning phone conversation, and then was summoned by Jacquier, who was being harried by phone calls from the Minister of the Interior and from the Prime Minister's staff. Jacquier later said in an unguarded moment in court that on 2 November 'everyone' of course knew Oufkir was involved. Even if he meant only everyone in SDECE, Le Roy's information was clearly more widely known among his colleagues than the official story suggests, and Jacquier himself admitted he had not told his ministerial masters all he knew or suspected. He did, however, instruct Le Roy to find out all available information on Figon and to draw up a note on Lopez's duties. (He was not told that the note existed already. It was never given either to the police or to the examining magistrate or to the court.) He also told Le Roy to go straight to police headquarters and offer every assistance; Le Roy, instead, went off to his lunch with Caille.

That afternoon Jacquier also sent to the Prefecture a delegation led by the assistant director of the counter-espionage branch, M. Camp, his subordinate M. Klein, and Le Roy. But Camp's detailed instructions from Colonel Beaumont were not to tell all that SDECE knew about the case but simply to pass on a summary of Lopez's report of 22 September—and to assure the police that SDECE had not organised this kidnapping. (Asked in court if it had organised many others, M. Camp said it was not for him to answer.) The summary, drafted not by Le Roy but by Camp's branch, was of little help; it mentioned the film and the 'unusual team', named but did not identify Lemarchand, gave none of the information available on

Chtouki, Figon or Bernier, mentioned Dlimi (by his office not his name) but not Oufkir or Lopez himself, and of course omitted all the new information from Lopez's phone call—the presence of Oufkir and Dlimi in Paris, their night at Lopez's house, and their comings and goings between Ormoy and Orly. Armed with this virtually worthless report, Camp and Klein—without Le Roy—called at 3 p.m. on the Director of the Sûreté Nationale, M. Godard, and left him, as he twice said in court, with the impression that they were seeking rather than offering information. Le Roy came in late from a quick talk with Lopez, which he rapidly summarised for his two colleagues—but out of hearing of Godard, the enemy.

At 4 p.m. the three SDECE men crossed the river to see M. Somveille, *Directeur de Cabinet* of the Prefect of Police—and found Caille there too. Here again, Somveille testified, the atmosphere was tense and embarrassed. Camp swore that SDECE knew nothing of the affair, Caille said, 'But suppose I prove to you that Lopez was in it?'; Le Roy replied that Lopez had denied it (in fact, Lopez had carefully denied only being involved in an 'attack' on Ben Barka), insisted that he was a most valuable informant, but added that if he was involved 'SDECE won't give protection'; was this remark, in conjunction with the note naming Lemarchand, Le Roy's counter-attack to Caille's charge against Lopez? Besides casting doubt on Caille as a source, Le Roy did not tell the Prefecture officials of Lopez's reports on Oufkir and Dlimi—though later he assured General Jacquier that he had done so. When Somveille urged him to send Lopez immediately to the Criminal Brigade of the police, he did not mention that he had seen Lopez just an hour before and was meeting him again at 8 p.m. that evening; when they met, he did at last tell Lopez to go to the police—next day. By then he knew his position was becoming untenable, for he said to Lopez 'I'm for the high jump, old man'. Yet even at this stage his superiors showed no disapproval of his conduct. In court Colonel Morvan professed astonishment that Le Roy had not fully informed the police; but counsel later suggested it was on Morvan's orders that Le Roy said nothing to the examining magistrate. And on the Wednesday morning Colonel Beaumont (without Jacquier's knowledge) instructed Le Roy to do nothing further about Ben Barka—that was a job for the police—but to report immediately any information about the Prefecture's attitude to Lopez. It was Colonel Beaumont himself who was selected by SDECE to conduct the internal inquiry into the organisation's failure to assist the official investigation.

By 2 November, then, General Jacquier at last knew most of what his subordinates had learned.[4] 'Everyone' in SDECE realised that Oufkir was

---

[4] 'This hive', a journalist who covered the trial wrote of SDECE, 'has at its head a drone: the Director-General. He does nothing, he knows nothing. From time to time he is got rid of, like

implicated—though to Jacquier's ministerial masters the very idea was quite inconceivable. By the same day, Commissaire Caille had also heard the story from his mysterious informer, as well as through Figon, and at his lunch with Le Roy he acquired new confirmation for his suspicions. On Wednesday the 3rd the case moved a stage further when M. André Simbille, Assistant Director of the Police Judiciaire, asked Souchon to get in touch with his friend Lopez, now so urgently wanted—and Souchon promptly confessed that he himself was implicated. Souchon's confession went straight to the Prefect of Police, Maurice Papon, and to the Minister, Roger Frey—but it was concealed from M. Bouvier the investigating detective and M. Zollinger the examining magistrate. That same afternoon, Lopez learned that Bouvier wanted to see him; he carefully explained that the message reached him at Orly—indicating quite clearly that it would not have been very hard to find him earlier. He presented himself during the afternoon to Simbille and Caille, and then had a long 'conversation' with Bouvier. As a result the police searched his villa at Ormoy and Boucheseiche's at Fontenay, finding very little and omitting to seal either building. (When they were phoning to Morocco just after Ben Barka came into their hands, Boucheseiche was overheard by an Orly employee asking Lopez if 'the house' had shutters. Later many questions were asked and no answers ever found about the possibility that Ben Barka was taken to a third building with which Boucheseiche was unfamiliar.) Bouvier showed no eagerness at this stage to record information about the policemen—either from Bernier about Voitot and the passport, or from Lopez about the approach to Ben Barka. Lopez also said he could at that very moment take the police straight to Oufkir and Dlimi—at the Moroccan Ambassador's reception. This embarrassing offer was not taken up, for Bouvier thought there was not nearly enough to go on; and he postponed till 1 a.m. the drafting of a statement which Lopez signed, after refusing to have SDECE or Lemarchand mentioned in it. The statement reached the Minister's desk about the time the Casablanca plane took off.

Roger Frey was later to explain in Parliament, reasonably enough, that the arrest of Oufkir might have had disastrous consequences for the French community in Morocco; he argued also that it could not be justified by scraps of unplausible information from shady and mentally unstable characters

General Jacquier, and another is summoned. The real authority belongs to the queen: that is the director of research, Colonel Beaumont': F. Caviglioli, *Ben Barka devant les juges* (La Table Ronde de Combat, 1967), p. 144. Later a former head of SDECE in Washington, who had resigned because of de Gaulle's anti-American policies, was to write of a meeting in December 1962: 'I was confident that Jacquier would put matters to rights. But I was to discover that suddenly he seemed to be overshadowed by his staff': P. Thyraud de Vosjoli in *Sunday Times*, 21 April 1968. On a similarly isolated director-general earlier in SDECE's history see above, pp. 40, 41.

like Figon. He did not explain why no action had been taken to dissuade or prevent Dlimi or the other Moroccans leaving the country; the answer doubtless lay in the busy week of diplomatic exchanges between Paris and Rabat, which failed to persuade King Hassan to take public responsibility for the crime by dismissing Oufkir. ('Tell the President', Hassan was said to have replied, 'that I'll drop my Minister of the Interior when he drops his'.) These transactions subsequently became the main semi-official explanation for the government's decision not to tell the examining magistrate of Souchon's confession until ten days later, and then to conceal the date it had been made; when M. Fernet, Director of the Police Judiciaire, was asked in court whether he had realised this decision was illegal, he replied 'And how!' Another possible reason for the delays was indignantly denied. On 4 November, almost the last legally permissible moment, President de Gaulle was to announce his decision to stand for re-election a month later. The Gaullists had just discovered from the opinion polls that his popularity was slipping, and had suddenly become alarmed at the electoral prospects even if he stood. But the revelation that the police were implicated might so disgust de Gaulle that he would change his mind and withdraw, with catastrophic consequences for his followers—and, in their minds, for the country.

Whatever the reasons, it was not until the day Oufkir and Dlimi had departed for Casablanca—first handing over money which presumably financed the gangsters' escape—that the first arrest took place, that of Lopez. Two days later de Gaulle, answering an appeal from Ben Barka's mother, assured her in a dignified message that the search for the missing leader would be conducted with the utmost rigour and diligence. One year later, Commissaires Caille and Bouvier were promoted.[5]

IV. THE SENSATIONS

During the next three weeks the small fry were arrested and charged: El Mahi on the 5th, Souchon and Voitot on the 11th, and Bernier on the 26th. Le Roy was not arrested until 10 February and then was charged only with 'failing to report a crime'. The authorities continued to act in a manner certain to arouse the maximum suspicion; thus on 12 November, the day after Souchon and Voitot were suspended, the press officer at the Ministry of the Interior denied to *Agence France-Presse* that two police officers were implicated in the case; later M. Frey explained to Parliament that this officer knew nothing

[5] M. Caille, who had been introduced to Figon under the name of Petitjean, turned his notoriety to account by publishing a detective story about a political kidnapping, entitled *Petitjean est au parfum.*

about what was going on. Then, under a law which has since been repealed, the decision to bring charges against the two police officers legally debarred the Police Judiciaire from assisting the examining magistrate; and since the police had failed to catch the gangsters or seal the two villas, and the SDECE, Prefecture and Ministers had withheld from him so much information, M. Zollinger's singlehanded efforts to unravel the mystery were inevitably slow and only partially successful. And even when the case came to court each key witness seemed to be both concealing evidence and using the threat of revelations to blackmail other participants.

Rigour and diligence, then, were not the most conspicuous features of the authorities' conduct. But though their obstruction prevented very embarrassing revelations for a time (covering the presidential election campaign) it did not do so indefinitely. For ten weeks after the crime Figon, unlike his fellow-gangsters, stayed in Paris happily cocking snooks at the police—getting *Paris-Match* to publish his photograph under Bouvier's office windows, and planting in *Minute* a wholly false story that Bouvier had arrested and then released him. His presence in Paris was widely believed to show that he enjoyed police protection. (Yet, as the Minister and Prefect both remarked, the British police, who have far more public sympathy than the French, were for months unable to trace the Great Train Robbers; and in Paris itself the OAS leader Sergent had also stayed at large for long periods, mocking the police—whose desire to catch him was undoubted—by getting himself ostentatiously photographed at the Trocadero.) Then *L'Express* of 10 January published a sensational account of Ben Barka's treatment at Fontenay and Ormoy, under the misleading headline 'I Saw Ben Barka Killed'. This was attributed to Figon, who promptly denied its authenticity, which became one of the most hotly contested issues at the trial. But Zollinger took it seriously enough to make a futile journey to inspect the two villas which the police had left unsealed so long before. On the 14th, Souchon after two months in prison wearied of his position. After a four-hour session with Judge Zollinger he told the examining magistrate of Lopez's reference to Foccart and of his own phone call from 'Aubert', and revealed that he had avowed his own part in the kidnapping to his superiors on 3 November, and had then confessed all over again on the 13th, obediently concealing his earlier confession.

It was about the same time that Figon, according to several of his friends (notably Mme Arnoul) suddenly lost his self-confidence and sense of security. Some of them said he was feeling trapped and blaming Lemarchand for not producing money and a passport for his escape; but perhaps he feared reprisals from the gangsters—or the Moroccans—for the revelations in the article in *L'Express*. On 17 January the police received (they said)

an anonymous tip that Figon was at a ground-floor flat in the rue des
Renaudes which he was preparing to leave within an hour; the house was
surrounded by a large force of police who broke in only to find Figon dead,
an overcoat over his clothes, a gun under his body and a bullet in his head.
Next day the authorities announced that he had certainly committed suicide.
Ben Barka's relatives were refused permission to associate the two cases, so
that Zollinger was not allowed to contribute to or see the results of the
Figon inquiry, which was closed within three weeks as 'no case for prosecution'—although inquiries into mysterious deaths in Paris often remain open
for months or even years.

French public opinion, mistrustful of policemen and politicians and
hardened by the experience of past scandals, is exceptionally susceptible to
conspiracy theories (few self-respecting Frenchmen believed that anyone but
a moron could take seriously the Warren Commission report on President
Kennedy's assassination). In whatever circumstances Figon had been found
dead, many people would have been sure the police had murdered him;
a typical reaction was the *Canard Enchaîné*'s revival of its 1934 Stavisky
headline—'Figon commits suicide with a pistol he has had fired at him at
point-blank range'. Yet suspicion was inevitably aroused by the long immunity followed by the sudden death, by the enormous force deployed at
the last minute, by the haste with which the suicide verdict was announced
and the case closed—and by the apparent determination of the authorities
to make the very worst of their difficult problem. There were contradictory
statements, first that the gun was fired at point-blank range, then 'at a very
short distance', about a centimetre by one official account, certainly less by
another. Nine experts saw the body, but one of the most distinguished of
them did not sign one autopsy report. Figon's hands were not given a
paraffin test to show if the gun had been fired (though when it was, it took
seven shots to produce a result, so this test could not have been conclusive).
The gun was in his hand but there were no usable fingerprints. A persistent
rumour, not confined to anti-Gaullists, claimed the wound was too large to
have been caused by that gun. It had no silencer, yet no one in the building
heard the shot—and when *Paris-Match* journalists re-enacted the death (as
the police never did), they found it should have been clearly audible. The
direction of the bullet, right-to-left and slightly forward and upward, would
have obliged Figon to hold the gun in a singularly awkward position—though
an expert in forensic medicine testified that this, though unusual, was by
no means impossible or even unlikely as suicides were quite unpredictable
in this respect. Figon's friends gave conflicting evidence of his state of mind
in the days before his death, and of the likelihood of his committing suicide
if trapped by the police; on the whole the weight of the testimony was that

he might have done so. The most dramatic revelation came from Mlle Coffinet, one of his girl friends—but not one who gave a general impression of great credibility—who was shown the gun and instantly screamed, 'It's not his!' His, she said, was a Unic with a blue barrel, this had a black one. A police expert tried with very little success to show that the barrel could look black or blue according to the light, and claimed never to have seen the model described; Mlle Coffinet's fiancé, M. Bal, was able to identify it by the simple expedient of telephoning the manufacturers.

With Figon there died the remaining witness to Ben Barka's fate, and the third Ben Barka affair began. For public opinion now began to view the events of 1965 in the light of the extraordinary developments of January 1966: first Souchon's revelations, then Figon's mysterious death, then the further sensations which crowded upon one another in the next month. Jacquier was prematurely 'retired', the SDECE was transferred from the Prime Minister's office to the Ministry of Defence, and yet another reorganisation of the police services was undertaken—not by Frey, the Minister normally responsible, but by Léon Noël, a distinguished old Gaullist now in retirement (but still a power in his former constituency of Yonne). M. Zollinger issued a warrant for Oufkir and Dlimi, and Commissaire Caille fell ill, finally refusing to name his informant when Zollinger pursued him to his sickbed. Lopez denied and Souchon reaffirmed the Foccart story; then on the 21st Lopez hinted it might be true, but Souchon suddenly withdrew the statement that he had given Foccart's name to his superiors. On the 22nd, on the radio, Lemarchand again denied he had seen Figon since the kidnapping; on the 24th he admitted that was a lie. The same day Boucheseiche sent the press a letter posted in Frankfurt, accusing the 'barbouzes' of murdering Figon. On the 27th a tape, found among Figon's effects, was played to a tense audience; it proved to be the script of a gangster film he had once thought of promoting, and not that of the *Express* story which (according to the journalist who recorded it, Jean Marvier) Figon had insisted on having back. But the current issue of *L'Express* had Marvier's account of Figon's weeks on the run, including his words to Marvier on the very day of his death 'Ah, Lemarchand and Caille, that pair, what wouldn't they give to see me rubbed out'. The next issue was to produce a new sensation: a charge by an alleged former Gaullist barbouze that the explosion in an Algiers villa which had killed twenty of his colleagues towards the end of the battle with the OAS had really been organised by their own leader, Lemarchand, because they all knew too much. Lemarchand's libel suits against *L'Express*, after long postponements, have not yet come to trial.

Figon's death suggested to many people, even to a leading Left Gaullist like Emmanuel d'Astier de la Vigerie, that 'not for the first time seven policemen entered a room and eight came out'. The government's behaviour certainly reinforced the public suspicion that it was determined to hush up the whole affair. A most distinguished judicial commentator, the *Monde*'s correspondent 'Casamayor', said so in print. 'Casamayor' is a judge, M. Serge Fuster, and the Minister of Justice promptly began disciplinary proceedings against him which the *Monde*'s editor ironically welcomed: '*Enfin des sanctions!*'. The disciplinary authorities refused to conform to the Minister's evident intentions and gave the lightest possible sentence, a reprimand.

After 'three months of suppression and three weeks of explosions', February 1966 was the peak period of agitation and the most dangerous moment for the Gaullists. On February 21 the President of the Republic, who had so often claimed to have restored the authority and dignity of the French State, himself tried to quieten public anxiety by a press conference. He publicly denounced the Moroccan Minister of the Interior as a criminal, and the French press for their indifference to 'the honour of the ship' of state. He dismissed the French part in the affair as limited to 'the vulgar and the subaltern'. He bid 'good citizens be reassured'. A journalist asked him why he had not chosen to inform the country of his government's actions before the presidential election, but had left the press to ferret out the information; he delighted much of his audience by his reply—'It's the fault of my inexperience'. Such was Charles de Gaulle's own summary of the results of the rigorous and diligent inquiry he had personally promised the mother of the victim a hundred days before.

V. THE TRIALS

The first trial of the accused opened in September 1966 and lasted six weeks; Lopez, Le Roy, Souchon, Voitot, Bernier and El Mahi were the only defendants in court. Some of France's leading lawyers were engaged: Me Floriot, an immensely successful defence counsel in criminal trials, for Souchon; Me Stibbe and Bâtonnier Thorp, well-known political lawyers of the Left, among the team representing the Ben Barka family (the *partie civile*); Me Hayot, who had also appeared in the Leakages case, and Me Biaggi, the extreme right-winger, for Lopez who soon added the redoubtable Me J. L. Tixier-Vignancour. But Tixier was much less successful in dominating the court than he had usually been in the past. The public prosecutor, M. Toubas, found little to criticise in the conduct of the authorities, readily accepted their view that all faults were committed by minor officials, and would not allow Tixier to exploit against the government his favourite techniques of innuendo and sensational irrelevance. At least twice Toubas challenged and routed his adversary, once by showing that the key to Figon's locked room, which Tixier had alleged was missing, had been found in the dead man's pocket by the examining magistrate.

The presiding judge, M. Perez, was not exactly unsympathetic to Tixier. Quite early on he warned the lawyer, 'Don't go too far, Maître', to which Tixier characteristically replied 'And don't you go too far, M. le Président'— adding at once, however, 'Anyway, neither you nor I have ever gone too far!' The judge closed the exchange with an equally conciliatory response, 'We come from the same area.' But Judge Perez would not permit the irrelevance which had allowed so many previous trials to turn into political displays with only the most tenuous relation to the case. His determination is understandable, for past abuses of the court rules had undeniably hampered discovery of the truth; yet this time it is arguable that the strict limits he imposed themselves crippled inquiry. When the cabinet refused to waive privilege and allow Pompidou and Frey to appear in person, counsel for the Ben Barka family submitted 33 questions in writing about the actions and inactions of the government. The judge disallowed eight of them, mainly about the information supplied to President de Gaulle and about the negotiations with Morocco, and objected to the form of others—even deleting a reference to the fact that the Prime Minister was at the crucial time the authority to which SDECE was responsible. In court, he allowed Caille to protect his informer while insisting that journalists must reveal their sources (English judges have sometimes taken the same line, as in the Vassall case). Perez would not allow questions on whether Lopez had once gone to Morocco on a mission for SDECE with Jo Attia, a well-known gangster and friend of Figon's; or whether Boucheseiche and the rest of the gang had belonged to an unofficial police force; or whether the police ever extended their protection to persons who had (like Ben Barka) declined it; or whether Papon did not think the arrest of Souchon and Voitot would have improved rather than worsened the French diplomatic position. When the Ambassador to Morocco refused to answer any questions at all and counsel for the Ben Barka family asked him if he was unwilling to help the court discover the truth, Perez intervened sharply and told him not to reply. Not surprisingly counsel commented, 'After the Reserved Domain of the military and the police we now have the Reserved Domain of the diplomatic corps.'

While the court tried hard to protect officialdom from the prying eyes of its enemies, several of the accused uttered an occasional hint, as quickly withdrawn, that if they were to be abandoned as scapegoats they might reveal some embarrassing information. When Souchon volunteered a description of the voice on the phone which showed it could not have come from the man he named, he plainly was not trying to incriminate Aubert himself. Was he telling the strict truth; or inventing the whole story; or was he giving a strong hint that he did have a highly placed protector whom—from loyalty to his old service or from hope of future aid and comfort—he would not identify? When Judge Zollinger asked him why he had not phoned the caller back to check his identity, Souchon said that a simple policeman like himself hesitated to bother an important man like Aubert. But when Judge Perez asked him the same question in court he gave a strange reply: 'It would have made no difference.' Asked to explain, his answer was stranger still. 'The Ministry is a big place [*une grande maison*] with many telephones—and I'd have been bound to get the same person on the line' (*sic*). Again this suggested a hint which no one sought to elucidate further.

Both the prosecutor and Frey, in his parliamentary defence, gave Souchon's delay in mentioning the phone call as ground for disbelief in its existence. But Souchon told Zollinger on 1 December that he had had his orders by telephone. He did not name Aubert until six weeks later—but he delayed just as long in mentioning 'Foccart est au parfum', the phrase which Lopez eventually admitted using, and in telling Zollinger that he had confessed to his superiors ten days before the date he was supposed to have done so. There is therefore no question that for two months he withheld from the examining magistrate information relevant to his defence but embarrassing to his superiors. Why? His wife told Zollinger that Fernet repeatedly advised her up to 14 January that her husband should keep his mouth shut; but when Fernet indignantly denied it, she promptly retracted her quite definite charge that she had been urged to advise her husband to keep silent about the date of his confession, while repeating that Fernet had told her to be patient and everything would work out all right. Souchon himself had said to Zollinger on 20 May, 'I didn't tell you—I followed their advice, I was patient'. And at other points he admitted that he had expected SDECE or the false 'Aubert' to intervene and rescue him if he duly played the game.

When Souchon finally told the story, he said that on 3 November he had referred to SDECE and had named Finville (Le Roy) and Foccart; but Fernet and Simbille then saw Zollinger and denied that any names had been mentioned. Souchon cautiously retracted: 'If he [Fernet] says I didn't cite names to him, I must accept that...Yet I was sure I spoke to him of MM. Finville and Foccart.' In court he was equally respectful and equally hesitant. 'If my Director in whom I have full confidence says I didn't mention M. Foccart's name, certainly that must mean I didn't mention it; there must have been a confusion in my mind.' *L'Express* (no impeccable source) reported him as having asked Zollinger, 'If I told you my instructions came from M. Simbille, what would happen?' 'He would join you in prison.' 'Even if he were only passing them on?' 'Yes.' 'In that case I prefer to keep silent.' When counsel asked him in court whether the 'Aubert' voice on the phone was not one very familiar to him, he replied 'Absolutely not'. Simbille was sure that Souchon would never knowingly have participated in a suspect or illegal act, and agreed that he might well have spoken on 3 November of 'assurances' and 'guarantees' that he had not done so.

Souchon's demeanour in court suggested as little as his record before the case or his conduct during it that he was searching for a way of escape at any cost. For example the Prefect of Police, Maurice Papon, averred that the incrimination of Aubert was 'something diabolical of which Souchon is quite incapable'. Judge Perez then asked Souchon if he would still reaffirm, in his old chief's presence, that the call happened as he had claimed.

Souchon: 'Yes, exactly so. I'd like to talk about that phone call. (Pause)...I love
    the force and I'd give my life for it.'
Perez: 'If you have any more to say, say it.'
Souchon: 'No, that's all.'
Papon: 'Say it—you were going to give us a fact about the phone call—say it.'
Souchon: 'I hesitated because people will think it's just to defend myself. But
    we did sometimes cut corners—I once talked to the Directeur de la Sûreté
    Nationale himself and your office didn't know. So a call from the Ministry
    didn't seem quite so strange.'

At Perez's question, the Prefect then repeated that Souchon would never have had orders except through official channels. Yet in the second trial, when Lopez mentioned that Souchon had once before come to Orly on an unofficial mission, Souchon readily agreed; it was to investigate an affair between a society woman and a public figure, at the request of the Prefect of Police himself.[6]

If Souchon really had invented the phone call, he could have caused enormous embarrassment by attributing it to Caille. He had plenty of encouragement to do so. His wife tape-recorded a conversation with one of his acquaintances, M. Garnieri, in which she asked whether the mysterious voice might not have belonged to a security officer in the Sûreté Nationale, a Resistance colleague of both men. But Garnieri replied heatedly, 'It's the opposite...I tell you it's Caille, Caille, Caille and Lemarchand.' ('An idea in the air', he explained in court—put into his head by the press.) When Madame Souchon tried to persuade her husband to name Caille, he indignantly refused: 'You're crazy to ask me to lie'. Then came a dramatic moment in court when the wife testified that someone there present, not Garnieri, had urged this course upon her. She refused to say who it was, then changed her mind as the judge was about to adjourn; he seemed inclined

---

[6] For confirmation that Prefects of Police have 'quite frequently' used the police for their private information see Théolleyre, *Le Procès des Fuites* p. 263.

to drop the matter, but she insisted in seeing him privately and when the court reopened next morning she identified the adviser as Lopez's counsel, Mᵉ Hayot. The lawyer denied it and the Bâtonnier accepted his denial. But she and Mme Voitot then claimed that Mᵉ Hayot had urged them both to replace their present counsel, Mᵉ Floriot, with his own colleague Tixier-Vignancour. When finally they said he had tried to enter the witnesses' room and the guard commander confirmed this, Mᵉ Hayot (who said he had been bringing sandwiches for Souchon) was obliged to withdraw from the case.

There was another dramatic incident one Saturday afternoon when Le Roy, showing signs of exasperation at being made a scapegoat by his superiors, suddenly appealed to Judge Perez: he could not defend himself without explaining the context of his work and that might mean revealing defence secrets. 'We'll see next week if I can go any further.' But, he asked, would the court protect him if he told all he knew and was promptly charged before the State Security Court? Perez told him he must manage his defence without revealing defence secrets—though the Minister of Defence, in refusing to give Le Roy the information he asked for, had said he was entirely free to defend himself in any way he thought fit. The weekend of reflection changed Le Roy's mind (as so often happened when an accused man showed signs of retracting his confession in a Stalinist court). By Monday Le Roy was again disciplined, submissive and taciturn.

Only one such incident was seriously followed up. This was during the Hayot affair; Voitot tried to defend his wife against Tixier's attack, and the lawyer turned on him in his most sinister bullying manner: 'Watch out, you, Lopez still has a story to tell.' Perez at once demanded to know what aspects of the truth Lopez was withholding from the court. Lopez said he had told all and at this point the usual recess occurred. But this time Tixier was not allowed to escape; as soon as the court resumed Toubas, supported by Perez, demanded an explanation. In full retreat, Tixier characteristically avoided total humiliation by borrowing a phrase used in equally inglorious circumstances by his hated enemy de Gaulle: 'It's the fault of my inexperience'.

Far more sensational than counsel's manœuvres was the totally unexpected arrival from Morocco of the second most important suspect at large. Mᵉ Floriot's defence speech for Souchon fell on deaf ears when the rumour, soon verified, suddenly swept the courtroom that Colonel Ahmed Dlimi had come to Paris to give himself up, claiming his sole purpose was to defend his personal honour. Instantly promoted and praised by his monarch, Dlimi succeeded in getting the entire long trial cancelled; the court adjourned without delivering a verdict *in absentia* against General Oufkir.

The second trial took place in the spring of 1967, with the same presiding judge and prosecutor but many changes among the lawyers. The Ben Barka family asked for a further postponement as three of their leading counsel had died suddenly; when it was refused they withdrew from the case. Lopez decided to dispense with the services of Me Tixier-Vignancour who often seemed to be acting for the Moroccans as well as for his client; with Dlimi in court, these two interests would be hard to reconcile. El Mahi's chief counsel also withdrew soon after Dlimi's arrival, disagreeing with his client about the line the defence should now take. Me Biaggi retired in sympathy with Tixier, so that the political lawyers of both sides had disappeared; and as political and public interest in the case had waned, the passions aroused were far less than on the first occasion.

The central figure of the new trial was Dlimi. Lopez had implicated him in the report of 22 September, had phoned him in Morocco on 19, 25 and 26 October, and had tried to do so on the day of the kidnapping. In Lopez's version of subsequent events, he had been one of the principals. In that version Dlimi arrived at Orly at 2 p.m. on Saturday 30th and went with Lopez to a restaurant near by to lunch with the gang (where according to Figon he proposed to get rid of Ben Barka forthwith and bury him in a small wood); he then went with Le Ny to Fontenay where Ben Barka was; when Lopez returned to his Ormoy home after 10 p.m. he found Dlimi there with Oufkir; they left but Dlimi phoned at midnight, Lopez collected them at Orly, and then drove them back to the airport at 5 a.m. (Two employees testified to seeing him there in company with three North Africans.) Dlimi affirmed, however, that his visit to Paris had no connection with the case. His government recalled him from Algiers; there was no direct plane so he flew by way of Paris. Lopez met him and took him to a restaurant but left him outside (though after the lunch was over he was briefly in the same car as two of the lunch party to whom he was not introduced). Then he went not to Fontenay but to a Paris hotel to see his wife who was there, and to await the night plane to Casablanca. But at 10 p.m. Oufkir arrived and asked him to stay overnight to discuss developments in Algiers. They dined together at a near-by restaurant and Dlimi then took his wife to a night-club, returning her to her hotel just after 6 a.m. and taking a taxi from central Paris to Orly. So little did he know about the case that he, the chief of police in Morocco, was not quite sure whether Ben Barka was under sentence of death.

Dlimi was more successful in finding corroborative evidence from Moroccan officials than from ordinary Frenchmen. The military attaché recalled taking him to the hotel—where the staff remembered his visit a few days later, but not his presence on the 30th. The night-club staff had no recollection of him, his wife, or the Moroccan tourist official who testified he had invited the Dlimis to his table—and was sure of the date because he had discussed the case with his wife soon afterwards (but wanting no trouble had waited sixteen months before speaking out to exculpate his compatriot). In response to an appeal from counsel, a taxi-driver came forward who could not remember his previous or subsequent journeys but was confident that he had taken Dlimi to Orly on the morning of the 31st, recalling also that they had stopped at a café—which, according to both the owner and the waiter, was always shut at the time he gave. Dlimi said there had been no Chtouki at the Moroccan Sûreté Nationale in his time—but it was proved that on 3 October Lopez's Chtouki had phoned from Paris to a Rabat number which, Judge Perez discovered from the Prefecture, belonged to the Moroccan Sûreté; Dlimi's counsel were assured by the Moroccan post office that it did not, but could not say whose it was. El Housseini was also totally unknown to Dlimi—although their names appeared on the same reservation slip both (with Boucheseiche and 'Cohen') for the night plane on 30 October which they did not take, and (alone) for the morning plane on the 31st which they did. These remarkable coincidences indicated to the booking clerks that they had registered together; but Lopez had helped with the first booking, and Dlimi's counsel suggested someone was trying to implicate their client by giving a false identity which admittedly was not checked at the counter—and yet another Moroccan official testified that Dlimi was travelling alone. Counsel were able to show one strange coincidence, the presence of a quite different M. Chtouki on the same plane (incidentally there was also a quite different M. Souchon on the same Geneva flight as Figon, Lemarchand and Bernier on September 20). The Paris dinner with Oufkir was corroborated by the restaurant staff; its times were barely consistent with Lopez's story of Dlimi's movements that night. Lopez maintained the night-time part of his account, but retracted his previous assertion that he knew Dlimi had gone to Fontenay in the afternoon (while characteristically hinting that the colonel still might have done so). Counsel pointed out that no one but Lopez had seen Dlimi at Fontenay or Orly, and that Lopez's evidence about Ormoy was contradicted by the taxi-driver.

According to *Le Monde*, the verdict delivered by the jury on 5 June surprised even the defendants—except Bernier. He, Dlimi, Le Roy, Voitot and El Mahi were acquitted; Lopez and Souchon were found guilty not of the kidnapping charge (which legally implied the victim had been held for at least a month) but of making an illegal arrest, and were awarded eight and six years imprisonment respectively. The three judges then sat alone to consider the absentee defendants, Oufkir, Chtouki and the gangsters, who were all given life imprisonment—a maximum sentence which could, however, be reviewed in a new trial if they gave themselves up.

VI. THE |VICTIM

The verdict of the court brought the case to a formal conclusion hardly more satisfactory than President de Gaulle's pronouncement. A prominent foreign politician had been kidnapped at mid-day in the streets of Paris, and probably murdered; one secret service agent and one police officer went to prison while neither the killers nor the instigators were caught. The enquiry had failed to elucidate any of the principal problems. In the 'first Ben Barka affair', we know for sure neither who organised the kidnapping and why, nor what happened to the victim and at whose hands. In the 'second Ben Barka affair', it is clear that some French public servants knew in advance a great deal of what was afoot; that, if they had understood its significance and alerted their colleagues early enough, the crime could have been prevented; and that, if they had done so only a little later, it could have been cleared up. But it is not so evident how far the confusion was due to muddle, misunderstanding and comprehensible failure to take strong action on weak evidence, and how far to the deliberate withholding of relevant information —or by whom it was withheld and why. In the 'third Ben Barka affair', similarly, after the event there was obfuscation, obstruction and interference with the course of justice, but it is again not clear exactly how much was being covered up, by whom, or for what motive.

The answer to the first set of questions—about the instigators of the plot— must be related to the political context. Had the King abandoned his attempt at rapprochement with the left-wing opposition, or did it continue into the autumn? Which did Ben Barka believe, and was his belief justified? Was he a stimulus or an obstacle to that policy? Was Oufkir acting for the King or on his own account? How did Ben Barka's role in organising the Tricontinental Congress affect his position in Moroccan and in international politics?

There is no doubt that in the spring the King was seeking a reconciliation with the opposition (Ben Barka had once taught Hassan mathematics, and one message ran 'I need my tutor back, I have an equation to solve'). But at the trial, counsel for the Ben Barka family argued that this had merely been a manœuvre to gain time, and brought many witnesses to confirm that by the autumn reconciliation was no longer on the agenda and Ben Barka considered himself a hunted man. However, this may have been an attempt to create a heroic political myth around the lost leader, who seems in fact to have believed in the King's goodwill. Ben Barka had plenty of enemies other than his own countrymen; and when his brother and his host first approached the police after the kidnapping they did not believe that the Moroccans were likely to have done it. Unless Ben Barka thought Souchon was taking him to a political negotiation it is difficult to account for his willingness to accompany the policemen without question, even when the car headed out into the suburbs; and despite the line taken by the *Partie Civile* in court there is good reason to believe he was thinking on these lines. One of his close friends among French politicians, Alain Savary, who had negotiated the independence treaty with Morocco in March 1956, saw Ben Barka in Cairo on 16 October, less than two weeks before his disappearance; and Savary found him very willing to meet in Paris where he now felt secure, and still closely interested in the possibility of a return to office by his party, though not by himself. And near the end of the trial Tixier-Vignancour—interested in showing that Lopez could reasonably have believed he was arranging a political meeting—dramatically produced a tape-recording of an account by El Azzemouri of his conversation with Ben Barka in the taxi which took them to St Germain: Ben Barka was talking animatedly about the prospects of returning home when the Tricontinental was over.

Frenchmen who knew of Ben Barka's April meeting with Prince Moulay Ali, and then learned of the subsequent Moroccan moves, might therefore have thought their object was another political rendezvous. But it was a rash belief even then, for phrases like 'special team', 'unorthodox means' and 'permanent objective' should have made them wary. Today that belief is no longer credible. Moulay Ali had arranged to meet Ben Barka without the complicated film scheme, the contacts with agents of foreign powers, the recruitment of gangsters, and the provision, apparently so carefully organised, of scapegoats—Bernier and probably Lemarchand—to be exploited or sacrificed after the event. These plans were too sinister, as well as too elaborate, for a simple rendezvous.

They were also too elaborate for a simple liquidation. If the objective was merely to remove Ben Barka from the scene it would have been much simpler and probably safer to kill him than to kidnap him, and for this there was no need to lure him to Paris when it had been attempted often enough elsewhere. But in Paris, where the Moroccans had their own agents, their French friends in high places and their ally at the airport, they had far better facilities than anywhere else for organising a kidnapping. The problem is therefore: who had an interest in seizing Ben Barka alive—and in taking the risk of kidnapping him in Paris at a delicate moment in Franco–Moroccan relations, just when the King was about to pay his official visit to President de Gaulle?

Oufkir and his subordinates might well have feared that the royal policy of reconciliation would lead to Ben Barka's return and endanger their own position and perhaps even their lives. But if so, the most brutal action— his death—would have been the final safeguard of their security. No doubt they had a professional interest in extracting information from him; among Figon's papers was a photocopy of a handwritten and elaborate questionnaire about the policy, organisation and contacts of the Moroccan opposition, presumably intended by its authors for the interrogation of Ben Barka—and by Figon himself for blackmailing the authors. Yet such an interrogation would be an unpropitious start to the King's political negotiation with Ben Barka; and if it led to the victim's 'accidental' death before Hassan could meet him, it is hard to see why the monarch gave the perpetrators his full protection, from the start of the French diplomatic mission a week after the kidnapping to the ostentatious encouragement of Dlimi when he left for Paris and the triumphal reception on his return. Hassan's fear of his over-mighty subject is a common but not very satisfactory explanation. But how else, if the King was still in favour of a rapprochement with the opposition up to the kidnapping, can his subsequent support for the perpetrators be explained?—especially when by acting just before his official visit to Paris, they had so seriously impeded his foreign policy.

The answer may perhaps lie in the peculiar political position of the victim and in the timing of the plot. Ben Barka had been in exile for several years and seems to have lost touch with his own country: his strong support for Algeria in the border war was highly unpopular in Morocco, and his own interests had shifted increasingly to his activities as the organiser of the Tricontinental Congress. But though his position at home had weakened (there was unexpectedly little protest at his disappearance), he was still a figure important enough for his party colleagues to fear entering the royal government while he remained outside it. The possibility of dissension between him and his party therefore complicates the situation still further. Pierre Clostermann, a Gaullist politician with good connections with the Moroccan royal family, argued at the second trial that Hassan might be glad to bring back a political leader who would divide the opposition and so weaken its bargaining power. Even Oufkir might have been reconciled to the possibility of Ben Barka's return if that would split the party and reduce the threat to his own position.

From the point of view of both the King and Ben Barka, however, the timing was crucial. Ben Barka, weaker in Morocco than before, remained a major figure there because of his status as an international revolutionary leader. This he would not abandon and when he talked to El Azzemouri it was about returning after, but not before, the coming Tricontinental Congress. But that would be too late for the King, who could not contemplate public reconciliation, still less acceptance as a minister, of the principal champion of the anti-American revolution in the third world. The King needed his old friend and present opponent back before the Congress if at all; Ben Barka would return voluntarily only after it. Here perhaps was the real equation that had to be solved.

One plausible account of the affair suggests that there was no solution. Since Ben Barka would not abandon the Tricontinental he had to be removed—not necessarily killed, but kidnapped and forced to give his captors access to his files in Geneva. Full information about the Tricontinental movement would be invaluable in many ways: for bargaining with the CIA and other secret services; intrigues and pressures in the Arab world; justification to the Moroccan public for the abandonment of the rapprochement policy; and, not least, the political (if not physical) elimination of Mehdi Ben Barka. But the same arguments can lead to a different answer; perhaps the equation could be solved after all. Not by murder—a bad solution which would delay and perhaps prevent a rapprochement with the opposition. Not by political negotiation—no solution at all, for Ben Barka would not willingly abandon his revolutionary role. But might it not be a different story if he had to make his decision under constraint? Then he could be faced with two alternatives. He could resign from the Tricontinental and return to Morocco loaded—and compromised—with honours from his sovereign; or he could be shipped off to prison and trial, after an 'interrogation' which would supply the authorities with useful details about the organisation of the Moroccan opposition movement and of the Tricontinental's plans. But while the King might have agreed to a proposal to face a captive Ben Barka with these alternatives, he and his Minister of the Interior might not have viewed the alternatives in exactly the same light.[7] Oufkir would have wanted to ensure that a reconciliation between the King and Ben Barka did not take place at his expense, and therefore might well have felt it necessary to discover Ben Barka's intentions for himself before letting the opposition leader and the monarch come face to face.

This would explain why Oufkir felt it necessary to come himself to Paris, but not why it took him so long to arrive. His presence was unnecessary and dangerous if Ben Barka was either to be killed in France, or to be shipped to Morocco for questioning; it made sense only if the negotiation or interrogation was to take place in France, whether to sound Ben Barka's intentions or to extract from him the means of access to the Geneva files. But if either was the motive it was essential to act quickly, before the French police and Ben Barka's friends in Geneva had discovered that he had disappeared. Yet Oufkir added to the extraordinary risk of coming personally to Paris the

[7] Another Moroccan Minister was in Paris at the time; Ahmed Balafrej, who was very close to the King, was in the city from 11 to 17 October and again from 26 October to 3 November for a medical check-up. By coincidence? For a rendezvous? Or to accredit the rendezvous story if anything went wrong?

extra risk of over 24 hours' delay—and in addition he came without money to pay the gangsters. This makes it impossible to believe that the plot worked out as the Moroccans had intended. It strongly suggests that though at first they had intended to work through Figon, they decided in September or October that he was dangerously garrulous and had better be dropped. (Perhaps their alternative plan involved the bogus arms deal with Ben Barka, hinted at by Tixier during the trial, for which the salesman Louis Nesmos was to be sentenced in March 1967.) This explanation would account for Figon's blackmailing letter to the Moroccans written soon after his return from Geneva in September—for the typist remembered doing it before the end of the month—but given to Lopez only on 10 October. It would explain why Figon, looking for a lucrative alternative to the blood money, was talking freely in early October—to Brigneau as well as to his usual friends—about the gangsters' scheme to kidnap Ben Barka on their own account and use him to blackmail the Moroccans. And it would explain why, learning two days before of Ben Barka's visit to Paris on the 29th, Figon seized the chance to face the Moroccans with a *fait accompli* and (as he said) blackmailed a reluctant Lopez into immediate action. By Lopez's own admission it was he who approached Chtouki on the 28th, not the other way round. If this was all the notice the Moroccans had, it is easier to understand both their unpreparedness and their extreme reluctance to pay off the gang.

For the second set of questions—about Ben Barka's fate—the answers again have to explain some puzzling features of the kidnappers' behaviour. If the evidence of the participants is disregarded as suspect, there are five certainties that have to be accounted for. First, around 4 p.m. on Saturday afternoon, only an hour before Oufkir landed and two hours after Dlimi did so, a group arrived at Orly to book four tickets for the 23.45 plane to Casablanca in the names of Dlimi, El Houssaini, Boucheseiche and 'Cohen', leaving a number (Fontenay 7) which was that of Boucheseiche's villa. The booking clerks recalled the group, and the police, after checking over 1,200 flight records, found no other suspicious note—though they admitted that Lopez could have arranged an unrecorded passage. Secondly, when Oufkir arrived at 5 p.m. he arranged for El Mahi to book him a Paris hotel room, ensuring that the reservation would be held until 1 a.m., but never used it—though given his reputation this is not very significant. Thirdly, Oufkir and Dlimi dined in Paris late that night, at a restaurant close to Mme Dlimi's hotel, and asked (as the waitress remembered) for a quick meal in order to catch a plane; Dlimi telephoned during the dinner. Fourthly, Lopez was seen at Orly both around midnight and again, with three men of North African appearance, between 5 and 6 a.m. Fifthly, when he left his family in Loiret to drive back to Ormoy he still expected to be back that night, for he warned the hotel he would be coming in about 3 a.m. At the second trial, Bouvier the detective pointed to the four unused tickets, the quick dinner and the two unused hotel beds (Oufkir's and Lopez's) as signs that something unexpected happened during the evening.

There are several possible hypotheses and there are objections to them all. The first is that the gangsters killed Ben Barka before Oufkir arrived. This was Tixier's line in court—rather to his client's distress—and it was supported by a letter supposedly from Le Ny, which the court did not take seriously, and by the article by Nadercine Challal mentioned below, though this part of Challal's statement was admittedly hearsay. He had heard that the body was buried in a wood and later disinterred and removed by the Moroccans; but like all similar stories this would make it hard to explain the presence of Oufkir (and Dlimi, according to Lopez) at Orly twice during the night. And if Oufkir found Ben Barka dead when he arrived, there is no explanation for the indications of a later change of plan pointed out by Bouvier.

A second hypothesis is that Oufkir left the suburbs to dine and spend the night in Paris, leaving behind him a live Ben Barka and believing that 'M. Cohen' was going to take the 23.45 plane more or less willingly. At 10 p.m. all was going well, and then something went wrong. It seems hardly conceivable that the General's subordinates would have maltreated Ben Barka against orders—but suppose that Oufkir left him in the gangsters' charge? These had committed a dangerous crime and when the General had arrived, he had not produced the payment they were demanding (according to Figon, Oufkir said Lopez's message had reached him on an official trip and he had been unable to obtain the money within a short time; at any rate we know that three of the gang were still hanging around the Moroccans for money four days later). Very shortly the gangsters' prize would walk out of their hands and on to a Morocco-bound plane. In the short time remaining, could they not at least extract from him the means of access to the Swiss bank where he must have kept the funds he administered for the Tricontinental Congress? Perhaps they also expected in any event to keep their blackmailing hold over Oufkir, who a week later swore to Clostermann that he had not committed the murder, adding furiously: 'They had me, they fooled me, I let myself be had.' This is perhaps the most plausible hypothesis. It would explain both the changes of plan noted by Bouvier, and the Moroccans' reluctance to pay up. Its main drawback is the fact that one of the gang, Boucheseiche, took refuge in Morocco after the crime. But none of the others did, and it is conceivable that Boucheseiche, whose links with the Moroccans were much older and closer than those of his associates, was not present and was unaware of their intentions.

The third hypothesis is that Oufkir left for dinner knowing that Ben Barka, dead or half dead, was in no condition to be sent on a regular flight (even if they could have taken a drugged or injured man with Lopez's help, that would have left Lopez too vulnerable to later investigation). This does not necessarily imply that Oufkir committed the crime personally. The evidence that he tortured (not that he killed) Ben Barka comes only from Figon. The story Figon told to Jean Marvier was reproduced by *L'Express* in circumstances quite as dubious as anything the authorities did. The journal gave it a baseless and sensational title ('I Saw Ben Barka Killed'), and claimed to have a tape of the account which the editors no longer possessed and knew in any case to have been inaudible. Nevertheless it seems clear that the tape had existed—a highly respected foreign journalist, Edward Behr, testified that he had lent his recorder to Marvier, heard the inaudible tape played back, and then taken notes from Marvier's account of it. Moreover, Figon had given a very similar account to several others: to the two *Express* journalists, Derogy and Kahn—he would not let them record it, but told them enough to enable them to persuade Marvier to let them use his notes; to Jean Vignaud (the dubious acquaintance he was to see for the last time just before his death); and most of the story to his old friend Mme Arnoul. None of this proves that his account was true, though for part of it there was corroboration; Judge Perez in the second trial revealed that the police had found Dubail's fingerprints on a glass in the room where Dubail, according to Figon, had guarded Ben Barka for a time. But that still does not validate the sensational parts of the story. Figon was a notorious romancer (and indeed told Vignaud that he often gave similar accounts of an event to different people with slight discrepancies in them, so that he would know which of his friends had betrayed his confidence). He lied frequently in order to embarrass or ruin Bouvier, and Lemarchand, and Caille; and he had an enormous grudge against Oufkir because he had not been paid. And the most convincing witness among his friends, Mme Arnoul, who thought most of the story genuine, was sure that he had never spoken to her of the torture.

But whether or not Oufkir himself played a part, he might have ordered Ben Barka to be killed on the Saturday evening and then gone into Paris to dine—and perhaps establish an alibi. This is said to be what happened by Roger Muratet in the fullest account of the case, *On a tué Ben Barka* (Plon, 1967). He gives a circumstantial description of how the body was shipped in a trunk aboard the 23.45 plane to Casablanca. But if this is true it is astonishing that the Moroccans should have carried out so risky an operation on an ordinary flight without having Lopez there to protect them. And Muratet mentions none of the signs mentioned by Bouvier as indicating a sudden change of plan; he ignores the booking of 'Cohen's' ticket for that plane with those of the three Moroccans, the no-show of all four, the desire of Oufkir and Dlimi for a quick dinner, and their appearances with Lopez (by his account) at Orly at midnight and at 5 a.m.—well after Lopez had expected to be back in Loiret. Nor is it much more plausible to assume that Oufkir had Ben Barka killed and planned to ship the body on the morning flight. For if he meant to be at Orly at 12 and 5 a.m. to supervise arrangements, why on earth should he go off to Paris for a dinner over which he then had to hurry? And if he went into Paris thinking his presence no longer necessary, why did he return to Orly?

Thus the third hypothesis—that Ben Barka was killed by Oufkir or on his orders—is hard to reconcile with a plan to ship out the body either by the night or the morning plane. But it is just conceivable that the Moroccans planned to send it on the former and that the plan failed—because Lopez thought it too risky, because the transport failed to arrive, or because the gangsters intervened again (not if Ben Barka was dead, but if he was barely alive, they might have wanted more time to extract information from him than departure by the night flight would have allowed). But whichever hypothesis is preferred it has to explain why Oufkir first went to dine in Paris, then unexpectedly returned twice to Orly in the middle of the night. For it seems clear that when the General left the suburbs for Paris he thought he had completed his mission—in one way or another—and had finished with the whole business; he would not have returned to Orly unless, after his departure, something had gone badly wrong.

VII. THE FRENCH RESPONSIBILITY

The 'second and third Ben Barka affairs' are concerned, no longer with the fate of the victim, but with the degree of responsibility of French officialdom for failing either to avert the crime, or rescue the prisoner, or arrest his kidnappers. Here one point is absolutely clear. The Gaullist government not only had no interest in Ben Barka's death, but had every interest in his survival. Ben Barka was a left-wing, anti-American, third-world nationalist leader with a lively admiration for General de Gaulle, and had been received at the Elysée some time before: a natural ally for Gaullist policy. Thus any official French connivance could have come only from some section of the State machine which was acting clean contrary to the wishes of the President. Despite much Gaullist rhetoric this hypothesis is at least as plausible under the strong Fifth Republican government as under its weak predecessors.

Suspicion of guilty foreknowledge centred on two groups which were bitter rivals: the unofficial but well-connected coterie of Lemarchand and the official but clandestine SDECE. In the early weeks of the case the evidence implicating Lemarchand was pretty tenuous. It was a fact that he was Figon's friend as well as his lawyer and the channel through which Figon was first contacted by the authorities; it was also admittedly a fact that he repeatedly lied about this contact both to the examining magistrate and in public. He had had some professional relations (their closeness was in dispute) with Le Ny, Vignaud, and another crook, Liwer, an associate of Figon's gangster friend Jo Attia. It was also universally believed that Lemarchand had been the organiser of the 'barbouzes' who ruthlessly fought the OAS in Algiers. But dubious associations do not prove complicity in the Ben Barka case. That charge arose from Lopez's evidence that Lemarchand had been on the 11 a.m. Geneva plane on September 20; from El Mahi's statement inspired by Lopez (though corroborated, if that is the word, by Figon) that he had been with the gangsters at the Résidence Niel on October 25; from Lopez's guess that it was to him that Chtouki telephoned on October 28; and from Lopez's claim to have recognised him at the scene of the kidnapping. The fourth of these statements was completely disproved and the third was, at best, only guesswork. The second was withdrawn by El Mahi when confronted by Lemarchand (while Figon's corroboration could be accounted for by his grudge: Lemarchand had not obtained the passport and money Figon wanted for his escape). The first was satisfactorily explained: Lemarchand was accompanied by a relative of his client at Geneva whom he said—and then proved—he was visiting; and his booking was made four days before while Figon had changed his at the last minute from an earlier flight. (Figon's own charges against Lemarchand can be disregarded; they were made only after he had conceived a grudge against his former protector.)

As in the case of Bernier, if Lemarchand was not guilty then he had pretty clearly been carefully placed in a highly compromising situation. For this there could be two reasons: an attempt to ensure that if anything went wrong, the threat of involving so close a friend of Caille and of Frey would persuade the authorities to hush everything up; or alternatively an attempt to implicate Lemarchand and through him his political friends and discredit the government as Tixier so obviously hoped to do. These two objectives—to involve Lemarchand as a protection for the criminals, and to involve him as a weapon against the Gaullists—were mutually incompatible in that no one person could want both; but anyone pursuing either end had a common interest in piling up evidence against him. Lopez, whose written report had not identified Lemarchand as lawyer, deputy and Gaullist underground organiser, claimed during the second trial that on seeing Figon and the barrister together he had at once concluded that Figon belonged to Lemarchand's organisation. 'Yes or no, did you report that?' asked Judge

Perez. 'Oh Monsieur le Président, you and your yeses or noes' was the only reply.

Quite apart from Lemarchand's own behaviour, however, there were two doubtful points in the conduct of his friends at the Ministry of the Interior at the critical moments. One was the phone call to Souchon, which was easily dismissed as an invention by Frey and by the Public Prosecutor— but not so clearly by Souchon's immediate superior or by the Prefect of Police, who both knew the character of the accused man. The other was the stubborn silence of Commissaire Caille about his informer whose name he would not reveal even in secret session of the court; in a case in which the Minister of Defence and secret service chiefs were prepared (at least inter- mittently) to authorise the revelation of defence secrets, Caille's protection of his sources remained uncompromising and unexplained—though he was vigorously encouraged in his course by both the Prefect of Police and the Minister of the Interior. One theory which might account for both these weak points was put forward very belatedly, at the very end of the first trial, in a *Nouvel Observateur* article by Nadercine Challal, a Moslem of Gaullist sympathies who had been a mayor in Algeria. He stated that in Algeria in 1961 he had come to know Lemarchand, whom he supplied with information against the OAS. Later, in Paris in May 1965, a Moroccan official had asked him to help arrange a clandestine political negotiation between a Moroccan government representative in France and Ben Barka, whose suspicions were to be overcome by having French policemen approach him; Challal was to persuade a friend of his who held a senior post in the Ministry of the Interior to phone the policemen and authorise them to act. He and his official friend were both reluctant, but agreed when Lemarchand urged them to do so. Lemarchand later discovered through Figon that the Moroccans' real aim was a kidnapping, but insisted that the plan should go on until, warned by Figon, the French police would intervene and rescue Ben Barka—thus securing a triumph for Gaullist prestige in the third world, making a valuable friend in Morocco, and incidentally paying back SDECE which had been anti-Gaullist in the OAS days and was now involved in the Moroccan plot. (Some adherents of this theory have added another motive: to discredit Oufkir who was too pro-American for the Gaullists.) Instead, Challal reported, Figon had sold out to the Moroccans and told Lemarchand nothing until his summons on 2 November. (Challal announced his willing- ness to testify in court but was never summoned—or perhaps never found.)

This account was belated, and Lemarchand denied all knowledge of its author. But it agreed closely with some evidence from Jacques Derogy of *L'Express*, one of the journalists who had interviewed Lemarchand. Derogy's story concerned Gerald Gohier, an acquaintance of both Lemarchand and

Figon, and a journalist on *Minute* at the time of the crime. According to Derogy, Gohier had said on two separate occasions—each time before a witness who was to support Derogy's account—that on 21 October, eight days before the kidnapping, Lemarchand had told him over lunch that Figon was involved in an affair concerning Ben Barka. Gohier had also said that the police had known about the plot and allowed it to proceed in order to intervene at the appropriate moment, but the Moroccans knew they knew and foiled them. In court Lemarchand denied both the lunch and the conversation, but in an earlier appearance he had admitted to dining with Gohier that day. Gohier admitted the meal with Lemarchand and the place, but not the date; he agreed he had talked to Derogy about Figon and Lemarchand, but denied that Ben Barka had been mentioned either by Lemarchand to him, or by him to Derogy. Apparently a particularly unconvincing witness, he also strenuously denied he was Caille's informer; but when asked the same question, Caille remained silent. Gohier reluctantly admitted that he had heard Figon's bar conversation on the night of 29 October, but said he had paid no attention to it.

Challal's theory is the one coherent (if far-fetched) explanation offered of why Lemarchand or the Ministry of the Interior might have had fore-knowledge of a plot they did not stop. Even this theory puts them on Ben Barka's side—although it attributes to them a curious way of showing their sympathy. Still more damaging are the charges against the SDECE, which was widely suspected of direct involvement in the conspiracy itself. A variety of motives have been suggested. One, much favoured especially among Left Gaullists, was collaboration with the CIA to eliminate the organiser of the Havana Tricontinental Congress. Another was that SDECE were obliging either Moroccan Intelligence as such, or Oufkir in a personal vendetta against Ben Barka, in return for services rendered in the past. There is no doubt that the Moroccans had frequently helped the French; Robert Buron, a prominent politician who had a clandestine meeting with Algerian nationalist spokesmen in Morocco in 1958, discovered soon afterwards that it had been fully reported by the Moroccan secret services to their French colleagues. Again SDECE might have had its own professional reasons for collaboration. Morocco was said to be central to all its African operations, which could hardly continue uninterrupted without at least the tolerance of the Moroccan authorities; and the top post that Lopez coveted in Royal Air Maroc (and for which the Moroccans were certainly pressing his claims) would obviously have widened the opportunities open to French Intelligence. Lemarchand even complained to Derogy and another left-wing journalist (separately) in January 1966 that the anti-Gaullist wing of SDECE had used the case to try to destroy him and Caille in reprisal for the part they had played in breaking the OAS.

That there were some SDECE officers who were violently opposed to Gaullist policy towards the United States, especially in Intelligence matters, is clear from the now celebrated 'revelations' of the former SDECE agent Pierre Thyraud de Vosjoli (the basis for the novel *Topaze* about a Russian spy in de Gaulle's entourage). Even if Vosjoli's story is exaggerated or untrue, the outrage that led him to write it would still show the bitter feelings of some people in the service. It was no secret that passions ran equally high over colonial policy, and that during the Algerian war the SDECE could not be used against the OAS. Indeed Georges Pompidou, who as Prime Minister had been responsible for SDECE, told the National Assembly on 6 May 1966: 'It must be admitted that having been, especially in recent years, occupied entirely by the Algerian war, that is the struggle against the FLN, the personnel of the SDECE were peculiarly badly placed to adapt readily to the situation produced by the Evian Agreement and even sometimes to accept Algerian independence.'

Yet it would be a mistake to regard SDECE as merely an efficient machine concentrated on the ruthless pursuit of antiquated colonialist politics. The antagonism between it and the police included a large element of purely professional jealousy. Thus M. Colon, chief of the airport police, gave evidence that Lopez was always boasting publicly about his secret service work which was 'the laughing-stock of Orly'. Le Roy replied that this proved only that Colon knew nothing about SDECE's real activities and that Lopez had been kept at Orly expressly to divert Colon's attention. Later at another session of the court, Le Roy, explaining why he had gone so early to organise General Jacquier's arrival, asserted that it was necessary to greet the head of SDECE in one particular reception room—the one without microphones. Lopez proudly intervened to say that he had discovered the 'bugs' and that this was the reason why M. Colon detested him, because he had found the microphone hidden behind the Picasso! Nor was the secret service always so security-minded as to overlook human feelings. When the Judge asked Mme Lopez whether she knew that her husband belonged to SDECE she replied 'Oh yes; they sent us a greetings card every New Year'.[8]

The conduct of the authorities during the critical days just after Ben Barka was kidnapped is perhaps more understandable than the critics allowed. SDECE claimed not very convincingly that its information was too incomplete and uncertain to be worth passing on. But if for whatever reason the secret service did not inform the police or the ministers, it would have been

---

[8] The rivalry between police forces also had its comic as well as its sinister side. Julien Le Ny was a passenger in the car which took Ben Barka to Fontenay; the court heard that Souchon had thought the gangster to be one of Lopez's SDECE men until he made a critical comment on the Prefecture's vehicles, when 'I concluded he was from the Sûreté Nationale'.

surprising if the latter had immediately concluded, on the evidence of Figon or the suspicions of Bernier, that the Minister of the Interior of a friendly country had come to France and personally murdered his political enemy. The reluctance of the authorities to close the frontiers is also understandable, and the fact that that dramatic step had been taken not very long ago—incidentally, against a chorus of protest at the time—made it harder not easier to repeat. The departure, unquestioned, of Dlimi is perhaps a little harder to explain, but not much; the decision to conceal the confession of Souchon and Voitot, pending diplomatic discussions with the Moroccans, had already been taken and even the most polite detention of the head of the Moroccan police would hardly have encouraged the Moroccan government to save French face by taking full responsibility. When counsel at the second trial asked Fernet, 'So if the Moroccans had dismissed Oufkir your police officers would never have been arrested at all?' Judge Perez pulled him up sharply for an 'inappropriately polemical question'.

In the 'third Ben Barka Affair' concerning the later stages of the enquiry, the authorities undeniably behaved in a way certain to raise the maximum suspicion. But this could be explained without assuming guilty foreknowledge, as the effect of clumsy and unscrupulous attempts at concealing their previous misdeeds. There is no question that they made such attempts. The concealment of Souchon's confession on the 3rd was explained by the diplomatic talks, and also by the suggestion that if Ben Barka was still alive in Moroccan hands, the revelation that French policemen were involved might incite his captors to kill him off and blame the French. But these motives, even if valid up to 12 November, cannot explain why the authorities never told Zollinger of the real confessions, but instead arranged sham ones after Souchon and Voitot were arrested, in order to mislead the examining magistrate who learned the truth only on 14 January when Souchon finally decided to tell him. This prolonged silence was plainly due exclusively to a political desire to conceal an illegal act from the judicial authorities—and from the electorate in the middle of a presidential campaign.

Many wild charges against the authorities were made during the case and believed for a time, only to be convincingly disproved: the story that Simbille was an old friend of Boucheseiche, which proved a simple case of mistaken identity; the story of the Ministry of the Interior plane which was supposed to have flown Ben Barka to Brest for transfer to a Moroccan ship, but which was shown to have made an entirely regular and innocent flight; the story of Alcayde's presence at the scene of the kidnap, produced by a lawyer (Biaggi) who could give no evidence for it. And some other sins of omission or commission may have been no more than blunders (e.g. the neglect to seal the villas) or forgivable failures (the inability to locate Figon) or the product of a desire to dispose too quickly of an embarrassing affair (the rapidity with which Figon's suicide was announced and the indecent haste to close his case without letting counsel for the Ben Barka family, or even M. Zollinger, see the file—why not, if Figon really had committed suicide?). Such incidents aroused doubt and sometimes positive suspicion even when taken singly; as they accumulated, disbelief in the good faith of the authorities inevitably spread. If, then, the Gaullist regime had no responsibility at all in the plot against Ben Barka, had it something to conceal over and above the natural desire of each of its services to cover up its own past blundering and negligence?

Here there are three possibilities. First, the desire to protect SDECE. Even governments which feel let down by the security services are never willing to expose their workings to prying eyes. 'Reorganisations without revelations' was the motto of the American government after the Bay of Pigs, and the British after Profumo and Philby. Gaullist ministers might struggle to bring a recalcitrant sub-government under their own control— but certainly not under that of Parliament or public opinion. They were more than ever reluctant to take that risk at a time when no one could be quite sure whether what was once called 'the *really* secret secret service' was actually working for King Hassan, for General Oufkir, for the CIA, or for the French crypto-fascist opposition, rather than for the government in Paris. For politicians and ordinary citizens would be bound to ask themselves, as counsel once asked the director of SDECE to the scandalised astonishment of Judge Perez, whether the secret service was 'legitimate or even useful'.

Secondly, some prominent Gaullists may have felt a need to protect themselves. Scandals have a tendency, above all perhaps in France, to search beyond the original questions and to drag skeletons out of many obscure cupboards in the process. The Gaullist movement was born in the secret organisations of the Resistance, and President de Gaulle himself commented, in his press conference on the case, on the survival of the underground 'networks' and the fierce hostility against them of their enemies from Vichy days and those of the OAS. 'Everyone knows', he declared, 'that the Resistance had its "specialist groups"'; and later in the Algerian quarrel 'everyone knows...that the authorities employed clandestine elements to inform themselves of subversive plots. Everyone knows that among the men who once belonged to these there may remain some nostalgia for their past activities.'

In Algiers in 1961, when the OAS were murdering regular policemen and army officers, the Gaullists fought them with their own weapons in a savage clandestine struggle. In that battle the men employed seem sometimes to have been as dubious as the means; and there were many bitterly resentful

Frenchmen—perhaps in the ranks of SDECE, certainly in the right-wing press and on the defence benches in court—who were only too anxious to expose both. It was rumoured persistently that Figon had been used as a barbouze either in Algiers or in the spectacular kidnapping of the OAS leader Colonel Argoud in Munich in 1963; but as Lemarchand pointed out without being refuted, Figon was in Portugal when Argoud was seized and in prison till near the end of the Algiers struggle. No such evidence was produced to contradict the equally persistent reports that Boucheseiche and his gang had interspersed their life of crime with two quasi-political wartime periods of unofficial police service—with the Gestapo against the Resistance and with the barbouzes against the OAS.

Thirdly, these charges could embarrass the Gaullists first in the unexpectedly difficult presidential election and then in the parliamentary campaign which in effect began immediately after (though that election was not due until March 1967). It was their proud claim to have restored, as the President of the Republic and all his followers tirelessly repeated, the dignity as well as the authority of the French State. But its dignity was hardly enhanced by the employment of the barbouzes, still less by the activities or the powers attributed to them by a conspiratorially minded public; how much worse an encumbrance was the charge that some of them had been recruited from notorious criminals. As for restored authority, this was not perhaps the most prominent feature of a regime whose secret service was accused by Gaullist leaders in private of working for foreign masters, Moroccan or American, and in public of sympathising with domestic crypto-fascists. When discussion of the case led to such embarrassing reflections it was hardly surprising that the Gaullists wanted it concluded with as little delay and as few revelations as possible.

Yet the sensational aspects of the case, though the most politically damaging to the regime, were not the real gravamen of the criticism of the Fifth Republic. Gaullists could plead that they had inherited the Algerian war from a previous administration, and so they had (though their own earlier record will not bear even cursory inspection, and de Gaulle's sedulously propagated myth that he was the great precursor of decolonisation is a distortion of history no less outrageous—though far more widely accepted—than any perpetrated by the late J. V. Stalin). Blame for the condition of the secret service was at least shared between the Gaullists and their predecessors, and blame for the form the Algerian war took in its last months lies primarily on the OAS terrorists. But it is the Gaullists alone who seven years after they came to power and three years after the war ended must bear overwhelming responsibility for the climate in which the civil, military and police services functioned.

One element of that climate was the bitter rivalry between official services —Sûreté Nationale against Prefecture, secret service against both—which recurs throughout this, like all other great French Affairs. A second element was the fondness for diversionary tactics illustrated by the repeated private attempts of Gaullist spokesmen (including ministers) to persuade journalists and other opinion-makers that the whole affair was the work of the CIA— a theory without a shred of evidence which, for once, even the French press did not swallow. A third element was the Gaullist ministers' attitude to their official positions. The attempt of the Minister of Justice to discipline a judge who (in his private capacity and under a pseudonym) wrote what perhaps nine-tenths of the country thought, was the only penal sanction imposed by ministers in connection with the case. General de Gaulle's Minister of the Interior neither offered nor was asked for his resignation, as his predecessor had resigned in 1934 when a foreign monarch was murdered in Marseilles. No contrast could be greater with the recent action when an important OAS prisoner had escaped and the departmental prefect, technically responsible for his custody, was instantly dismissed.

A fourth element was the repeated willingness of senior officials to impede judicial inquiry. SDECE would not produce its file on Ben Barka, and General Guibaud would not discuss how the service was organised (even though General Jacquier had done so). The heads of the police helped to conceal Souchon's confession on 3rd November from M. Zollinger, not only in the first week when ministers could plausibly say the public interest required silence, but later when all the ministers were protecting was their own reputations. Morvan of SDECE and Caille of the police both had the misfortune to fall ill just when their evidence might have been useful, and Caille protected his mysterious informer to the end as M. Frey publicly encouraged him to do. For the officials of course took their example from higher up. Derogy alleged that Lemarchand (who denied it) had said that Frey had asked him to conceal his 2 November meeting with Figon from the examining magistrate. The Ministry of Defence would not produce the SDECE questionnaire which Lopez took to Morocco in May, and it was the Minister, not the head of SDECE, who would not allow Judge Perez to call the officials who heard Le Roy's instructions to Deshaurmes on 22 October.

Another element in the climate of the case was the discovery by the general public of the squalid associations of some representatives of the new moral order. This was not without precedent: as Sir Denis Brogan remarked about the Stavisky case, 'The "republic of pals" meant that rigorously honest men were on good terms with fairly honest men, who were on good terms with shady men, who were on good terms with despicable crooks.' (Here, as in more respectable political spheres, some Gaullists apparently thought reform could be ensured by the elimination of the intermediaries.) Liwer, the currency crook and associate of Jo Attia, was alleged (but not demonstrated) to have been one of Roger Frey's constituency election agents. A respected court correspondent of *Le Monde* asked on 20 March 1966

What can policemen do who have just arrested well-known criminals carrying revolvers and sub-machine guns in their car, when a little later a senior official on orders from circles higher up goes to the police station to ask for them to be freed on the pretext that their job is to protect the Gaullist billstickers in the presidential election?

Maître Pierre Lemarchand was, politically speaking, an obscure Gaullist deputy with a wide acquaintance on the fringes of the law, who had been elected to the National Assembly a week after the providential arrrest of the only serious opposition candidate (on a charge which was dropped immediately afterwards), and whose involvement in the Ben Barka case led to his disbarment—reduced on appeal to three years' suspension. But within the Gaullist ranks he was not just a back-bencher remote from the seats of power; he was a close friend of the Minister of the Interior and he had rendered services in the Algerian crisis which earned him the solidarity of his *compagnons* of the UNR parliamentary party. One of the most painful parliamentary scenes of the Fifth Republic occurred over an attempt to amend the amnesty bill to bring the then disbarred Lemarchand within its scope. Opposed by the government, the entire opposition, the Left Gaullist chairman of the relevant committee and the UNR's Conservative allies, the proposal was supported by 90% of the UNR deputies and failed by only 47 votes.

Service rivalries, political diversions, face-saving ministers, subordinates who cover up for them, and politicians with dubious connections are not phenomena which made their first appearance with the Gaullist regime; each can readily be paralleled from other countries and other Republics. Nothing new—but the Gaullist boast was precisely that they had founded a new Republic, '*pure et dure*', truly expressive at last of '*la grandeur de la France*'. Instead the worst features of the despised old *République des camarades* were revived, more dangerous than ever, in the purified new *République des compagnons*.

The last example of the Ben Barka climate is therefore, though the least sensational, by no means the least striking. Louis Souchon had by common consent had an admirable record before joining the force and, as his retirement approached, an exemplary reputation in it. There was no evidence that this model policeman acted for personal gain when he broke the law to carry out what he thought was a political operation organised by his superiors for extraneous reasons which were no concern of his. Roger Frey maintained that Souchon had invented the phone call from the Ministry of the Interior which the policeman said he regarded as the final guarantee that his conduct had official approval. But the less backing that a man like Souchon felt he needed for his actions, the more complete the disintegration of discipline which they revealed.

'I thought it was official...I was fooled. But when someone tells you that M. *X* or M. *Y* of the Elysée is behind it, you believe them.' The speaker was not Souchon but a former barbouze from the war against the OAS, testifying in one of Lemarchand's libel suits (the only one to come to trial) on how the Gaullists attracted recruits for their own operations outside the law. Thus an officer of Souchon's character was prepared to act quite illegally in the way he did, either (as he said) because one of his superiors told him to help the secret service, or (as Frey argued) merely because a known secret service agent asked him to do it. The second hypothesis illustrates even better than the first that twilight of legality which was one hall mark of the Fifth Republic.

Even since 1940 General de Gaulle had been convinced, as he once said, that he 'incarnated legitimacy' in France. If a legal regime was illegitimate then Gaullists felt morally justified in using any means to uproot it—beating the imperialist drum overseas, undermining political stability in France, scavenging for scandal in the press, organising subversion in the army. The men who employed these weapons to come to power did not all share their leader's lofty conception of the purposes to which it was to be put. After seven years of Gaullist government, with its confusion between State and party, its official patronage and its secret subsidies, its underground networks and its parallel police, the most respectable servants of the Fifth Republic no longer knew where, in a political case, their duty to the Republic lay. President de Gaulle had some justification when he accused the press—so much less docile than his controlled television, so tiresomely inquisitive in illuminating the dark corners of the Ben Barka affair, but sometimes so reckless in its charges against men and institutions—of disregarding the 'honour of the ship'. But was not that concept already in jeopardy when the respected editor of *Le Monde* could write in reply, 'In France as in Morocco there are men who, in circumstances of exceptional violence, show themselves just as capable of rendering services on the fringes of the law as within its boundaries...in France, as in Morocco, one should think twice before making these men ambassadors, deputies, ministers or confidential advisers...'? A month before, as the revelations broke, the President himself was reported to have fumed to his cabinet, 'There is no State—and I am at the head of it'.

PART III

LEGACY OF EMPIRE:
WAR IN ALGERIA

7 The Fourth Republic: murder or suicide?[a]

I. SOURCES

In May 1958 France went through a cold revolution. In form it was common-place. Not only the law but the constitutional conventions were observed; the National Assembly merely elected a new prime minister by an unusually comfortable majority, and conferred on him emergency powers of exceptional scope. Yet a bare month earlier the deputies would not have dreamed of accepting either the man or the powers. They gave way because they feared the intervention of the army, and knew that no effective force—official or popular—would defend the legal government. Georges Bidault said that De Gaulle needed only ten words for his speech to the Assembly: 'Messieurs, entre la Seine et vous, il y a—moi.'

We now possess several accounts of the crisis. Books have been written by two deputies who flew to Algiers, Pascal Arrighi, and Raymond Dronne; by the settlers' leader and director of *L'Echo d'Alger*, Alain de Sérigny; and by a number of journalists. Henri Pajaud, of Algiers, and Dominique Pado of *L'Aurore* are wholly favourable to the movement; Serge and Merry Bromberger, of *Le Figaro*, and Paul Gerin of *Paris-Presse* are sympathetic; Jean Ferniot of *France-Soir* is critical; J. R. Tournoux of the *Progrès de Lyon*, though occasionally influenced by his close links with M. Pleven, is generally objective; André Debatty provides a useful anthology of contemporary comment.[1] Dronne, Sérigny, Pajaud, and Gerin deal almost entirely with events in Algeria; Arrighi and Ferniot concentrate on Paris; Pado, the Brombergers, Tournoux, and Debatty cover both. All except Gerin discuss the Corsican *coup* (Ferniot and Tournoux very briefly). Nearly all print full or partial texts of the principal statements made during the crisis;

[1] P. Arrighi, *La Corse—atout décisif* (Paris: Plon, 1958). R. Dronne, *La révolution d'Alger* (Paris: Ed. France-Empire, 1958). A. de Sérigny, *Le révolution du 13 mai* (Paris: Plon, 1958). H. Pajaud, *La révolution d'Alger* (Paris: Les 4 Fils Aymon, 1958). D. Pado, *Le 13 mai: histoire secrète d'une révolution* (Paris: Ed. de Paris, 1958). M. & S. Bromberger, *Les 13 complots du 13 mai* (Paris: Fayard, 1959). P. Gerin, *L'Algérie du 13 mai* (Paris: Gallimard, 1958). J. Ferniot, *Les ides de mai* (Paris: Plon, 1958). J. R. Tournoux, *Secrets d'Etat* (Paris: Plon, 1960); also *Carnets secrets de la politique*, Paris: Plon, 1958). A. Debatty, *Le 31 mai et la presse* (Paris: Colin, 1960).

[a] From *French Historical Studies*, 3.1 (Spring 1963); originally entitled *How the Fourth Republic died: Sources for the Revolution of May 1958*. The appendices are new (though the first two were written with the article). Sub-titles have also been added.

the most useful are those in Debatty, Tournoux, Gerin and Pado (and in *L'Année Politique* 1958, cited as *AP*). Debatty, Pajaud, and Sérigny have good photographs.

Tournoux is the most reliable; his material was carefully checked with the participants. The Brombergers seem to have won the loquacious confidence of every conspirator on either side of the Mediterranean, and their account of the plots coincides broadly with Tournoux. But they are confused, repetitive, and sensationalist, and on events and attitudes in Paris Ferniot is far better. Gerin is good on the mood of Algiers and the army; he has less than Pajaud on the preparations for the 13 May. Both are first-hand witnesses for the attack on the Gouvernement-Général (GG); Sérigny, though present before and after, was discreetly absent at the critical point. Pado is comprehensive in scope but brief, sketchy and inaccurate in treatment. Dronne, though careless and ingenuous, reveals a good deal (usually unintentionally). Arrighi was the nominal leader of the Corsican *coup*. He too suppresses tiresome facts and is very slipshod about dates and times, but his propaganda is more plausible than the others. Sérigny, except on his own activities, is worthless; in his pages the spontaneous unity of all patriotic Frenchmen is unsullied by planning and unmarred by dissension.[2] Debatty's sources are all in print; he is useful for foreign (including FLN) reactions, for the atmosphere in Algiers, and particularly for events elsewhere in Algeria.

There are many good accounts of particular aspects. In February 1958 Jean Planchais of *Le Monde* published a most perceptive book on the mood of the army. The events of the 13 May are described from the insurgents' viewpoint in the *Bulletin du Mouvement Populaire du 13 Mai* ('M.P. 13'), and in the Poujadist journal *Fraternité française*; also from the official side in a report by Lacoste's assistant Chaussade. There are many articles on events, movements and atmosphere in Algeria, notably in *France-Observateur* and *L'Express*; a short book by Albert-Paul Lentin of *Libération* is also useful. The behavior of the Republic's leaders in Paris is criticized with asperity by Pierre Viansson-Ponté in *Esprit*, and with more sympathy by the right-wing deputy Jacques Isorni. A Socialist meeting in July 1958 heard full reports by Robert Lacoste, Guy Mollet, Jules Moch, and others; Moch summarized his very frank account elsewhere. The breakdown of the government's counter-measures after Corsica and the negotiations with De Gaulle were described at the time by two well-informed American reporters, Walter Kerr and Edmond Taylor. There are several circumstantial accounts of the

[2] Sérigny suppresses the army's plans to invade France (pp. 145–6) and implies that Salan and Massu had no foreknowledge of the Corsican *coup* (pp. 115–16); Arrighi insists (p. 71) that the 13 May was spontaneous and unplanned. There are all too many other instances of bias and distortion.

various plans for insurrection, while the activities and outlook of the Gaullists in France are recounted by two young militants, Jacques Dauer and Michel Rodet, and (in a novel) by Antoine Dominique,[b] who was also closely involved. André Le Troquer has published his own account of his crucial interview with De Gaulle. A general book on the Algerian problem by the American journalist Joseph Kraft gives a detailed account of the May days. Though one source is fictional and the others are mostly anti-Gaullist, there is reason to believe them all well-informed. Evidence about De Gaulle's own part began to appear only when *Algérie française* supporters started denouncing his betrayal of the cause; in books by Claude Paillat of *Paris-Presse* (reflecting his military sources) and by Jacques Soustelle, and at the trials of Alain de Sérigny and of the conspiratorial generals, Petit, Jouhaud, and especially Salan.[3]

All these reports overlap. They reproduce many of the same speeches, communiqués, and anecdotes. But often they supplement one another, and their contradictions are as revealing as they are exasperating. By checking one against another, a fairly accurate picture can be obtained.

II. CONSPIRATORS

Algiers has always been a conspirational city. On 6 February 1956 the extremists organized a riotous European mob to greet the new Socialist premier, Guy Mollet, and alarmed him into changing his policy and his Minister for Algeria. In subsequent weeks they built up 'counter-terrorist' societies to fight the FLN's nationalist terrorists with bombs and kidnappings.

---

[3] J. Planchais, *La malaise de l'armée* (Paris: Plon, 1958). *M. P. 13, Bulletins* no. 2, 4 and 5; *Fraternité française* (henceforth *F-F*), 25 October 1958 on the preparations for the insurrection and 1 November 1958 on the events of 13 May itself; extracts from Chaussade's report in *France-Observateur* (henceforth *F-O*), 18 September 1958, and the full report in Tournoux, *Carnets*, pp. 87–99. The *Monde* correspondent's story appeared from 27 May to 1 June 1958 (and see *ibid.* 15 May); *F-O*, 29 May has an excellent account of the first ten days in Algiers; *L'Express*, 15 May, has Jean Daniel's account of the events of the 13th, and on 22 May, 29 May, and 31 July it deals with plots and plotters. A. P. Lentin, *L'Algérie des colonels* (Paris: Eds. français réunis, 1958); P. Viansson-Ponté, *Esprit*, September 1958; J. Isorni, *Ainsi passent les Républiques* (Paris: Flammarion, 1959). *Bulletin intérieur du parti socialiste SFIO* (henceforth *SFIO*), no. 105, 6 July 1958; Moch also wrote in *La Nef*, July-August, and in *Midi Libre* in June. Kerr in *New York Herald Tribune*, 16 June 1958; Taylor in *The Reporter*, 26 June. For the insurrection plans, *L'Express*, 12 June 1958; *F-O*, 12 June, *L'Humanité*, 31 October (for Paris), *Le Canard Enchaîné*, 2 July (for the south-west); J. Dauer and M. Rodet, *Le 13 mai sans complots* (Paris: Pensée moderne, 1959); A. Dominique, *Le Gorille en révolution* (Paris: Gallimard, 1958); A. Le Troquer, *La parole est à André Le Troquer* (Paris: La Table Ronde, 1962); J. Kraft, *The Struggle for Algeria* (New York: Doubleday, 1961); C. Paillat, *Dossier secret de l'Algérie* (Paris: Le Livre contemporain, 1961); J. Soustelle, *L'espérance trahie* (Paris: Ed. de l'Alma, 1962). See *Le Monde*, 24 October 1960, for Sérigny's statement at his own trial, and 9 June 1961 for Delbecque's evidence at Petit's trial; also *Le Procès d'Edmond Jouhand* (Paris: Albin Michel, 1962) and *Le Procès de Raoul Salan* (Paris: Albin Michel, 1962).

[b] Pseudonym of Dominique Ponchardier, later French Ambassador to Bolivia.

In December 1956 a general, Jacques Faure, was arrested for conspiring to seize power in the city. A month later a bazooka shell was fired into the office of the Commander-in-Chief, General Salan, whose ADC was killed.

One extremist group was associated with the Poujadists; their chief was the intellectual of the movement, Dr Bernard Lefèvre. Another was the 'Christian Fascist' *Union française nord-africaine* (UFNA), whose leader Robert Martel was interned for a time by Lacoste. Both were involved, along with the Gaullist adventurer Biaggi, in organizing the riots of 6 February 1956. Both supplied recruits to the counter-terrorists, whose chief organizations were the CRF (*Comités de la Renaissance française*, dissidents from UFNA) and the ORAF (*Organisation de Résistance de l'Algérie française*, linked with the Poujadists).[4] ORAF's leader was a doctor and champion swimmer of Hungarian origin, René Kovacs; he was associated with General Faure's plot[5] and responsible for the bazooka attempt against General Salan. Arrested, he tried to escape punishment by boasting of his powerful political and military protectors; brought to trial soon after De Gaulle came to power, he conveniently escaped abroad.[6]

Both UFNA and the Poujadists dreamed of using a revolt in Algiers to destroy democracy in Paris. Martel of UFNA was in touch with a counter-revolutionary secret society in the capital, the 'Grand O', which was inspired by Dr Félix Martin, the sole active survivor of the pre-war Cagoulard conspiracy. Its leaders were a former commander-in-chief in Algeria, General Cherrières (who had left in 1955 after quarrelling with Governor-General Soustelle) and a former air force commander in Indo-China, General Chassin, who was now President of the *Anciens d'Indochine*, a turbulent body of ex-servicemen under violently anti-democratic leadership.[7]

More respectable settlers' leaders, like Sérigny, had less ambitious aims. They wanted a 'Government of Public Safety' dominated by their 'quartet' of parliamentary allies, Jacques Soustelle, Georges Bidault, André Morice,

---

[4] Brombergers, pp. 33–5, 78–9, 83–4, 89, 95–8; Tournoux, pp. 121–3; Pajaud, pp. 32–4; Lentin, p. 17; *Le Monde*, 26 Sept. 1958.

[5] On it, Brombergers, pp. 87–93 (put in wrong year *ibid.* p. 282); Tournoux pp. 197–8; Kraft, pp. 159–61; Arrighi, pp. 14–16; *L'Express*, 31 July 1958.

[6] Brombergers, pp. 61, 94–103 (put in wrong year, *ibid.* p. 48); Gerin, pp. 117–20; Kraft, p. 161; Arrighi, pp. 131–2; *L'Express*, 31 July 1958; *F-O*, 16 Oct. Kovacs said he took his orders from a Committee of Six including Soustelle, Debré, Arrighi, and General Cogny; Brombergers, p. 103, suggest that he knew (from General Faure) that the Gaullists were intriguing to replace Salan by Cogny, and therefore used these Gaullist names as blackmail. At his trial Salan accused the Gaullists; Mitterrand (Minister of Justice in 1956–7) spoke of the political conspiracy, and Debré gave a categorical denial: *Procès Salan*, pp. 77, 231–5, 276–9. Kovacs' accomplices were freed from prison by the insurgents of January 1960; in 1962 the chief of them was arrested as an OAS terrorist leader.

[7] Tournoux, pp. 121–4, 180–204 (all his unspecified quotations are from *Secrets d'Etat*); Brombergers, pp. 80–4, 121–3; Kraft, pp. 177–8; *L'Express*, 29 May, 31 July 1958; cf. Dauer and Rodet, pp. 50–1 (for *Anciens*); Lacoste, *SFIO*, p. 16 (for Dr Martin).

and Roger Duchet. Although Sérigny had been an ardent Pétainist in the war, he had recently financed and organized an Algerian section of Soustelle's largely Gaullist *Union pour le Salut et le Renouveau de l'Algérie française* (USRAF).[8] And he was in constant touch with the Resident Minister, Robert Lacoste (appointed after the riots of 6 February 1956). Lacoste had long been warning Paris that a change of policy would mean an outbreak in Algeria; by May 1958 this prospect no longer wholly displeased him, for his fellow-Socialists had thrown him over and accepted a change.[9] Finally, a tiny handful of Gaullists were resolved to use the expected rising to bring the General back to power.

There were very few Gaullists among the Europeans of Algeria. In the army (which now enjoyed wide powers of civil administration as well as decisive force) there could be no hope of success. Because part of the officer corps rallied to them, the Gaullists seized the leadership of the movement in Algeria from their locally stronger rivals. Because of their wide military, police, and administrative contacts in the French governmental machine, they were able to enforce a revolutionary transfer of power. And because of De Gaulle's personal prestige they were able to achieve their objectives without bloodshed in France, and with unexpected Moslem goodwill in Algeria.

The political crisis opened in September 1957. The Radical Prime Minister Bourgès-Maunoury introduced a mild Algerian reform bill, the '*loi-cadre*', which set up a single electoral college and so deprived the Europeans of their privileged political position. A hostile demonstration was called for 16 September; General Massu stopped it. Sérigny then called on his parliamentary friends, who overthrew the government; Massu called this 'a crime...which will probably lose us Algeria'.[10] The ministerial crisis lasted the record time of 37 days. From it emerged another Radical premier, Gaillard, who put through a still milder bill. The ex-servicemen and the Students' Union (AGEA) called another demonstration, which was a failure, and Lacoste retaliated by deporting some of the leaders and drafting the president of AGEA—who was succeeded by a more extreme character: Pierre Lagaillarde.[11]

---

[8] The caretaker government planned to arrest him for inciting to violence (in 1960 De Gaulle did so; he was acquitted). On his activities, Sérigny, pp. 6, 12–13, 45; Brombergers, pp. 61, 105, 154; Ferniot, p. 37; Tournoux, p. 261 n.; *Le Monde*, 24 Nov. 1960. On USRAF, also Ferniot, pp. 41–3; Dauer and Rodet, pp. 62, 168; Daniel, *L'Express*, 22 May 1958; Brombergers, pp. 58–60; Pajaud, p. 34; E. Michelet, *Le Gaullisme passionnante aventure* (Paris: Fayard, 1962), pp. 139–40, 170—he says it was quickly swamped by pro-Vichy elements.

[9] Lacoste, *SFIO*, p. 13. Arrighi, p. 16; Brombergers, p. 114; Kraft, p. 173; Daniel in *L'Express*, 15 May 1958.

[10] On Massu, Daniel in *L'Express*, 22 May 1958, Lacoste, *SFIO*, p. 13, Tournoux, p. 209, Brombergers, p. 42, note 87 below; on Sérigny, Gerin, pp. 148–9; on both, Ferniot, pp. 37–8.

[11] Pajaud, pp. 37–8; Dronne, p. 193; Brombergers, pp. 80 and 108–9; Sérigny, pp. 63–4.

In February 1958 the crisis became acute. Exasperated by Tunisian aid to the FLN, army leaders—without governmental authorization—bombed the frontier village of Sakiet. Ministers feared to offend the army by disciplinary sanctions, but they bowed to international opinion by accepting the 'good offices' of British and American mediators. Civilians and soldiers in Algeria feared this would entail a humiliating capitulation to the FLN. In Algiers the temperature mounted, and in Paris the Right overthrew another cabinet, their third in twelve months.

Both the Right and the army had miscalculated. Instead of stiffening the government's Tunisian policy, the Sakiet raid had weakened it. Now Gaillard's fall further undermined the influence of the friends of Algiers—even in their own parties. President Coty's first nominee for the premiership was Georges Bidault of MRP; the party president, Pflimlin, demurred. The Radicals would not join a Pleven cabinet which was to include the right-wing Radical leader André Morice. The Socialists would enter no government at all; this ensured the eviction of Lacoste from the Ministry for Algeria. The crisis, provoked by the settlers, was used to eliminate the men the settlers wanted. Finally Coty put forward Pierre Pflimlin, the man who had vetoed Bidault and had even talked of negotiating with the FLN.[12]

The Assembly was to vote on Tuesday 13 May. That same afternoon in Algiers, military chiefs and civilian crowds were to assemble at the War Memorial to commemorate three French soldiers executed by the FLN in Tunisia. On previous occasions, army and populace had clashed; this time it was different. The change was due mainly to the Gaullists, and in particular to Léon Delbecque.

Many Gaullists believed that the General could be brought back to power only through a tremendous psychological shock, which could come only from Algiers. In November 1957, at the suggestion of Soustelle, Delbecque—an old Gaullist who had served in Algeria as a reserve officer—was taken on the staff of the new Gaullist Minister of Defence, Jacques Chaban-Delmas. By April he had made 27 trips to Algeria. There he fostered contacts between soldiers and civilians and forged an instrument intended to turn to De

---

[12] Tournoux, pp. 245–50; Ferniot, pp. 2–4; Sérigny, pp. 22–4; Arrighi, pp. 18–21; Soustelle, pp. 15–16; J. Fauvet, *La Quatrième République* (Paris: Fayard, 1959), pp. 342–5. Also, on suspicions of Pflimlin, Dronne, pp. 56–8, Sérigny, p. 44, Gerin, pp. 16 and 76, Ferniot, pp. 14 and 72, Debatty, p. 42, Isorni, p. 139; on his defense, Brombergers, pp. 158–60; on the Socialists, Lacoste, *SFIO*, p. 14, Arrighi, p. 25. Coty ruled out Mitterrand and Mendès-France because Algiers would revolt: Ferniot, p. 4; Fauvet, p. 344n.; Brombergers, p. 130, cf. Tournoux, p. 245. De Gaulle, when approached secretly, refused to accept the nominating procedure: Brombergers, pp. 11 and 17–18; Fauvet, p. 345; cf. Tournoux, pp. 242–4; A. Dansette, *Histoire des Présidents de la République* (Paris: Amiot Dumont, 2nd ed. 1960), pp. 340–1.

Gaulle's account the explosion which he saw as inevitable.[13] After Gaillard's fall, he founded a Vigilance Committee (embracing 22 parties, student groups, and ex-servicemen's leagues) to canalize the popular discontent.[14]

Only at the last minute did Lacoste learn of these activities, which were concealed from him by the head of the telephone-tapping service.[15] Promptly he demanded that Gaillard have the conspirator withdrawn; otherwise he would appeal to President Coty.[16] But Delbecque managed to return (to a military airfield not controlled by Lacoste) and organized a large orderly demonstration on 26 April which showed he had his following well in hand.[17] At first Lacoste had thought the rally might strengthen his own position in Paris, but Peccoud, the Director of Security, feared it would get out of control and persuaded him to ban it.[18] But the army leaders, who had enforced his ban on the September march, declared themselves unable to do so this time.[19] The demonstrators denounced Pleven and called for a Government of Public Safety. There was no mention of De Gaulle.[18]

As Pleven gave up his attempt to form a government on 8 May, the tension in Algiers mounted. Fanning the flames, Lacoste was proclaiming everywhere the imminence of a 'diplomatic Dien Bien Phu'.[20] Sérigny and Delbecque were now working together; they saw him (separately) on 9 May and, at Soustelle's suggestion, pressed him to put himself at the head of the movement for a Government of Public Safety, assuring him that De Gaulle

[13] Tournoux, pp. 220–1, 230–1; Dronne, pp. 22–4, 51; Brombergers, pp. 45–7, 105–8; Pajaud, pp. 24, 39; Gerin, pp. 78–81; Ferniot, pp. 38–9; Fauvet, p. 344; Kraft, pp. 175–6; *F-F*, 25 Oct. 1958; *F-O*, 29 May 1958; Daniel in *L'Express*, 22 May 1958. Chaban-Delmas neither knew the details nor played his part on 13 May: Brombergers, pp. 43–51, 60, 69, 234, cf. Tournoux, p. 238—though Dronne (p. 24) claims Chaban knew nothing, *F-O* (29 May) says he knew everything, and he himself in the 1958 election boasted of his responsibility (*Le Figaro*, 21 Nov. 1958).

[14] Gerin, pp. 80 and (full list) 206; Brombergers, p. 108; Lacoste, *SFIO*, p. 14; Debatty, p. 41.

[15] Brombergers, pp. 46–7, 113.

[16] Lacoste, *SFIO*, p. 14, Tournoux, p. 238; Gerin, p. 80; Pajaud, p. 24; Brombergers, pp. 71 and 113.

[17] Estimated at 10,000 by the authorities and 30,000 by Delbecque: Tournoux, p. 238n.; cf. Lacoste, *SFIO*, p. 14; Brombergers, pp. 63 and 112. Pajaud (p. 21) and Arrighi (p. 62) agree 10,000; Debatty (p. 41) says 15,000. Delbecque's decisive role is stressed in an official telegram published by Tournoux, p. 475 (extract given by Lacoste, *SFIO*, p. 14); and by Lacoste, *Procès Salan*, pp. 314–15.   [18] Sérigny, p. 14. For Peccoud, Pajaud, p. 22.

[19] Lacoste, *SFIO*, p. 14; he anticipated this in an official telegram published in Tournoux, pp. 473–4. General Allard even authorized his troops to protect marchers from the police by force: Brombergers, p. 112. This was needless, as the Prefect Baret shared his views: *ibid.* pp. 147, 164. Cf. Sérigny, pp. 29, 71 on Baret; Daniel in *L'Express* (22 May 1958) on both men.

[20] Jouhaud, *Procès Jouhaud*, p. 19 (cf. Brombergers, p. 133); *SFIO*, p. 13; Gerin, p. 74; Pajaud, p. 24; Sérigny, p. 32; Arrighi, p. 18n. (six different examples); cf. Tournoux, p. 236, Ferniot, p. 55; but not, as often stated, in *L'Express*, 2 May 1958. On 8 May his office said his departure was 'the FLN's most resounding victory since the beginning of the rebellion...can lead only to a sell-out...not only inopportune but catastrophic': *SFIO*, p. 15 (cf. *ibid.* p. 28). He is said to have told an Algiers senator to 'have a fine demonstration and sack the town hall' (he loathed the liberal mayor, Chevallier): Sérigny, p. 38, Brombergers, p. 141, Lacoste denied it. See also Gerin, pp. 207–8; Pajaud, p. 25; Daniel in *L'Express* (22 May 1958); *M. P. 13*, no. 2; and p. 137 below.

would come out in their favor.[21] Delbecque organized Vigilance Committee delegations to reinforce their plea. Lacoste hesitated; he favored an *Algérie française* demonstration but not a revolt against the Republic. Finally he refused, and on the 10th he left for Paris, to the intense wrath of the Europeans of Algiers. Disappointed, Sérigny now turned to De Gaulle (of whose integrationist opinions he had been assured by Soustelle). In an editorial on Sunday 11 May he appealed to the General to speak out.[22]

Originally Delbecque had intended to act in August.[23] But he seized the opportunity Lacoste had created. From the 9th, USRAF was distributing tracts demanding a Government of Public Safety. Over the weekend, preparations were hardly concealed. For the 13th, Delbecque in Algiers and Biaggi in Paris decided to organize simultaneous demonstrations culminating in the setting up of CSPs, Committees of Public Safety. (The Paris rally was to prove an utter failure.) The Algiers CSP, composed of Vigilance Committee members and led by Soustelle, would take over Lacoste's office in the Ministry of Algeria (better known as the Gouvernement-Général, 'GG') and launch an appeal to De Gaulle. However, a rival plot was being hatched under Delbecque's nose. For the Fascist 'ultras' had formed a Committee of Seven including Lagaillarde, Martel and Dr Lefèvre, which meant to steal the Gaullists' revolution as Delbecque was stealing Lacoste's riot. The ultras would attack the GG first, at 6 p.m. on the 13th; the army would have to join them or shoot them. They had no doubt of its choice, especially as their candidate for power was the army itself.[24]

[21] Clearly De Gaulle would not take power illegally, but Delbecque believed he would if offered it legally: Tournoux, pp. 231–4, 251–3, 261, 263–5, 302; Brombergers, pp. 25–6, 69; Gerin, p. 82; cf. for what De Gaulle knew, Ferniot p. 43, n. 83 below; for Soustelle, Soustelle p. 34.

[22] Sérigny, pp. 25–32; Brombergers, pp. 130–7, 141, 146; Lacoste, *SFIO*, pp. 15–16; Gerin, pp. 20, 74, 207–8. Cf. Pajaud, pp. 24–5; Pado, p. 44; Debatty, pp. 233, 307n.13. Soustelle's letter of 28 March 1958 (to Sérigny about De Gaulle's views) was published in *Le Monde*, 24 Nov. 1960; cf. also Soustelle, pp. 18, 30–3. Sérigny's editorial in *Dimanche-Matin* is cited in Sérigny, pp. 36–8; Debatty, p. 50. Lacoste's departure upset his own calculations by alienating European sympathies: cf. note 66 below.

[23] Brombergers, p. 46, Ferniot, p. 55. Sérigny told Jouhaud that night that Delbecque's plan was for a long demonstration ending (after Pflimlin's probable defeat) with Soustelle haranguing the crowd and appealing to De Gaulle: *Procès Jouhaud*, pp. 191–2. This was Soustelle's wish: Soustelle, p. 35 (cf. p. 17), Brombergers, pp. 140–1; and an officer told Lagaillarde as he broke into the GG, 'Stop, you're wrong, it's for tomorrow!': *ibid.* p. 156. If Pflimlin won, the *émeute* would prevent the arrival of Lacoste's successor; cf. *ibid.* pp. 153, 164–5, 190, Ferniot, p. 55, Gerin, pp. 53 and 58–9, Daniel in *L'Express*, 15 May 1958, and *F-F*, 25 Oct., Pajaud, p. 8, Debatty, pp. 49 and 73. Biaggi, who was planning a simultaneous Paris demonstration, was convinced that Delbecque also meant to drop paratroops at once on Paris: *Procès Salan*, p. 382. On this plan cf. Brombergers, pp. 48, 147, 154–5, 160, 190, 274; Tournoux, pp. 311–12. *Ibid.* pp. 262–6 says that he envisaged *either* sending paratroops *or* a peaceful occupation of Lacoste's office to influence the Assembly's vote: see also Brombergers pp. 155–6, 189, *M. P. 13*, no. 2, and Pajaud, pp. 39–40, 56–7 (who says they were to act at 8 p.m.; cf. *ibid.* p.112). See also Kraft (pp. 176–7) on the changes of plan.

[24] For the ultras, Brombergers, pp. 108–11, 160–6; Tournoux, pp. 241, 269–70, 275; Kraft, pp. 177–9; *M. P. 13*, no. 2. In the absence of General Cherrières they fell back on Salan: *ibid.*,

For the army was no longer willing to obey the government unconditionally. Salan and Massu were not themselves plotting, and indeed the Gaullists meant to arrest them.[25] But several of their subordinates were involved with the Gaullists or with the ultras (Colonel Thomazo with both).[26] And the whole army opposed negotiations with the FLN. Lacoste stiffened their hostility, bitterly upbraiding the generals on 8 May for their 'cowardly' silence.[27] Thus encouraged, Salan warned President Coty next evening that the election of a 'sell-out government' would produce incalculable results among his forces. General Ely, chief of staff in Paris, supported his protest.[28] And when Lacoste finally decided to ban the 13 May demonstration, Salan once again refused to enforce the order.[29]

III. MALICIOUS WOUNDING

On the morning of the 13th the activists distributed their leaflets. USRAF charged that Pflimlin meant to hold peace talks during the summer holidays; Algiers must stop his election and demand a Government of Public Safety under the 'quartet'.[30] At 1 p.m. a general strike began; it was complete.

also Brombergers, pp. 122, 183. Their strategist was Lefèvre: *ibid.* p. 121, Kraft, p. 178. The Committee of Seven also included Crespin (UFNA), Maître Baille, and two Poujadists, Goutailler and Ortiz (of the January 1960 barricades); Colonel Thomazo often attended. Delbecque did suspect their intentions: Tournoux, pp. 261, 274. On Paris, Brombergers, pp. 139–41, 155–6, 201–6, cf. pp. 59, 63; Tournoux, p. 290; Dauer and Rodet, p. 107.

[25] Brombergers, pp. 47–8, 143, 154, 196, 301; Tournoux, pp. 261, 263 (but cf. 257); Kraft, pp. 175, 177; Lacoste, *SFIO*, p. 16, Lentin, p. 64, *F-F*, 1 Nov. 1958, *L'Express*, 22 May 1958, *F-O*, 29 May 1958; Ferniot, p. 49, Gerin, p. 51; cf. note 77 below. Delbecque testified he had orders from the Gaullist leaders to 'replace' Generals Salan, Allard, and Jouhaud if necessary: *Procès Jouhaud*, pp. 184, 188.

[26] The Gaullists (notably Allard and Jouhaud) had been won over by General Petit of the General Staff with an assurance that Soustelle would lead and de Gaulle endorse the movement: see Brombergers, pp. 143–5, 196; Tournoux, pp. 260–1, 273; cf. Delbecque's evidence at Petit's trial (*Le Monde*, 9 June 1961). Officers were being chosen for Algeria on political grounds: Brombergers, pp. 48 and 156–7; Ferniot, p. 53; military spokesman quoted in the London *Daily Telegraph*, 16 May 1958, p. 22. The chief ultra officer was Lieut.-Colonel Trinquier, whom Lacoste had removed from Algeria but who was sent back (apparently at Salan's instigation) and whose regiment moved (out of turn) to Algiers on 11 May on orders from Paris: Lacoste, *SFIO*, p. 15; Chaussade in Tournoux, *Carnets*, pp. 91 and 98; Brombergers, pp. 49–50, 146–7, 164; Tournoux, p. 279 n.; Lentin, p. 24; Ferniot, p. 39. This was Delbecque's doing: Kraft, p. 176. On Thomazo see note 34, also Brombergers, pp. 45, 123–4; Tournoux, pp. 189–91, 204, 239, 241; Kraft, pp. 175, 177. On others see notes 38 and 51 below.

[27] Brombergers, pp. 129, 132–3.

[28] Text of Salan's telegram in *AP*, pp. 529–30, Ferniot, pp. 8–9, Sérigny, pp. 30–1; extracts in Debatty, p. 46, Arrighi, p. 20, Brombergers, pp. 137–8. Cf. Tournoux pp. 257–8, Sérigny, p. 35, Arrighi, p. 23. Jouhaud and Allard helped Salan draft the telegram and Lacoste approved it: Allard, *Procès Salan*, pp. 187–8. Salan himself (*ibid.* p. 78) misdates the telegram as 7 May.

[29] Sérigny, p. 71, Ferniot, p. 18, *F-O*, 29 May 1958; cf. Brombergers, p. 143.

[30] Text in Gerin, pp. 19–20, Pajaud, pp. 41–2 and Kraft, p. 174 (less full). Other leaflets in Gerin, pp. 209–11, Debatty, pp. 47 and 56, *M. P. 13*, no. 2; for loudspeaker slogans (see below), Gerin, pp. 26–7; Sérigny, p. 55; Dronne, pp. 62–3.

Soon the streets filled with youths. They sacked the American Cultural Center, but paratroops stopped them wrecking the offices of the mildly liberal *Journal d'Alger*.[31] At 5 p.m. the Vigilance Committee loudspeaker began spreading incendiary slogans: treacherous politicians and intellectuals in Paris were the real murderers of the three executed soldiers, show them not your scorn but your anger, we will accept no government of the System, no sell-out government, only a Government of Public Safety. After the ceremony at 6 o'clock, the army leaders returned to their headquarters and the crowd began to disperse. Neither realized that a revolution was in progress not far away.[32]

This revolution was not very well organized, since the operation Lagaillarde and Martel had planned for the end of the ceremony was anticipated by their rivals. It was not wholly serious, since these rivals were the schoolboys of AGELCA (*Association générale des élèves des lycées et collèges d'Algérie*).[33] And it was not too risky, since the paratroop colonels were sympathetic or privy to the plot.[34] Yet the Hungarian rising was also made largely by students and schoolboys.

Even before the ceremony began, the *lycéens* were climbing the broad stairway from the War Memorial up to the Forum, the open square in front of the GG. The top was held by riot police (CRS), who threw tear-gas grenades which infuriated the crowd. AGELCA loudspeakers denounced the CRS provocation; and the under-20s charged the steps. As schoolboys toured the city on their scooters spreading the word, the crowd swelled.[35] Suddenly the CRS withdrew into the building. Maisonneuve (Lacoste's assistant) protested to the prefect Baret, and was told paratroops would replace them. None had come. He ordered the CRS to make a sortie; they cleared the Forum, and he phoned Lacoste in Paris that it was all over. But

[31] Gerin, pp. 24–5, Sérigny, p. 52, Brombergers, pp. 168–9, Kraft, pp. 179–80, cf. Pajaud, pp. 43–4. The morning papers reported an official apology for the sacking of two other American Cultural Centers—by Arabs in the Lebanon: Debatty, p. 58.

[32] Lagaillarde described the assault in Sérigny, pp. 63–9; Brombergers, pp. 175–6. Martel's account is in *M. P. 13*, *Bulletins 2, 4*, and 5, and in Tournoux, pp. 275–8; cf. *F-F*, 1 Nov. 1958. That of Chaussade, Lacoste's assistant, is in Tournoux, *Carnets*, pp. 88–99, and (in part) in *F-O*, 18 Sept. Gerin (pp. 27–36) and Pajaud (pp. 49–58) were eye-witnesses; Brutelle, *SFIO*, p. 4, and the Constantine Socialist Krief, *ibid*. p. 18, quote others. (Krief is not named in *SFIO* but is identified by Tournoux, p. 338n.) For the crowd's dispersal, Gerin, pp. 27–8, Pajaud, p. 50, Brombergers, pp. 177 and 192–3, Dronne, p. 64.

[33] Gerin, pp. 10, 28–30, 53, 81; Brombergers, p. 170; *F-F*, 1 Nov. 1958, Brutelle, *SFIO*, p. 4, Krief, *SFIO*, p. 18, Ferniot, p. 16; but Tournoux (pp. 278–9) points out that the crowd did include more formidable revolutionaries, cf. Gerin, p. 37, Brombergers, p. 177.

[34] Thomazo disapproved of the attack, but did not tell Massu who later reproached him: Brombergers, pp. 161–2 and 166, Tournoux, pp. 269 and 276, Lacoste, *SFIO*, p. 16. See also note 26. For Trinquier, *ibid*. For Godard and Vaudrey, see below, note 38; for Ducasse, note 51.

[35] Pajaud, pp. 49–51; Gerin, pp. 28, 33, 53; Sérigny, pp. 57, 64; Brombergers, pp. 170–2; Debatty, p. 72; *M. P. 13*; *F-F*, 1 Nov. 1958. The CRS commander denied throwing the first grenades: Pajaud, p. 50.

at the War Memorial, as the generals left at 6:05 p.m., Lagaillarde was shouting 'Tous au GG contre le régime pourri'. Now, half an hour late, a few paratroops arrived and took their place on the stairway; they allowed the crowd to break through to the square.[36]

At 6:15 the attack began; fewer than five hundred took part.[37] The CRS were stoned and drew back behind the gates of the GG.[38] Outside, the schoolboys fell furiously on the parked cars of the GG officials, the only people not on strike; by 6:30 more intrepid *lycéens* had broken into the library at the corner of the building. Senior officers appealed for calm; without loudspeakers they were quite inaudible (later, they wrote on a board).[39] The parachutists stood by as one of their own trucks was used as a battering ram against the gates;[40] about 6:45 these gave way.[41] More tear-gas grenades were thrown from the windows, and a few shots fired; most of the crowd retreated, but a few broke through into the building, including Lagaillarde who, protected by his parachutists' uniform, climbed to an upper floor and vigorously (but inaudibly) urged his followers on. The CRS had disappeared, and the crowd began sacking the offices and flinging the files from the windows. The demonstrators hoisted their own flags, notably that of the Poujadist UFF.[42]

[36] Chaussade in *Carnets*, pp. 91–2; Brombergers, pp. 172–3; Sérigny, pp. 57–8, 71; Pajaud, p. 50; Kraft, pp. 180–1. Also on the CRS withdrawal, *M. P. 13*, no. 2; on the sortie, SFIO, pp. 4 and 18; on Baret, note 19 above; on the paratroops, *F-O*, 29 May 1958, Tournoux, p. 279n., Pajaud, p. 52, Gerin, p. 37.

[37] Brombergers, p. 177, Lentin, p. 64 (200–300), cf. Debatty, p. 62. Photos in *ibid.* pp. 61–5.

[38] 'On—il y a beaucoup de "on" dans cette histoire—les a fait retirer et le Forum est libre... une compagnie de CRS qui, de façon assez inexplicable, a été ramenée derrière les grilles': Gerin, p. 29, cf. *F-O*, 29 May 1958. Colonel Godard and Lt. Col. Vaudrey were maintaining order, the CRS were ordered to withdraw by the military, and the order was given on two separate occasions: Brombergers, pp. 173–4 (cf. p. 196); Tournoux, p. 279n. For Godard, see also Chaussade in *Carnets*, p. 91; cf. Pajaud, p. 52; Gerin, p. 31. Krief, *SFIO*, p. 18 says specifically that a paratroop colonel gave the order; cf. Daniel in *L'Express*, 22 May 1958; only Kraft, p. 181, names Godard; the episode is suppressed in Sérigny, p. 58. By 1962 Godard and Vaudrey were both OAS leaders on the run.

[39] Gerin, pp. 29–33 and 39, Sérigny, pp. 58–9, Brombergers, pp. 173–5, Pajaud, p. 51.

[40] 'Les hommes peints nous poussaient en faisant semblant de nous retenir', said a demonstrator: Brombergers, p. 177. On their passivity, *ibid.* pp. 174 and 196; Tournoux, p. 279n.; *F-O*, 29 May 1958; Daniel in *L'Express*, 15 May 1958; cf. Lentin, p. 24; on the truck incident also Chaussade in *Carnets*, p. 92, Gerin, p. 32; Sérigny, pp. 58 and 65 (who does not say it was a paratroop truck); *F-F*, 1 Nov. 1958.

[41] Sérigny, p. 68, Brombergers, p. 174 (6:45); Pajaud, p. 52 (6:50); cf. Gerin, pp. 32 and 52; Debatty, pp. 65 (6:30) and 294 (7 p.m.); *F-F*, 1 Nov. 1958 (before 7).

[42] Gerin, pp. 32–6; Pajaud, pp. 50–3; Sérigny, pp. 59 and 65; Ferniot, p. 17; Brombergers, pp. 175–6; Debatty, p. 308 n. 24. Vital offices and police and security files were protected by the paratroops: Gerin, pp. 32 and 36; Ferniot, p. 17; Sérigny, p. 68; Brombergers, p. 179. But all police files on economic offences disappeared (Brombergers, p. 194); and Pajaud, p. 54, says '...les services qui furent saccagés, ne présentaient aucun intérêt, seuls, quelques hommes qui savaient ce qu'ils avaient à faire, pénétrèrent dans les locaux de la sûreté nationale, d'où ils emportèrent tous les dossiers qu'il leur était utile de récupérer'. Peccoud left the bazooka plot file on his table for Salan to study (there were suspects on the CSP): Brombergers, pp. 184–5; cf. Gerin, pp. 119–20.

The Committee of Vigilance were still sitting not far away, unaware that they were being robbed of their revolution.[43] Massu arrived at 7:30, followed by Salan, who came by the subway from military HQ through which the senior officials (and apparently also the CRS) later escaped from the building.[44] Massu was furious, exclaiming 'Quel bordel', upbraiding Peccoud for using tear-gas and Lagaillarde for 'disguising himself' as a parachutist.[45] Before long Paris telephoned, and Lacoste warned Massu against promoting sedition; the story persists that Massu asked whether to fire on the crowd.[46] Lagaillarde and the riot leaders were urging him to become president of a Committee on Public Safety (CSP); he told a press conference next day that he agreed in order to keep them under control (Salan said nothing; the crowd had howled him down when he tried to speak).[47] The committee,

[43] Delbecque had been warned by Martel at 5:30 but had apparently not taken him seriously: Tournoux, p. 276, Brombergers, p. 170, *M. P. 13*, no. 2. Delbecque could not reach Soustelle, and some of the Vigilance Committee were jibbing at forming themselves into a CSP: Brombergers, pp. 188–9, Tournoux, p. 274. See also *ibid.* p. 281; Gerin, pp. 47 and 81; Kraft, p. 188.

[44] For Massu: Gerin, p. 36; Pajaud, p. 55; Brombergers, p. 180; Debatty, p. 62; *F-F*, 1 Nov. 1958; cf. Kraft, p. 182. Salan had taken his time, for an SOS had reached him at 6:45: Sérigny, p. 60, Brombergers, pp. 182–3, cf. p. 282. For the subway: *ibid.* pp. 182–3; *F-F*, 1 Nov. 1958; also Pajaud, p. 54; and Gerin, p. 49 (officials); implied *ibid.* pp. 34, 36 n. (CRS); Delbecque's associate Lieutenant Neuwirth had earlier arrived this way with an escort of territorials provided by Thomazo: Tournoux, p. 281.

[45] Gerin, p. 42; Pajaud, p. 56; Brombergers, pp. 181–2 (for Peccoud); Pado, p. 18; Dronne, p. 66; *F-O*, 29 May 1958; cf. Sérigny, p. 68 (for Lagaillarde, who was a parachutist reserve lieutenant); Mannoni in *Le Monde*, 29 May 1958; *F-F*, 1 Nov. (for all).

[46] Lacoste spoke by phone to his subordinates during the attack, and to Massu long afterwards. His subordinates may have asked him whether to fire; he certainly warned Massu against joining the CSP. Most accounts confuse the two calls.

Brombergers, pp. 175, 177–8 say Chaussade asked whether to fire; Lacoste asked Gaillard and Bourgès-Maunoury, his Minister of the Interior, who said no. (But Chaussade in *Carnets* does not mention it.) Ferniot, p. 20, says Gaillard, in the late afternoon, gave a 'don't shoot' order. (But the CRS commander told Pajaud he never received one.) Salan testified that he phoned Ely at 8:30 p.m. and said there could be no question of firing on the crowd: *Procès Salan*, p. 79. Massu is named as asking for orders in all other accounts (as in Ferniot in *L'Express*, 22 May 1958; *Paris-Match*, 24 May, quoted Debatty, p. 64).

That Massu asked whether to fire *after* the GG was occupied is surely improbable. Arrighi (p. 68) says he did so earlier, but contradicts himself, *ibid.* p. 32. Brutelle, *SFIO* (p. 4) and Viansson-Ponté (p. 197) say the same, but wrongly suggest he was at the GG. Because he was not, Gerin (p. 52) disbelieves the whole story (though he quotes it in its most popular form, that neither the outgoing nor the incoming premier would take responsibility for ordering troops to fire).

Lacoste describes his call to Massu in *SFIO* (p. 16) with no mention of firing; also (fuller) in Tournoux, *Carnets*, pp. 75–6; Debatty, pp. 63–4. The call came from Paris: Tournoux, *Carnets*, p. 74; Sérigny, p. 70; Gerin, pp. 45–6; Brombergers, p. 187; Pado, p. 20; Arrighi, pp. 32–3 (contrast Debatty, p. 63; Viansson-Ponté, p. 197). Gerin puts it at 9:24 p.m. (but does not mention Lacoste); Pado (p. 21) puts it earlier; Viansson-Ponté (p. 197) gives three incompatible times in one paragraph—before the attack, an hour before Massu announced the CSP, during Montel's speech in the Assembly (i.e. after the CSP was formed). *F-F*, 1 Nov. 1958, claims Massu said angrily to Lacoste, 'Then you want me to fire on the crowd?' and handed over the phone without awaiting a reply.

An order to fire would probably have been disobeyed: see Gerin, p. 37; Brombergers, pp. 177–8; Arrighi, p. 69; cf. Dronne, p. 64.

[47] For Massu, Sérigny, pp. 68–9; Pado, pp. 21–3; and for the press conference, note 60; for

formed about 8:45, was very unlike that envisaged by Delbecque and the Vigilance Committee.[48] The seven unknown individuals occupying Maisonneuve's office were all members; they proved to be Fascist sympathizers.[49] Three parachutist colonels were added, and (at the army's suggestion) four Moslems; Delbecque, who arrived soon afterwards,[50] was—as Soustelle's representative—made vice-president and, amid violent scenes, several Vigilance Committee members were brought in.[51] Outside the door a determined youth protested that it was 'inadmissible' to form one without him—his boys had entered the GG first, hadn't they? He was Jacques Roseau, president of AGELCA. He was made a member, voted with the extremists, and as President of the Youth Committee demanded postponement of the summer exams and abolition of the oral.[52]

In Paris the news produced a sensation. The deputies, absorbed in the ministerial crisis, had shown little concern for Algerian reactions to their decisions (though Serge Bromberger in that day's *Figaro* had given an amazingly accurate forecast of events).[53] Returning one by one from dinner, members were plunged at once into feverish agitation. But Algiers had again miscalculated. The demonstration to stop Pflimlin converted a very doubtful vote into a certainty; the Communists decided to abstain, and probably a few defiant members swung to his side. He was elected by 274 to 129. With

Salan, Chaussade in *Carnets*, p. 92; Pajaud, p. 57; Gerin, pp. 43 and 68; Martel in Tournoux, p. 278; Brombergers, pp. 182–3, Kraft, p. 182, Dronne, p. 67, Pado, p. 21, Ferniot, p. 17; *Le Monde*, 15 May 1958 (*ibid.* 30th differs); *F-F*, 1 Nov. 1958—suppressed by Sérigny (though cf. p. 71).

[48] For the time, Gerin, p. 44, Sérigny, p. 62, Brombergers, pp. 185–6; cf. *Le Monde*, 15th and 29th May 1958, Ferniot, p. 18 (earlier); Pajaud, p. 58, Debatty, p. 294 (later); Lagaillarde (Sérigny, p. 68) says 'about 8'. For the composition, Pajaud, p. 54 and p. 112; Brombergers, p. 186; Gerin, p. 82; Pado, p. 29; *F-O*, 29 May 1958.

[49] They were Baudier, Jolivet, Lagaillarde, Montigny, Moreau, Parachini, and Perrou: Sérigny, p. 61; Lagaillarde in *ibid.* p. 69; Arrighi, p. 68, Brombergers, p. 185. (Pajaud (p. 54) wrongly names Martel and Merlo, who however were added almost at once: Sérigny, p. 62; Martel himself in Tournoux, p. 278; *F-F*, 1 Nov. 1958, is slightly inaccurate.) Sérigny (p. 61) says the seven belonged to no political organization; Brombergers (p. 185) confirms (except for Lagaillarde, and Montigny of UFNA). Perrou, a commercial traveller from Morocco, soon dropped out; next October the other four (with Ortiz of the January 1960 insurrection and Roseau of AGELCA) demanded a general strike against De Gaulle, so did Lagaillarde at first but Montigny was against it: *Le Monde*, 24 July, 17 and 18 October 1958.

[50] By 9 p.m.: Brombergers, p. 190; Lacoste, *SFIO*, p. 16; Lagaillarde, *loc. cit.* He was absent when the CSP was formed (*ibid.*); so not before 9 as implied by Pajaud, p. 56, Gerin, p. 42 (before Salan) and p. 82 (just after Salan). But he spoke to the crowd between 9:10 and 9:24, after a quarrel with Salan (*ibid.* pp. 45–6); so not at 10 (as Sérigny, p. 62; Arrighi, p. 69; *F-F*, 1 Nov. 1958), 10.30 (as Kraft, p. 188), or 11 (as Paillat, p. 39, *M. P. 13*, no. 2).

[51] Tournoux, pp. 277, 282; Paillat, p. 58; Sérigny, p. 62 and (full list) pp. 164–5. The colonels were Thomazo, Trinquier, and Ducasse (who was rather favorable to the ultras: Paillat, pp. 60–1). Massu wanted Moslems to form half the CSP: Brombergers, p. 256.

[52] Gerin, pp. 44, 53–4; Lentin, p. 19; for his votes, see note 49. Under De Gaulle he was drafted, despite bitter ultra protests.

[53] Cited Arrighi, pp. 23–4 (fuller); Debatty, p. 51; for other warnings, *ibid.* pp. 47–53. Cf. Ferniot, p. 10.

the Communists and fellow-travellers against him, he would have a majority of one.[54]

The vote was taken about 3 a.m. Fifty minutes later the cabinet met at the Elysée, and in a sitting of an hour and a half took several grave decisions: to break off communications with Algeria, arrest some extreme Right leaders and dissolve their parties, place Soustelle under police guard, and reinforce the gendarmerie in Paris. The Minister of the Interior spoke of 'starving Algeria out', the Minister of Defense swore to 'smash the revolt'.[55 c] But the government also decided (unanimously) to gamble that Salan and Massu had really only joined the movement in order to control it, and they confirmed the delegation by Gaillard of civil authority in Algiers (*not* Algeria) to Salan.[56] At 6:30 a.m. President Coty as commander-in-chief ordered the army by radio proclamation to obey the legal government.[57] And at dawn, when the crowd had left the Forum and one foreign observer thought the government might have recovered control of Algiers,[58] the prime minister went to bed.

The cabinet's policy was fatally contradictory; it alarmed the army leaders by threats, while soothing public opinion by professions of confidence in the generals.[59] Yet without regaining their allegiance there was no hope of recovering control of Algeria. The premier was encouraged to try by a long telephone call from Salan on the morning of the 14th, and a mild press conference by Massu that afternoon, in which he insisted that his aim was to keep the civilians from getting out of hand, that the army was still in control, and even that the CSP would remain only until a new Minister for Algeria arrived. 'Including Pflimlin's Minister?' he was asked. 'My reply

[54] Ferniot, pp. 20, 27, 56; Arrighi, pp. 25–7, 33; Kraft, p. 192; Soustelle, pp. 17, 35; Brombergers, pp. 204–7, cf. pp. 198, 213, 216; Debatty, pp. 67–9, 307 n.19; Sérigny, p. 41; Gerin, p. 39; Tournoux, p. 289; Pajaud, p. 26; *Le Monde*, 15 May 1958.

[55] Ferniot, pp. 28, 57–9; Arrighi, pp. 27, 30–3; cf. p. 52n.; Brombergers, pp. 199, 213–14; Tournoux, pp. 289–92; Gerin, pp. 56, 85–6; Sérigny, pp. 74, 83–4; Pado, pp. 24, 30; Dronne, pp. 144–5.

[56] Though several ministers distrusted him: Brombergers, pp. 221–3. Gaillard's telegram arrived at 9:35 p.m.: Sérigny, p. 70, *F-F*, 1 Nov. 1958 (quoting text). He had asked Pflimlin: Brombergers, p. 191, cf. p. 213: contrast Ferniot, p. 26. At 1:15 Pflimlin after consulting Mollet, Gaillard and Duchet (Viansson-Ponté, pp. 199–200) attacked the generals in the Assembly as insurrectionaries; and about this time a second telegram (Salan's staff say a verbal message) restricted the scope of the first: Brombergers, pp. 198, 223; Ferniot, p. 26. Salan's powers now extended only to the department of Algiers: Sérigny, pp. 79 and 83; Brombergers, pp. 223 and 227; Arrighi, p. 41; cf. Debatty, p. 308 n. 25 ('the region'); Brombergers, p. 198 ('the zone'); not to all Algeria as Salan pretended (and as Kraft, p. 195), nor merely to the city as Ferniot, p. 26; Debatty, p. 74 (quoting the government communiqué next day). The dispute greatly influenced Salan's conduct: cf. notes 59 and 69.   [57] Text in *AP*, p. 534; Pado, p. 139; Ferniot, pp. 28–9; Debatty, p. 73.

[58] The *Messagero* correspondent, quoted Pado, p. 28; Debatty, p. 70; cf. Brombergers, p. 217.

[59] Tournoux, p. 292n.; Brombergers, pp. 199, 221–3, 228–30; cf. Kraft, pp. 194–5; for public opinion, note 115 below.

c Interior: M. Faure (Radical). Defense: P. de Chevigné (MRP).

was quite clear. Until a new Minister for Algeria takes over the GG.'
Delbecque's press conference just afterwards was less reassuring; he claimed
that the CSP did not recognize the Pflimlin ministry, and would sit till
France had a Government of Public Safety under General de Gaulle. Later
that evening Massu declared he had been 'misunderstood'; the CSP would
remain till a new Minister could take over with the consent of the people.[60]

More disquieting developments were taking place in Paris. General Chassin
escaped arrest, took to the maquis with a dozen men, was photographed by
the London *Daily Express* (which credited him with 15,000), and on the
16th led an abortive attack on the St. Etienne prefecture.[61] Two members
of General Ely's staff, air force generals Challe and Martin, were removed
under arrest from Paris; a third, General Beaufort, was told by the premier,
'You are all mutineers.'[62] On the 16th Ely himself resigned in protest; he
was not allowed to visit De Gaulle or publish a statement.[63] Rumours of
soldiers marching on Paris alarmed the government. On the afternoon of the
16th the Assembly voted a state of urgency by 462 to 112; the Communists
voted for Pflimlin, though he repudiated their support.[64]

Attempts to strengthen the cabinet had begun even before it took office.
The CNI (Conservatives), who had no love for Pflimlin, urged him to make
way for a government of national union under Mollet, whom they had themselves ejected just a year before. Mollet himself, Lacoste, Bourgès-Maunoury,
and Gaillard seemed favourable, but neither Socialists, Radicals, nor MRP
would retreat under fire.[65] Pflimlin then tried to recruit the two chief party

[60] For Salan: Tournoux, p. 295; Brombergers, p. 215; Ferniot, p. 29; Pado, pp. 33–4; Dronne,
p. 76; cf. Kraft, pp. 188–9. For Massu: Pajaud, pp. 75–81 (fullest); Gerin, pp. 50–1 and 60–1;
Debatty, pp. 77–9; Dronne, pp. 71–4, 78, 195–6; Kraft, p. 189; Ferniot, pp. 33–6; Brombergers,
pp. 219–20; Arrighi, pp. 70–1 (for the GG: Pajaud, pp. 78–9, Mannoni in *Le Monde*, 30 May 1958;
for the 'misunderstanding', *F-O*, 29 May 1958, cf. Pado, p. 37, Brombergers, p. 220; for both,
Gerin, pp. 60–1). For Delbecque: Pajaud, pp. 81–2; Gerin, p. 61; Debatty, p. 79; Dronne, pp. 78–9
and 196. Massu himself had read at 4 a.m. a violent CSP denunciation of 'Pflimlin's sell-out
government...elected with the complicity of Communist votes', appealing to De Gaulle, and
saying the army, linked to the people by the CSP, 'takes power until the final victory': quoted in
full, Pajaud, pp. 64–5; Sérigny, pp. 74–5; Debatty, p. 66; Ferniot, pp. 31–3.

[61] Brombergers, pp. 275–8; Tournoux, pp. 289, 322–3, 329; Kraft, pp. 187–8; Pado, pp. 60–1;
Ferniot, p. 94 for St. Etienne, cf. also Dominique's novel. Above p. 132 for Chassin's record.

[62] Challe had sent troop-carrying planes to Algeria, claiming they might be needed in Tunisia:
Brombergers, pp. 235–6. Martin had been to Bonn but the Minister mishearing Bône (Algeria),
thought he had been plotting: *ibid.* pp. 244–5. Cf. *ibid.* pp. 145, 154, 232; Pado, p. 60 (for Challe);
note 118 below (for planes); Arrighi, p. 45 (for Beaufort).

[63] Brombergers, pp. 235, 245–8; Tournoux, p. 302; Arrighi, p. 45; Pado, p. 61; Ferniot,
pp. 80–1; Gerin, p. 152. His successor Lorillot disseminated his statement in the army: Brombergers, p. 310. For its text, *ibid.* p. 247; Pado, p. 140; Gerin, p. 152n.

[64] Ferniot, pp. 66–7; cf. Arrighi, pp. 46, 49.

[65] Ferniot, pp. 21, 24–6; Arrighi, pp. 30–2; Viansson-Ponté, p. 199; Brombergers, pp. 206,
236. CNI rules required a two-thirds majority to forbid members joining Pflimlin's cabinet; his
opponents were one vote short: Isorni, pp. 139–40; cf. Ferniot, p. 5 (two short); Sérigny, p. 43.
(For Lacoste, *ibid.* pp. 39–40.)

leaders. But the CNI would not let Pinay join unless Lacoste returned to Algiers and Bidault came in, while the Radicals opposed Lacoste and the Socialists vetoed any sympathizer with the insurgents.[66] On Wednesday 14th, Mollet accepted a vice-premiership, and two days later his colleagues followed, Jules Moch replacing Maurice Faure at the Interior, Max Lejeune becoming Minister for the Sahara, and Albert Gazier, at Information, taking responsibility for the strict censorship which was soon imposed on radio and press.

Meanwhile in Algiers events had taken a decisive turn. On the morning of Thursday 15th Salan spoke to the crowd in the Forum. His position was most disagreeable. The mob suspected him of republicanism, and on Tuesday night they had howled him down. The Gaullists had tried to take his job, and the ultras his life—though both factions were now protesting their devotion and warning that the others meant to arrest or shoot him.[67] He knew that as Pflimlin's official representative, still in touch with Paris, he was suspected by the whole CSP of playing a double game;[68] yet his trust in the government was as fragile as its confidence in him. On the 15th he took his first step towards open revolt.[69] Ending a skilful and successful speech in traditional style, 'Vive l'Algérie française, vive la France!',[70] he stepped back amid cheers to face Léon Delbecque. After a moment's visible hesitation he came forward again. 'Et vive De Gaulle!'[71] Hitherto, the Liberator's name had aroused little enthusiasm.[72] Henceforth it dominated the crisis.

[66] Ferniot, pp. 61–4; Arrighi, pp. 31, 37, 42–3; Brombergers, p. 225; Pado, pp. 38–9; *L'Express*, 29 May 1958. Algiers had turned against Lacoste since his departure.

[67] Brombergers, pp. 199–200; cf. p. 260; *ibid.* pp. 47–9, 191 (Gaullists); above, p. 132 (ultras); n. 47 (crowd). After Sakiet, Salan needed political support against ministers who wanted to make him a scapegoat. He turned to the *Anciens d'Indochine* (above, p. 132), having been their president before Chassin; they had links both to the respectable CNI and to the counter-revolutionary 'Grand O': Brombergers, pp. 121–3, cf. pp. 49, 219; Kraft, p. 178; Tournoux, pp. 192–3, 283–4. Grand O were Martel's allies (above p. 132) and the CSP badly needed goodwill from the commander-in-chief who was himself now at odds with both Republicans and Gaullists: Brombergers, pp. 198–199, cf. pp. 216–17. So at 3 a.m. on the 14th Martel told his men, 'Get them shouting "Vive Salan!" and never mind why': *ibid.* p. 199.

[68] Tournoux, pp. 294–5, 308–11, 313–16; Dronne, pp. 100–1, Pado, pp. 30–1; Gerin, pp. 48 and 60; Brombergers, pp. 219 and 230.

[69] On the night of the 13th he had refused to appeal directly to De Gaulle: Brombergers, p. 197; Kraft, p. 188; Tournoux, p. 287 (text of his telegram, *ibid.* pp. 288–9). But the blockade of Algeria and the attempt to limit his powers made him suspect the government's intentions: above, n. 56. Cf. Pado, pp. 35–6, 47–8; Arrighi, p. 66. Sérigny testified that Jouhaud won Salan over: *Procès Jouhaud*, p. 193 (also counsel, p. 302).

[70] Text in Gerin, p. 213; Dronne, pp. 82–3; Pajaud, pp. 84–5.

[71] Tournoux, pp. 298–9; Pado, p. 47; Ferniot, p. 45; Gerin, p. 69; Dronne, p. 83; Brombergers, p. 230; Arrighi, p. 72; Kraft, p. 189; *M. P. 13*, no. 2; no pause in Pajaud, p. 85. Soustelle, p. 37; Paillat, p. 12 claim that with the approval of his entourage (apart from his wife) he had decided on the appeal to De Gaulle before he began speaking. Others say he later denied uttering the words, which were omitted from the draft official communiqué but restored by one of the Gaullists: Tournoux, p. 299; cf. Kraft, p. 189.

[72] On the popular reaction, Gerin, p. 25; Mannoni in *Le Monde*, 28 and 31 May 1958 (quoted Debatty, p. 96); Pajaud, pp. 102 and 114; Pado, p. 41; contrast Dronne, pp. 62 and 69 but cf.

Six hours later De Gaulle replied with his first public statement, concluding, 'I am ready to assume the powers of the Republic.'[73] Algiers was delighted. Next day, amid general surprise, Mollet—an old enemy of the Gaullists—expressed both admiration for the General and anxiety about his intentions. Did he recognize the legitimacy of the legal government? would he disavow the CSP? and if offered the premiership, would he stand in the usual way and withdraw if defeated?[74]

The cards had been distributed; it remained only to play them. Suppose Salan had not appealed to De Gaulle, or he had not responded? Conceivably the movement in Algiers would have collapsed.[75] But its driving force came from junior officers who were quite out of touch with opinion in France;[76] far more likely the civilian and military extremists would have arrested Salan and Massu and launched an attack on the mainland.[77] The successful appeal to De Gaulle ensured that the movement would neither crumble nor fall under Fascist control.[78] It attracted support from Moslems, whose wholly unexpected demonstrations in Algiers on the 16th, and later elsewhere, seemed at last to offer a hope of reconciliation.[79] It won maximum sympathy in the metropolitan army and administration. And it neutralized republicans

ibid. pp. 53, 164, 193, and Brombergers, p. 197. The enthusiasm was for Soustelle: *ibid.* pp. 190, 192; Kraft, pp. 175, 179; Mannoni, 28th; Sérigny, pp. 72–3. On previous appeals to De Gaulle, above p. 136 and n. 60; Gerin, p. 46; Debatty, p. 67; Brombergers, p. 197. Salan later claimed to have called for a De Gaulle government when he telephoned Ely on the 13th (see note 46 above).

[73] Text in *AP*, p. 534; Ferniot, p. 65; Sérigny, pp. 85–6; Pajaud, p. 86; Brombergers, p. 231; Pado, pp. 139–40; Kraft, p. 195.

[74] The questions were put in the lobby to Jacquinot (pro-Gaullist), and published in the next day's *Populaire*: Ferniot, pp. 69–70; Brutelle, *SFIO*, p. 5; Pado, pp. 58–9; Arrighi, pp. 47–8; and Viansson-Ponté, p. 205 (inaccurate); Brombergers, p. 243. (All quote, Ferniot and Brombergers fullest.) Mollet was persuaded by Chaban-Delmas (*ibid.* pp. 241–2), but he had kept in touch with Guichard, De Gaulle's secretary, since *before* May 13: Ferniot, p. 114; cf. *ibid.* p. 87.

[75] For the leaders' dismay at Pflimlin's election and Soustelle's absence: Sérigny, p. 75; Tournoux, p. 289; Brombergers, pp. 198 and 260; Arrighi, pp. 40 and 71–2; Gerin, p. 49; Ferniot, p. 31; *F-O*, 29 May 1958; cf. Kraft, pp. 188–9.

[76] Gerin, pp. 11 and 149–52; Viansson-Ponté, pp. 202–3; Planchais, Ch. VII, and in *L'Express*, 15 May 1958; Brombergers, pp. 43, 126–7, 148, 224, 253, 263, 301, 308–10; Dronne, pp. 94–5, 98; Krief, *SFIO*, p. 19; Isorni, p. 135; Ferniot, p. 54; cf. note 77.

[77] Biaggi, *Procès Salan*, p. 383; Tournoux, pp. 284–6, 294–5, 298, 313, 316. Cf. above, note 25, and below, note 145.

[78] Tournoux, pp. 308–9; Brombergers, p. 260; Ferniot, p. 71; *F-O*, 29 May 1958; cf. Pado, pp. 35, 48.

[79] They were organized by the army, but developed spontaneously; many Moslems were curious, attracted by De Gaulle, or amazed to find a European crowd fraternizing instead of lynching. For sceptics who were impressed, Mannoni in *Le Monde*, 18–19 May and 1–2 June 1958; Daniel in *L'Express*, 29 May; Kraft, pp. 184–5; *F-O*, 29 May 1958; Debatty, pp. 285–6, 308–9; even Lentin, pp. 39–41, 66–8 concedes (p. 67) that nearly half the demonstrators came voluntarily. See also Gerin, pp. 90–1, Brombergers, pp. 256–60, Dauer and Rodet, pp. 128–34, Debatty, pp. 200–1 (balanced); *ibid.* pp. 178–80, 210 (sceptical); *ibid.* pp. 102–5, 156, Pajaud, pp. 89–96, Sérigny, pp. 91–8, Salan's official telegram in Tournoux, pp. 483–4 (enthusiastic); cf. Dronne, p. 53. Soustelle made full use of these events: cf. Arrighi, pp. 173–7. De Gaulle told Auriol they determined his own conduct: Tournoux, p. 396.

who would not believe that De Gaulle aimed at dictatorship.[80] Finally, Mollet had opened the dialogue between the General, who would not come to power unconstitutionally, and the Socialist Party, without whose support he could not be legally elected.

Now the joker was slipped into the pack; Soustelle escaped from his police guard.[81] Friends chartered a Swiss plane, and at 1:30 p.m. on the 17th he arrived unheralded at Algiers. The surprise was total. Delbecque had indeed announced his impending appearance on the very first evening;[82] but Soustelle had waited for the Assembly debate, the escape plans had miscarried,[83] and his friends had given him up—Sérigny went to the airfield expecting to meet a prominent Moslem integrationist, Sid Cara. The military shared their astonishment but not their pleasure. Salan feared both that Soustelle's arrival would deter Pflimlin from resigning, and that so popular and powerful an ally would challenge his own authority. The newcomer nearly had to take off again for Switzerland. The civilians, however, insisted that Salan telephone Pflimlin and discover his intentions; Soustelle agreed to leave at once if the premier meant to resign. At 3:45 p.m. Salan learned that Pflimlin was determined to stay. A dramatic and emotional meeting of the two leaders was then staged before a crowd quite unaware that they had been thinking of arresting one another a couple of hours before.[84]

The soldiers showed their suspicion of politicans whenever a deputy arrived at Algiers. Two more were reluctantly accepted, the Gaullist Raymond Dronne and the right-wing Radical Pascal Arrighi, member for Corsica (who prudently informed Soustelle and not Salan of his arrival). But the Conservative J.-L. Vigier was rejected as an emissary of the prime minister, and the army expelled or interned five politicians of the extreme Right (three of whom unwisely arrived in company with suspects in the bazooka plot against Salan).[85 d]

[80] L. Hamon, *De Gaulle dans la République* (Paris: Plon, 1958), Part I, has the best analysis of De Gaulle's political assets.   [81] Cf. Soustelle, pp. 35–7.

[82] Tournoux, p. 283; Brombergers, p. 192; Sérigny, pp. 69 and 72; cf. Gerin, p. 46.

[83] When he decided to leave, the airfields had been closed. De Gaulle had refused to advise him; Soustelle said he would wait for the generals to act, and Biaggi retorted 'That phrase can be spoken only in Spanish'. Debré offered to go in his place. See Tournoux, pp. 261–2, 273–4, 319n.; Brombergers, pp. 152–5, 188, 284–5; cf. Kraft, p. 177 (generals), Paillat, p. 14; Soustelle, pp. 35–6.

[84] Tournoux, pp. 314–16; Brombergers, pp. 290–8; Sérigny, pp. 104–7, Pado, pp. 70–5; Dronne, pp. 15–16 and 107–8; Arrighi, pp. 58–9 (his times are wrong as usual). The hopes of Pflimlin's resignation arose from a misunderstanding with the premier's envoy Bolotte: same sources, respectively pp. 317n., 290 and 296, 104 and 106, 73–4, 108, 59. For Soustelle's fear of arrest, Soustelle, p. 36; Brombergers, pp. 293–4; for Salan's, *ibid.* pp. 294 and 297; Tournoux, pp. 315–16; Ferniot, p. 78 (he told Pflimlin of it); for Soustelle's possible expulsion, also Kraft, p. 190; Dronne, Pado, *F-O*, 29 May 1958. Sérigny (p. 106) hints at a minor discord which he himself soon smoothed over; Soustelle (pp. 36–8) also confines himself to hints.

[85] Dronne, pp. 103–4; Arrighi, pp. 66–7 (cf. pp. 55–6); Pado, pp. 92–3; Sérigny, pp. 102–3;

d On Vigier see above, p. 55, and on Pesquet (n. 85), above, p. 74–7.   [*over*]

Nor were these the most serious signs of dissension between the civilians and the military commanders. The territorial tank unit (UTB) was recalled from operations on the 14th to protect the CSP from the army, and on the 17th it moved to the airport to defend Soustelle against Salan.[86] Later on, Delbecque proposed that Soustelle, Massu and Sid Cara should form a political directory to advise Salan; Massu—who had not forgiven Soustelle for defeating the *loi-cadre*—promptly and publicly denounced any attempt to undermine the authority of the army. When the CSP for Algeria and the Sahara was set up, the junior officers insisted that it should have a military co-president, Massu, as well as Sid Cara. Yet in the end Soustelle's mere presence in Algiers, even without official status, widened immeasurably the breach between the C-in-C and the government.[87]

IV. WITHERING AWAY

In Paris the second week of the crisis opened with a cabinet meeting on Sunday 18th. Some ministers were anxious to act strongly against the generals and Soustelle, and even against De Gaulle; their proposals were vetoed by the prime minister.[88] Next day, at 3 p.m., the General held his tensely awaited press conference at the Palais d'Orsay.[89] He indignantly denied that he would ever infringe the fundamental liberties he had himself restored fourteen years before; he recalled the socialistic achievements of his government in 1944–6; he referred by name only to two persons, 'my friend' Lacoste and Mollet 'whom I esteem'; and he recalled with emotion an unforgettable (though unfortunately quite imaginary) meeting with the latter

Debatty, pp. 194–5; Tournoux, pp. 310–14; Brombergers, pp. 320–1, 353–4. The five were Biaggi (interned but escaped), Pesquet (interned), Berthommier, Le Pen, and Demarquet (expelled); machine-guns were brought up to force the last two to leave: *ibid*. p. 321. *Le Monde* (23 May 1958) says they landed three times, each time being welcomed by civilians but forced to take off again by the military. For their (and Biaggi's) denials concerning the bazooka plot, *Le Monde*, 21–2 and 24 September 1958. For Biaggi: Kraft, p. 190.

[86] Pajaud, p. 59; cf. *F-F*, 1 Nov. 1958; Brombergers, pp. 217–18 (14th); Delbecque defied an order demobilising it: *ibid*., Tournoux, p. 311. Brombergers, p. 295 (17th). The UTB had been set up by Thomazo, then serving under General Faure, who relied on the territorials for his own plot: *ibid*. pp. 87, 89; Tournoux, pp. 189–90; Arrighi, p. 63; Pajaud, p. 40; *L'Express*, 31 July 1958. On it cf. Gerin, p. 22; *F-O*, 29 May 1958.

[87] Soustelle, p. 38; Brombergers, pp. 300, 325–6, 331–2; Kraft, p. 190; Debatty, p. 152; Dronne, pp. 113–17. Massu's statement in *ibid*. p. 114; Debatty, p. 188; for his suspicion of Soustelle, cf. Dronne, p. 115, Tournoux, pp. 313–14, *F-O*, 29 May 1958 (but omitted by Soustelle, p. 41). For the very liberal tone of Soustelle's speeches, cf. his broadcast to France of 23 May cited *ibid*. pp. 267–9 (wrongly dated, no sign to show that the Gaullist peroration is omitted), Arrighi, pp. 173–177, extract in Debatty, pp. 205–6.

[88] Proposals to end the generals' civil powers, stop their speeches, remove their HQ from Algeria, prosecute Soustelle and ban De Gaulle's press conference: Tournoux, pp. 318–20, Ferniot, pp. 79–80; cf. Brombergers (p. 302) and (on Pflimlin) *ibid*. p. 324; Tournoux, pp. 303–6.

[89] Text in *AP*, pp. 534–6; Pado, pp. 140–8; cf. Ferniot, pp. 84–7; Brombergers, pp. 318–19; for press comments, Debatty, pp. 158–74.

in 1945. But he adroitly avoided condemning the Algiers leaders; he praised the action of the army; and while saying in answer to Mollet that he would take power only from the Assembly, he demanded an exceptional procedure. The balancing act was so skilful that both sides were dissatisfied; the Algiers extremists felt De Gaulle had betrayed them and was compromising with 'the System', and their confidence returned only when the Socialists denounced him for flouting the constitution.[90]

The Communists had called for a general strike to take place at the moment the General was to speak. It was a total failure; the other unions refused to join in, and the workers did not follow.[91] At the Renault works less than four per cent came out; in the provinces the collapse was even more complete. It was the first of many demonstrations that there would be no popular opposition to De Gaulle.

In public the cabinet's only reaction was to press on with constitutional reform proposals to take the wind out of the General's sails. But behind the scenes a race now began between the preparations for insurrection developing in the country, and negotiations being set on foot between Paris and Colombey. On Wednesday 21st the prime minister and President Coty both saw Pinay, an old anti-Gaullist; next day the CNI leader visited the General's home and returned enthusiastic.[92] Piette, Socialist deputy and close friend of Mollet, followed on Friday. (His Resistance name had been 'Colonel Personne'; when Mollet denied meeting De Gaulle, his critics said 'Personne y était'.)[93] But at the weekend the apparent lull ended abruptly. The new CSP for Algeria and the Sahara was set up, and demanded for the first time not merely a new government but a new regime. Massu told the London *Evening News* that within a week De Gaulle would be in power.[94] And on Saturday 24th came the real challenge; the seizure of Corsica.

Soustelle has claimed that the operation was intended to shatter the govern-

---

[90] Pado, pp. 86–7; Brombergers, p. 320; cf. *F-O*, 29 May 1958.

[91] Tournoux, p. 324 and n.; Pado, pp. 87–8; Brombergers, p. 320; Ferniot, p. 82; Debatty, p. 158; *L'Express*, 29 May 1958; on the Renault workers cf. *ibid.* 5 June.

[92] Ferniot, pp. 98–101; Brombergers, pp. 333–5 (cf. Arrighi, p. 126); Pinay had feared that a Popular Front government would follow De Gaulle, to whom he thought of offering the Ministry for Algeria (*ibid.* p. 334, cf. p. 284). But Jacques Bloch-Morhange, *Les Politiciens* (Paris: Fayard, 1961), pp. 227, 235–44, claims to have inspired Pinay's decision on 10 May to meet De Gaulle and facilitate his return to power. The author says Coty and Pflimlin discouraged Pinay (cf. Brutelle, *SFIO*, p. 7); all agree they refused to give him an official mission.

[93] Arrighi, pp. 126–7 (for 'Personne', *ibid.* p. 139); cf. Viansson-Ponté, p. 208. Contrast Bloch-Morhange, pp. 243–4: on Saturday morning Piette, in Mollet's name, was refusing any direct contact with De Gaulle. But Mollet was in close touch with the General's secretary Guichard: *ibid.* p. 243, Ferniot, pp. 87 and 114, Kraft, p. 197, Brombergers, pp. 333, 358, 363, 367 (they say he agreed on Saturday to a meeting, but called it off on Sunday because of Corsica).

[94] CSP names in Sérigny, pp. 166–8; statement quoted fully *ibid.* pp. 169–71; partially Debatty, pp. 188–9; Massu, quoted *ibid.* p. 196; for both, also Ferniot, pp. 103–4.

ment's resistance quickly without an airborne attack on Paris.[95] The island was garrisoned by parachutists who were stationed alternately at Calvi and in Algeria.[96] More Corsicans live in North Africa than at home, and the insurgents could count on local sympathy.[97] Henri Maillot, a distant cousin of De Gaulle and Resistance leader in the island, had made contact with Algiers, where Massu was already seeking reliable Corsicans.[98] On the 19th Pascal Arrighi reached Algiers; two days later he broadcast to his compatriots.[99] On Thursday 22nd there was a demonstration in favour of the police superintendent, removed for permitting a previous rally. Maillot's friends met at 9 p.m. on Friday night and resolved to seize the Ajaccio prefecture next evening;[100] Algiers may not have expected such quick action.[101] At 5:15 a.m. on Saturday, Arrighi, with three companions chosen by Massu and an order from Salan, landed in a military plane at Calvi and won over the police and army. The Ajaccio demonstrators met at 6 p.m., the paratroops arrived from Calvi at 6:35, and ten minutes later they held

[95] Soustelle, p. 44; Tournoux, p. 332; Debatty, pp. 233–4, Brombergers, pp. 328–9 and 373–4; the last add (p. 328) and Soustelle hints that he, Delbecque and Massu used it to force Salan's hand. Tournoux (p. 332) says it was planned in Paris on May 14 and a woman messenger took the orders to Algiers a week later. Arrighi testified: that the Gaullist leader (later minister) Roger Frey had told him on May 21 that De Gaulle had ordered Guichard on the 18th to bring Corsica over to the insurgents, and that a woman (Mlle de la Loyère) had brought the order to Algiers on the 21st; that plans were then made by the Gaullists, not the military, nothing having been prepared previously; and that Massu told him on the 23rd that Salan had just agreed at last: *Procès Salan*, pp. 318–19. By 1962 Arrighi wished to acquit Salan and discredit De Gaulle; contrast notes 98 and 101, and Soustelle (p. 44) for evidence that Algiers was spontaneously preparing the Corsican coup before the 21st. Yet Sérigny (p. 123) pretends and Arrighi (p. 120) implies that the *coup* occurred unplanned, without contact with Algiers. However, the alleged signal broadcast on the 23rd, 'La chapelle s'illuminera ce soir', was just psychological warfare by Frey. (Frey had failed to get to Algiers on Errol Flynn's yacht and had had instead to hire the boat of an English ex-naval officer turned smuggler: Brombergers, pp. 262–3; cf. Dronne, p. 13; Pajaud, pp. 117–19.)

[96] Arrighi, p. 84; Pado, p. 94.

[97] Over 100,000 in Algeria: Arrighi, pp. 107–8, Brombergers, p. 327; Debatty, p. 313; cf. *ibid.* p. 217; Sérigny, p. 122; Pajaud, p. 127 (250,000 in North Africa).

[98] Maillot: Pajaud, pp. 127–8; Debatty, p. 217 (he set up a 'Republican Committee for the Safeguarding of Constitutional Institutions in Liberty and National Grandeur'). Massu: Arrighi, pp. 79–80; Brombergers, p. 321; Pado, p. 93.

[99] Arrighi, pp. 54–5, 79; Brombergers, p. 321; Dronne, p. 135; Debatty, p. 211. He was the only Corsican deputy who had never held office, and had just lost his departmental council seat (probably more relevant facts than his alleged links with the bazooka plot). His broadcast (on the 21st, not the 23rd as Kraft, p. 191) is in Arrighi, pp. 177–9.

[100] Debatty, pp. 217–18; Arrighi, p. 87; Brombergers, p. 342; Pajaud, p. 128; Dronne, p. 138; Sérigny, p. 120.

[101] 'L'événement se produisit avec *une soudaineté* qui nous stupéfia': Sérigny, p. 115 (my italics). Cf. Brombergers, pp. 327–8, 340; Arrighi, p. 91; Ferniot, pp. 108, 119. But Sérigny implies (pp. 115–16) that Salan and Massu had no foreknowledge; this is untrue: Arrighi, p. 79; Pado, p. 93; Brombergers, pp. 328–9 and 335–7; cf. note 95. Plans were laid before Arrighi arrived: Dronne, p. 135; Pado, p. 93; Debatty, p. 217; Brombergers, p. 321; Kraft, p. 191; cf. Arrighi, pp. 79–80. General Miquel at Toulouse was told a day ahead: Brombergers, p. 335. A locally popular general on Chaban-Delmas' staff had perhaps won over the army: Casalta, *SFIO*, p. 23.

the prefecture.[102] Delbecque and Sérigny flew over next day with a CSP delegation; Colonel Thomazo came for the ride at the last minute, led the troops in singing bawdy songs, and was appointed military governor by Salan during the flight.[103] At Bastia there were three distinct CSPs, a determined Socialist acting mayor (Casalta), and a pro-government municipal council; but only a hundred people came out to demonstrate.[104] No one would die, or even march, for the Fourth Republic. The National Assembly itself refused to expel Arrighi—was he not accredited by Pflimlin's own representative in Algiers?—and agreed only to withdraw his immunity.[105]

Corsica showed that the government was no longer obeyed.[106] The prefect indeed stayed loyal, the sub-prefect of Sartène did not meet the new authorities till Pflimlin had resigned, and the military commander Colonel Prigent, finding Arrighi had misled him, returned in disgust to the mainland. But the other five sub-prefects, the police and the gendarmerie all went over.[107] The Bastia sub-prefect said pathetically to Casalta, 'I don't know which side will fire me', and the Colonel, 'I don't know which side will shoot me'.[108] The Calvi parachutists acted with the tacit connivance of their mainland headquarters;[109] the other troops followed their lead. Forewarned by the prefect, Moch flew in CRS from Nice—using Air France planes lest military aircraft take them to Algeria.[110] But the CRS were met by the paratroops on arrival, and promptly changed sides.[111]

Encouraged by reports from Bastia, the cabinet met at 9:30 on Saturday

[102] Arrighi, pp. 83–99; Brombergers, pp. 339–45; Sérigny, p. 120; Dronne, p. 139.

[103] Sérigny, pp. 116–17, quoted Debatty, pp. 214–16; Arrighi, pp. 111–15; Pado, pp. 99–100; Brombergers, pp. 349–50.

[104] Arrighi, pp. 100–2, 108–9, 115–17; Casalta, *SFIO*, p. 226; Brombergers, pp. 345–52; Tournoux, pp. 333–4; Sérigny, pp. 120–1; Pado, pp. 100–1; Pajaud, p. 130; Dronne, pp. 140–1; Debatty, p. 219; fine photo of Casalta in *ibid.* p. 221.

[105] Arrighi, pp. 127–35, especially pp. 133–4.

[106] Though it offended even friends of Algiers in Paris, it demoralized the government by displaying their impotence and by threatening national unity: Pado, p. 103; Pajaud, p. 133; Isorni, p. 161; cf. Dronne, p. 138; Debatty, p. 233 (quoting Lacoste). For comments, *ibid.* pp. 209–34.

[107] Moch, *SFIO*, pp. 11–12; Casalta, *ibid.* pp. 23–6; Arrighi, pp. 90–1, 97–8; Tournoux, pp. 333–334; Brombergers, pp. 342–4. Also for Sartène, *ibid.* p. 352; Arrighi, p. 118; for the gendarmes at Ajaccio, Pajaud, p. 129; for those at Corte, Debatty, p. 213, Dronne, p. 141 (but contrast Arrighi, p. 100); for Colonel Prigent, Sérigny, p. 122, Casalta, *SFIO*, p. 25 (Arrighi conceals his defection). It was not revolution which bothered the Colonel, but taking orders from the Tenth Military Region (Algiers) when he was subordinate to the Ninth (Marseilles): Arrighi, p. 90; Brombergers, p. 341.

[108] Casalta, *SFIO*, p. 25; cf. Brombergers, pp. 346–50; Dominique's novel *passim*.

[109] Arrighi, p. 93; Moch, *SFIO*, p. 12; Brombergers, pp. 341–2.

[110] Arrighi, p. 96; cf. Tournoux, p. 335; Brombergers, p. 356.

[111] Were they disarmed as the press reported? Yes: Ferniot, p. 105; Brutelle, *SFIO*, p. 6; Viansson-Ponté, p. 206. No: Arrighi, p. 96; Pado, p. 97; cf. Sérigny, p. 118; Pajaud, p. 129; Brombergers, pp. 343–4. According to a Canadian journalist eye-witness, their arms were stacked but guarded by one of their own NCOs. They numbered under 100 (Arrighi, Brombergers); 150 (Pajaud); 180 (Dronne, p. 138).

night and decided to retake the town before dawn on Monday. CRS were sent to the south coast, and orders given to the fleet. But at 5:30 on Sunday afternoon Admiral Nomy saw the prime minister and President Coty, and the cabinet meeting half an hour later overruled Moch and cancelled the operation. Ministers feared to deplete their few reliable forces; the army would not undertake to hold Bastia against airborne reinforcements from Algeria; the navy, though not mutinous, was clearly reluctant; even the meteorologists sent false warning of Mediterranean storms.[112] Communications with Corsica (where supplies were low) soon had to be reopened because the Marseilles prefect feared trouble among the many Corsicans in the city.[113] The government's total inability to react to the loss of the island displayed their impotence before the world—and above all to themselves. Asked in his press conference what Algiers would do if the government used force in Corsica, Salan's spokesman replied, 'What force?'[114]

The Corsican collapse completed the withering away of the French state. For years disastrous policies had repeatedly been imposed on Paris by colonial administrations (supported by Gaullist and Conservative politicians who simultaneously deplored the weakness of government). Then the army acquired a taste for local policy-making. Now all governmental authority disappeared, even in metropolitan France. Certainly ministers encouraged confusion by pretending that Salan was their loyal agent.[115] But this alone cannot explain the passive disobedience and active sabotage which confronted them everywhere.

The Navy, once a bulwark of Vichy, was non-committal.[116] The air force was Gaullist;[117] it showed its sympathies symbolically by flying its planes in Cross of Lorraine formation—and practically by sending to Algeria the troop-carrying aircraft needed for an airborne invasion.[118] The army was in 'moral rebellion'.[119] With difficulty the cabinet found a general willing to replace Ely as chief of staff: Lorillot, who promptly assured Salan that his sole aim was to save the army's unity, told generals to discuss Salan's order

---

[112] Taylor, pp. 8–9; Kerr (see note 3); Tournoux, pp. 334–7; Ferniot, p. 109; Brombergers, pp. 356–7; Arrighi, pp. 103–4; cf. Debatty, p. 209. Moch (quoted Tournoux, p. 337) says the operation was rejected at 7 p.m. on Sunday; this discredits Brombergers, pp. 357, 366 (Monday) and the story quoted in Debatty, p. 312 n. 43, that Pflimlin told his party that the navy had thwarted his plan to retake Ajaccio (*sic*).

[113] Arrighi, pp. 110–11; Casalta, *SFIO*, p. 25.

[114] Dronne, p. 147. (Not in the *Echo d'Alger* report.)

[115] Cf. Debatty, p. 234; Moch quoted Tournoux, pp. 305–6; Ferniot, p. 30; cf. note 59 above.

[116] Taylor, p. 9; Brombergers, p. 357; Arrighi, p. 103; Tournoux, pp. 324–5.

[117] *Ibid.*; Moch, *SFIO*, p. 11.

[118] Tournoux, p. 266 and n.; Brombergers, pp. 145, 154, 235–6, 238, 310; *L'Humanité*, 31 October 1958.

[119] Moch: *La Nef*, July 1958, p. 10. Chevigné: Ferniot, p. 66; Tournoux, p. 325. Challe had warned Mollet (*ibid.* pp. 300–1; Brombergers, pp. 233–4) and Ely Chevigné (refs. in n. 63 above).

of the day with their officers, distributed Ely's censored message of resignation, and later personally deciphered messages between De Gaulle and Salan without informing the cabinet.[120] Marshal Juin publicly gave Algiers his blessing, and privately warned Coty and Pflimlin that the army was united.[121] Four of the nine regional commanders openly sided with Algiers; Miquel, at Toulouse, was so ostentatious that the mayor and prefect refused to speak to him (though his 'M. le Préfet, je ne suis pas ici pour défendre votre préfecture mais pour la prendre' is no doubt apocryphal).[122] The IGAMEs (regional prefects) warned ministers that attempts to arrest political suspects might merely precipitate their own arrest.[123]

The civil service, according to Moch, frustrated cabinet decisions by 'inert opposition'.[124] In the Ministry of the Interior, the republican holy of holies, his own subordinates disobeyed orders, withheld information, or exaggerated it to intimidate him. The Paris police were notoriously unreliable; only two months earlier they had staged an ugly anti-parliamentary and anti-Semitic demonstration outside the Assembly, inspired by a former police chief turned extreme-Right deputy, Jean Dides.[e] The gendarmerie (controlled by the Ministry of Defense) reacted like the army. The colonel of firemen—so useful in riots—reported that his men could be counted on only to put out fires—'and in the Palais Bourbon, they wouldn't bother'. Even the CRS, the riot police created by Moch himself eleven years before against Communist insurrectionary tactics, were affected. The government thought half of them reliable enough to provide the defense of Paris on the critical 27 May. But the plotters themselves believed that the CRS was eager to join the revolt; and certainly they neither could nor would have opposed the army.[125]

---

[120] Sérigny, pp. 139–40; Brombergers, pp. 310–11, 337, 384; also Pado, p. 62 (on Salan's order); Ferniot, p. 155 (on deciphering).

[121] *Ibid.* p. 119 (Pflimlin); Pado, p. 62, Brombergers, pp. 279–80 (Coty); Pajaud, pp. 113–14 (quotes open letter).

[122] Four of nine: Moch, *SFIO*, p. 10, quoted Ferniot, p. 140; Arrighi, p. 122. They were Miquel, Lecoq (Bordeaux), Descours (Lyon), Widerspach-Thor (Dijon); the general at Rennes sympathized, but not those at Paris, Marseilles, and in Germany who were to be replaced (in Germany by his second-in-command, General Faure of an earlier plot): Brombergers, pp. 248–50; 378–9; Tournoux, pp. 372–6. Miquel had long been in touch with both the ultra and the Gaullist plotters: *ibid.* pp. 186, 202. His command included all the paratroops in France (Brombergers, pp. 68, 304) whom Moch wanted sent to Algeria: *SFIO*, p. 11; cf. *L'Express*, 12 June 1958.

[123] Moch, *SFIO*, p. 10 (quoted Ferniot, p. 141). He mentions (*loc. cit.*) the 'constant fear of incidents like those of Corsica'. One IGAME reported, 'I am on a powder-barrel'; another, 'on a volcano'; a third, 'the army will not obey'; a fourth, 'the general says he will soon be in my place': Ferniot, pp. 94 and 141; Brombergers, p. 332; Moch quoted *L'Express*, 29 May 1958; cf. Lacoste, *SFIO*, p. 16; Kerr (see note 3); Arrighi, p. 123.

[124] Moch in *La Nef*, July, p. 10.

[125] *Ibid.*; also *SFIO*, p. 11; Tournoux, pp. 325–7; Pado, pp. 123–4; Dronne, pp. 164–6; Taylor, p. 10; Arrighi, pp. 121–2 and 158–60; Dominique's novel *passim*; Brombergers, pp. 208,   [*over*]

[e] On Dides see above, chap. 4 *passim*.

At that night's cabinet Pleven summed up: 'We are the legal government, but what do we govern? The Minister for Algeria cannot enter Algeria. The Minister for the Sahara cannot go to the Sahara. The Minister of Information can only censor the press. The Minister of the Interior has no control over the police. The Minister of Defense is not obeyed by the army.'[126] Said a left-wing Gaullist in the Assembly, 'You are not abandoning power—it has abandoned you.'[127]

Deserted by their own forces, some ministers considered transferring the government to the Belgian border and perhaps arming the miners of the northern coalfield.[128] But an appeal to the workers would have aroused little response. The strike of May 27th failed as disastrously as that of the 19th, the non-Communist unions again refusing to co-operate;[129] and at the September referendum the Communists lost most support in the working-class 'red belt'—their followers would not even vote, let alone fight, against De Gaulle. About 200,000 marched from the Place de la Nation to the Place de le République on 28 May—but they were in no civil war mood.[130]

Resistance was absurd without the Communists, impossible with them; for that alliance would have alienated most of the nation and broken up the cabinet itself.[131] As the third week of the crisis opened, therefore, some determined Ministers were seeking, not to keep De Gaulle out at all costs, but to obtain from him an honourable alternative to bloodshed, military

306, 315–17, 376–8, 381–2, 406–7, 418–19. Also for Dides and the March police riot, Isorni, pp. 142–3, *L'Express*, 12 June 1958, Arrighi, pp. 3–7; for the firemen, *ibid.* p. 45, Tournoux, p. 354; for the CRS, *ibid.* pp. 354–5, 375 n., Gerin, p. 37, Pado, pp. 120–1, Kerr (note 3); for the Ministry of the Interior, Soustelle, p. 38 n. (he used its switchboard when telephoning from Algiers to France!).

[126] Tournoux, p. 361; Ferniot, p. 144; Brombergers, p. 393; Kraft, p. 200.

[127] Jean de Lipkowski, *JO*, 27 May 1958, p. 2538; Ferniot, pp. 136–7 (fuller); Arrighi, p. 142.

[128] Moch, *La Nef*, p. 12; Kerr (note 3); Tournoux, pp. 302–3; Brombergers, pp. 379, 382, 421. On May 19 Moch obtained Defense Ministry arms for the CRS, which Algiers wrongly suspected were really for arming Communists: Tournoux, pp. 353–4; Brombergers, pp. 316–17 (date), 382; Sérigny, p. 84 (wrong date); Dronne, pp. 144–5; Soustelle, p. 44; see also note 131 below. Chevigné later won a libel suit against a local editor who had accused the Pflimlin government of arming Communists: *Le Monde*, 11–12 March 1961.

[129] Moch quoted Tournoux, p. 362 n.; Brombergers, p. 387; Pado, p. 110; cf. *L'Express*, 29 May 1958 (but 70% of the Nord miners came out: *AP*, pp. 211–12).

[130] Arrighi, p. 148 (Gaullist), and Ferniot, p. 146 (anti-) say 200,000; Viansson-Ponté (p. 212) and Brutelle, *SFIO* (p. 7) (anti-) put it just above. Pado (pp. 117–18) has eight press estimates, varying with the paper's politics from 500,000 to 55,000; the last purports to be the Prefecture's estimate, which was under 100,000 (Tournoux, p. 363); was halved by pro-Gaullist officials to influence Moch (Dominique, p. 174, Gaullist). For 'accurate estimates by specialists', Dronne, p. 155 (40,000); Dominique, p. 175 (124,000); *L'Express*, 5 June 1958 (200,000). For the mood, Brombergers, p. 401, Arrighi, pp. 148–9 (Gaullist); Ferniot, p. 147, Moch quoted Taylor, p. 11, Debatty, pp. 245–7, Viansson-Ponté, p. 213 (anti-Gaullist); Tournoux, p. 363.

[131] For cabinet divisions, Moch, *La Nef*, pp. 10 and 12; Tournoux, pp. 321–4, 353–4, 358–61; Ferniot, pp. 141–3.

rule, and an ultimate pro-Communist reaction. Always avoid civil war, said Moch wryly, especially when you are sure to lose. Mollet agreed: 'It would have been the war in Spain—without the republican army.'[132]

V. 'RESURRECTION'

These Ministers proposed to test De Gaulle's purposes by demanding first (in vain) a disavowal of the Corsican *coup*, later (successfully) an acceptance of the customary parliamentary procedure for coming to power. In France, where symbols are taken seriously, this latter concession both assured legal continuity and formally affirmed De Gaulle's loyalty to the Republic.[133] On the afternoon of Sunday the 25th, Mollet gave to Guichard a six-page letter for the General stating the Socialist doubts and scruples, which he showed the premier next morning.[134] Pflimlin then asked his party colleague Maurice Schumann (former Free French radio spokesman in London) to visit Colombey on his behalf.[135] But De Gaulle had already answered Mollet and, by the local prefect, asked both Pflimlin and Mollet to meet him that night—this invitation to be published if they refused.[136]

The two leaders agreed at once, though Mollet was later persuaded by Moch not to go unless De Gaulle repudiated the Corsican coup.[137] The General and the prime minister both shook off the journalists, and met about midnight at the house of an old Gaullist, the curator of the château of St. Cloud. Thinking of Parliament, Pflimlin asked De Gaulle for a disavowal of Corsica; thinking of the army, the General replied while he would

---

[132] Moch: Taylor ('civil war': p. 9), cf. *La Nef*, pp. 10 and 12. (But Brombergers, pp. 368, 380, 389–90 suggest he switched only later, on the 27th.) Mollet: *SFIO*, pp. 43–4 ('Spain': *ibid.* p. 44; Tournoux, p. 364; Ferniot, p. 171).

[133] Hamon (cf. note 80), pp. 3 and 6–9; Tournoux, p. 345; Taylor, p. 9; Brombergers, p. 368. For De Gaulle's dislike of Fourth Republican procedures, *ibid.* pp. 17–18, 388, 397.

[134] Published with the reply in *Le Monde*, 16 Sept. 1958 and *AP*, pp. 537–8, summarized by Brombergers, pp. 363–4; he argued that a government imposed by the army would be followed by one controlled by the Communists. Cf. *ibid.* pp. 365–6; Mollet, *SFIO*, p. 43 (p.m. 25th); Ferniot, p. 115; Pado, p. 115; *Le Monde*, 19 April 1962 (Guichard). Misdated by Arrighi (p. 127) and by Viansson-Ponté (pp. 208–9), whose mistakes in timing make everyone's behaviour incomprehensible.

[135] De Gaulle invited Schumann to come as Pflimlin's representative; on Sunday afternoon Pflimlin said he must go as an individual (lest the Socialists think themselves betrayed). Then Schumann found out that Mollet was already in touch with Guichard; and next day when Mollet told Pflimlin of his letter, the premier told Schumann to go officially after all: Brombergers, pp. 358–60, 366; Ferniot, pp. 107–8, 114–16; cf. Taylor, p. 9.

[136] *Ibid.* pp. 116–18; Tournoux, p. 344; the prefect arrived at 4 p.m. Cf. Viansson-Ponté, p. 209; Brombergers, p. 367; Arrighi, pp. 136–7; Pado, p. 107; Taylor, p. 9.

[137] Taylor, p. 9; Ferniot, pp. 120–1; Brombergers, p. 368; Mollet also had to reverse his party's support for next day's general strike: *ibid.* (last two), also Viansson-Ponté, pp. 209–10; for Moch's persuasion, also Brombergers, p. 368; Arrighi, p. 137; cf. Tournoux, p. 344; Pado, p. 107; Moch, *La Nef*, p. 10. Piette went instead, and saw Guichard: Arrighi, p. 139; cf. Bloch-Morhange (*Les Politiciens*), p. 244.

never take power illegally, to disavow as a private citizen would merely destroy for nothing his usefulness as an arbiter. As president of MRP, Pflimlin offered to arrange a meeting with the party leaders, which De Gaulle welcomed; but as nominee of the Assembly, the premier would not abandon the post entrusted to him. De Gaulle was unwilling to announce a disagreement. They parted at 2 a.m., Pflimlin now convinced of the General's bona fides.[138] So at midday he was thunderstruck to read De Gaulle's third public statement, 'I have begun the regular process of forming a republican government', with its appeal to all, particularly the armed forces, to maintain order.[139] The premier dared not deny the untruth, and therefore seemed to have betrayed his colleagues and supporters.[140]

What had happened? De Gaulle had found that Algiers' planned Operation Resurrection was to go into effect that night.[141] Four days earlier General Miquel had approved a 32-page timetable for a paratroop descent on the 27th. The aerodromes of Le Bourget and Villacoublay were to be occupied by tank units of the Paris garrison. From the south-west, 2,500 men were to fly in from 2:30 a.m., reinforced from 5:30 by another 1,500 from Algiers. Most of the few fighting troops in France were involved in the plan, and in controlling the capital they were to be supported by recalled paratroop reservists and Indo-China veterans—and by the police and CRS with whom the government hoped to oppose them. All these auxiliaries were to wear military (mainly parachutist) uniforms. In eighty provincial towns there were CSPs ready, based on Gaullists, Pétainists, or Poujadists, paratroop and Indo-China reservists, or expatriates from North Africa. As they took over the southern prefectures at 5:30 p.m., the army would stand by benevolently to 'preserve order'. And the original military conspirator of 1956, General Faure, was second-in-command of the army in Germany and thus con-

[138] Moch, *SFIO*, pp. 10 and 12; cf. *La Nef*, pp. 10–11; Taylor, pp. 9–10; Tournoux, pp. 344–6; Ferniot, pp. 121–4; Brombergers, 369–72 (on legality, cf. pp. 388, 397; note 146 below); Arrighi, pp. 137–8; Pado, pp. 108–9; Viansson-Ponté, p. 210; Kerr (see note 3). Times from Moch and Tournoux; others differ slightly.

[139] Ferniot, pp. 125–6; Brombergers, pp. 383–5; Arrighi, pp. 140–1; Tournoux, p. 347; Moch, *SFIO*, pp. 10 and 12 (cf. Brutelle, *ibid.* p. 7); Taylor, p. 10; Pado, p. 109 (text in first three and in Sérigny, p. 146; *AP*, p. 539). Released 12:25 (Moch, cf. Pado) but Guichard let Pflimlin know earlier, and at 11:30 De Gaulle (using official channels through Lorillot) ordered Salan to await instructions (text in Tournoux, p. 351).

[140] Coty persuaded him not to deny: Tournoux, pp. 348–50; Viansson-Ponté, p. 211. On Pflimlin, also Moch, *SFIO*, p. 12 and *La Nef*, p. 11; Taylor, p. 10; Brombergers, p. 385. Ferniot, p. 135 (cf. p. 126) hints Mollet knew in advance; in *L'Express*, 25 May 1958, p. 6 he affirms it; Brombergers (p. 387) denies. Arrighi, p. 141 (alone) says Pflimlin had promised De Gaulle to resign on Thursday 29th; Moch denies (*La Nef*, pp. 10–11).

[141] For De Gaulle; Brombergers, pp. 312, 362–3, 370, 383. For 27th: Moch, *SFIO*, p. 12; Moch quoted Tournoux, p. 349; Dauer and Rodet, p. 123; Brombergers, pp. 312, 335, 362 (but *ibid.* pp. 375–6, 383 say 28th, cf. 385); Kerr (n. 3). Arrighi alone (pp. 123, 138, 141) says Pflimlin told De Gaulle.

veniently placed to cut the government off from its proposed sanctuary in the northern coalfield.[142]

At 10 a.m. on the decisive Tuesday, Moch learned from a friendly diplomatic source that the strike was for that night, and took precautionary measures.[143] Moreover, General Beaufort—who was to command the revolt in Paris—kept President Coty informed of his own plans and deadlines.[144] The army leaders all hoped that the threat alone would suffice; it does not follow that they—let alone their subordinates—were merely bluffing.[145] Ministers did not think so, and Moch, on reading the General's communiqué, at once concluded that De Gaulle had acted to keep open the legal road to power, which an invasion would close forever.[146] He was right; the communiqué led Algiers to postpone the operation. But De Gaulle, pouring oil as well as water on the flames, was also encouraging the insurrection which at the time he claimed he alone could avert, and later he condemned as a 'military usurpation'.[147]

[142] Tournoux, pp. 265–6, 375, 378 and n.; Brombergers, pp. 305–7, 335, 376–8 (and cf. pp. 251, 310, 381, 407); Dauer and Rodet, pp. 122–3; Kraft, pp. 191–2; Ferniot, p. 120; Kerr (note 3); *L'Humanité*, 31 October 1958, *Le Canard Enchaîné*, 2 July 1958, cf. Taylor, p. 10. *L'Express*, 12 June for ex-paratroops (175,000 in France, 6,000 armed and ready) and provincial CSPs. For the northern coalfield, note 128 above; for Faure, Brombergers, p. 250, and note 122 above.

[143] Moch, *SFIO*, p. 12; *La Nef*, pp. 10–11; cf. Ferniot, p. 120. Source: the American Consul at Algiers: *ibid.* p. 139; Tournoux, p. 343; Brombergers, pp. 376 and 394; cf. Kraft, p. 199. Precautions: Parisian and south-western aerodromes blocked with barbed wire (but the air force would clear them) and occupied by CRS with orders to fire on unauthorized planes (but would they obey?); Kerr (note 3); Ferniot, p. 110; Tournoux, pp. 352–3; Brombergers, pp. 305, 377.

[144] '"L'intoxication" de l'Elysée, de l'hotel Matignon, du Palais-Bourbon par le général de Beaufort...devait aboutir à une victoire psychologique qui permit l'économie de l'opération militaire véritable': Brombergers, p. 312 (cf. p. 376); cf. Taylor, *loc. cit.* p. 10. For similar warnings by Abdesselam, a Kabyle member of the CSP: *ibid.* pp. 326 and 364; Tournoux, p. 342 and n.; Ferniot, p. 139; cf. Arrighi, pp. 75–6; Abdesselam, *Procès Salan*, p. 203.

[145] Tournoux, p. 377 (Beaufort), cf. p. 356. Brombergers, pp. 233 (Challe); 248, 311–12 (Ely); 274, 300–1, 303, 328 (Salan); 308, 432–5 (Miquel); 263, 301, 363, 371, 373, 405 (junior officers ready to take over); 126, 143, 308–9, 404, 427, 429, 433–5 (juniors not Gaullist, so De Gaulle could not restrain them). Cf. Tournoux, pp. 368, 400; notes 25 and 77 above.

[146] Kraft, p. 199; Tournoux, pp. 348–50 (views of Pflimlin, Moch, Mollet); but cf. *ibid.* p. 400. Brombergers, pp. 312 (of others), 380 (of Moch and Mollet; Chevigné did not believe in a *coup*). Cf. Moch, *SFIO*, p. 12; *La Nef*, p. 11. On legality, Brombergers, pp. 388, 297. De Gaulle's Paris staff opposed the *coup* and put pressure on Algiers: *ibid.* pp. 315–16, 359; Tournoux, pp. 367–9, 390; Dauer and Rodet, p. 126; cf. Soustelle, p. 47. But on 24 May Guichard told Professor Marçais of Algiers that an airborne *coup* might be necessary: Marçais, *Procès Salan*, p. 264. He also told General Miquel's envoy that while De Gaulle did not want an invasion he 'would take the situation as it might present itself': Miquel, *ibid.* p. 217; cf. note 164 below. This casts doubt on the Brombergers' statement (p. 312, cf. p. 359) that De Gaulle was victim as well as beneficiary of the plot.

[147] Usurpation: broadcast, cited *Le Monde*, 10–11 June 1962, p. 2. Postponement: Abdesselam, *Procès Salan*, p. 204; Algiers' telegram to Miquel p.m. May 27th, 'proposed action no longer envisaged for the moment'—Brombergers, p. 384; note 139 above. Encouragement: on the morning of May 28 De Gaulle was visited by Salan's envoy General Dulac (whom journalists mistook for General Catroux: Arrighi, p. 147; Brombergers, p. 405; Sérigny, p. 143 n.; cf. Tournoux, p. 351 n.; Ferniot, p. 154; Soustelle, pp. 45–6). He told Dulac to tell Salan that while he regretted the necessity, 'what he has done and will do is for the good of France'; Dulac concluded that

In political circles De Gaulle's announcement stiffened the opposition. At a joint meeting that afternoon the Socialist parliamentarians and executive were violently critical of Mollet (who was in cabinet) and voted by 112 to 3 never to accept De Gaulle. MRP too came out against the resignation of the government, and many Radicals were strongly anti-Gaullist. For once a parliamentary majority was struggling desperately to keep a reluctant cabinet in office. It was expected that Pflimlin would make the vote on the constitutional reform bill a pretext for resignation; so more than two-thirds of the deputies (408 to 165) voted the bill. But the CNI, against Pinay's advice, instructed their Ministers to resign (Mutter, Minister for Algeria, refused).[148] On this excuse, despite Socialist protests, the premier resigned at 4:13 a.m. on the 28th.[149]

The crucial role now fell to President René Coty. Early in May he had secretly approached De Gaulle, but found the General unwilling to accept the normal parliamentary procedure.[150] Now he sent to Colombey his assistant Merveilleux de Vignaux, a close associate of Bidault and in 1958 (unlike 1940) a keen Gaullist.[151] That afternoon, as the demonstrators were assembling near the Place de la Nation, Coty summoned Pinay, Mollet, and Teitgen of MRP and told them that he would send for De Gaulle rather than risk a Popular Front.[152] He chose three men to see the General on his behalf: his predecessor Vincent Auriol, André Le Troquer the Socialist President of the Assembly, and Gaston Monnerville, the colored West Indian Radical who has presided over the upper house ever since the war. As Auriol declined, Monnerville and a reluctant Le Troquer went alone to a stormy midnight meeting at St Cloud. The General, who had sworn twelve years

Salan had a free hand to decide whether to invade: Dulac, *Procès Salan*, p. 376; Salan, *ibid.* p. 79. The accounts differ in detail. De Gaulle told Dulac Salan should command himself (instead of Massu) and bring more men (Paillat, pp. 24–6)—yet Salan was to have come anyway (Soustelle, p. 44). De Gaulle thought the numbers of troops inadequate, and said 'Do the necessary' (Soustelle, pp. 45–6). A telegram to Jouhaud on 29 May said: De Gaulle agrees, we expect you at 2:30 a.m. on the 30th (counsel at *Procès Jouhaud*, p. 302). Soustelle and Frey were pressing for invasion, Salan resisting them: Jouhaud, *ibid.* p. 21; Salan, *Procès Salan*, p. 79. However, Salan was satisfied at Dulac's report: Abdesselam, *ibid.* p. 204. Cf. note 164 below. Colonel Trinquier, an ultra sympathizer, claims that De Gaulle told Dulac he wanted a larger force, but for pressure not for use; and that on Dulac's return the plan was provisionally shelved: *Le coup d'état du 13 mai* (Paris: L'Esprit nouveau, 1962), pp. 180–2, 188–90.

[148] Ferniot, pp. 128–37; Kraft, p. 199; Brombergers, pp. 387–92; cf. Arrighi, pp. 143, 156; Pado, pp. 111–12, 125; Viansson-Ponté, p. 212; Le Troquer, pp. 187–8. The first and last two give the Socialist text (cf. Brutelle, *SFIO*, p. 7); the majority given (respectively) as 117, 111, 111, 117, 112, 112, 117, unstated.

[149] Cabinet debate in Tournoux, pp. 357–62; Ferniot, pp. 138–45; Brombergers, pp. 393–7. *Ibid.* pp. 368, 389; Moch and Mollet feared that a premature resignation would bring in, not De Gaulle, but Mitterrand and the Popular Front. Cf. Taylor, p. 10; Brutelle, *SFIO*, p. 7; Pado, p. 113.

[150] See note 12 above.

[151] Arrighi, p. 147 (on him, cf. Ferniot, p. 145).

[152] Ferniot, p. 148; Arrighi, pp. 145–6; Pado, p. 116; Tournoux, *Carnets*, pp. 82–3.

before never to set foot in the Assembly again, demurred at appearing for the investiture debate as Le Troquer insisted, and demanded not only prolonged exceptional powers but also the right to draft a new constitution. Le Troquer was indignant, De Gaulle exasperated, Monnerville conciliatory but firm. They separated in anger, and at 1 a.m. the two Presidents reported back to Coty.[153]

Next morning, Le Troquer spoke most gloomily to a Socialist meeting; and in Algiers the invasion plans were resumed for that night.[154] At 2:30 p.m. Moch (unknown to Pflimlin) ordered the prefects to take to the maquis if attacked.[155] Half an hour later the deputies met, standing to hear their President read the first and last special message from a President of the Fourth Republic. Coty warned that only a De Gaulle government could prevent civil war. If his nominee were rejected, he would resign and transfer his powers, under Article 41 of the Constitution, to Le Troquer as President of the Assembly.[156]

Le Troquer read very fast, making his disapproval obvious. When he came to the threat of resignation, the Communists and many Socialists sat down; at the end, first the Left and then the Right sang the *Marseillaise*. Oppressed by the knowledge that invasion was only ten hours away, Coty had gone far beyond the President's normal role. But he had alienated instead of persuading the Socialists—without whom there could be no parliamentary majority for De Gaulle.[157]

Two developments later in the afternoon changed their minds. First, it became known that Monnerville's interpretation of De Gaulle's position differed sharply from that put about by President Coty's putative successor.[158]

[153] Le Troquer, pp. 190–9. Also Ferniot, pp. 148–52 (cf. p. 178); Tournoux, pp. 382–5; Arrighi, pp. 149–50; Brombergers, pp. 409–13; cf. *ibid.* p. 421; Taylor, p. 9; Pado, pp. 119–20 (inaccurate). He asked for one (or two) years' special powers, Le Troquer offered three months, they agreed on six—proposed by Monnerville who said little else (Brombergers, p. 411); whose role was crucial (Tournoux). On the importance attached to procedure, note 133 above.

[154] Le Troquer: Tournoux, p. 387, and *Carnets*, p. 85; Brutelle, *SFIO*, p. 7; Pado, p. 121; Brombergers, p. 419. Invasion: *ibid.* pp. 402, 415–16 (at 1 a.m. on 30th); Jouhaud's counsel, *Le Monde*, 15–16 May 1962, p. 3 (2:30 a.m.); Dauer and Rodet, pp. 124–5 (3 a.m.); Pado, p. 120; cf. Dominique, p. 162 (8 p.m. 28th); Tournoux, pp. 390, 399, 405, contrast 370.

[155] *Ibid.* pp. 391–2, and Arrighi, pp. 181–2 (both have text); Arrighi, p. 50 and Soustelle, p. 44 (both imply a wrong date); Ferniot, p. 154; Brombergers, p. 422.

[156] Tournoux, pp. 386–8; Brombergers, pp. 415–18; Ferniot, pp. 155–7; Arrighi, pp. 151–2 (long extracts in last two, text in *AP*, pp. 539–40, Pado, pp. 150–3). The idea and the draft were both Coty's own. Pflimlin and Lecourt (Minister of Justice, MRP) countersigned despite some constitutional scruples: Tournoux, p. 388 n.; Brombergers, p. 418. If Le Troquer had become acting President as he fully expected to, he would have nominated Naegelen (who would, however, have refused the premiership): on this and other names canvassed, see also Tournoux, *Carnets*, p. 85 n.; Ferniot, p. 164; Arrighi, pp. 136 and 154–5.

[157] Ferniot, pp. 157–9; Arrighi, pp. 153–5; Brombergers, pp. 422–3; Pado, pp. 121–2; Tournoux, p. 389; Isorni, pp. 163–4.

[158] All *ibid.*; also Brombergers, pp. 419–21 and 423–4; Isorni, pp. 165–6; Pado, p. 51; Dronne, p. 160. For Le Troquer's defence, Le Troquer, pp. 190–9; also *Le Monde*, 6–7 July 1958; extracts

Secondly Vincent Auriol obtained from the General (and the censor) permission to publish De Gaulle's very conciliatory reply to his letter of three days before. It changed the climate at once. By 62 to 29 the Socialists accepted Auriol's letter as a basis for negotiation.[159] At 7:30 p.m. De Gaulle entered the Elysée and agreed to form a government.[160] He asked to see a Socialist delegation, and next day (Friday 30th) first Auriol, then Mollet and Deixonne—president of the Socialist deputies—flew to Colombey. Deixonne went an opponent and returned a supporter. That night on the Champs Elysées Communists clashed with Gaullists who—as in the 'motor-horn demonstration' the previous evening—were openly supported by the police; at Toulouse extremists, resenting any compromise with the System, vainly urged General Miquel to launch Operation Resurrection after all.[161]

On Saturday afternoon the General met twenty-six party leaders at the Hotel Lapérouse; the Communists refused to attend. The Socialists (and Coty) persuaded him to appear before the Assembly, though not to submit to the normal barrage of questions—on everything from European union to the price of cider—by which prospective premiers were always assailed and sometimes entrapped. He outlined his constitutional proposals; the politicians showed anxiety about ministerial responsibility to Parliament and over his attitude to the CSP.[162] At 6 p.m., the Socialists resolved by 77 to 74 to support De Gaulle (but not impose party discipline). Deputies and executive members were still hostile, but the senators—who knew and trusted their President—swayed the decision.[163] On Sunday, June 1, at 11 a.m., Guichard telephoned to Salan to be ready to invade if necessary.[164] Four

in Ferniot, p. 151 n.; cf. Brombergers, pp. 437–8; the sequel did not disprove his account, cf. *ibid.* pp. 423–4.

[159] Ferniot, pp. 159–63 (with extracts); Arrighi, pp. 155–6 (with De Gaulle's text); Brutelle, *SFIO*, p. 8; Tournoux, p. 395; Brombergers, pp. 420–5. Mendès-France's friend Georges Boris had urged Auriol to write: *ibid.* p. 410. Both texts in *AP*, pp. 538–9; Pado, pp. 148–50. Also for the effects, *ibid.* p. 122; Isorni, p. 162.

[160] His communiqué in Arrighi, p. 157. Also Tournoux, p. 389; Ferniot, p. 165; time differs in Brombergers, p. 425; Pado, p. 122; Dauer and Rodet, p. 125.

[161] Brombergers, pp. 426–35; Arrighi, pp. 158–9; Pado, pp. 123–4; also for Socialists, Ferniot, pp. 167–8, Tournoux, pp. 394–5; for Resurrection, *L'Express*, 12 June 1958; Tournoux, p. 390; Dauer and Rodet, pp. 125–6; Moch, *La Nef*, p. 11. Miquel was most unhappy about De Gaulle's intentions, but at Algiers on 2 or 3 June, Salan persuaded him not to act: Miquel, *Procès Salan*, pp. 217–18; cf. Paillat, p. 22.

[162] Ferniot, pp. 165–6, 169–70; Brombergers, pp. 426–7, 436–7; Brutelle, *SFIO*, p. 9; Ramadier, *ibid.* p. 66; Arrighi, pp. 160–1. Names of the 26 leaders: *ibid.* 160n. He promised (but did not give) a job to a Poujadist: Isorni, p. 77 n. He gave a precedent (Laniel) for rejecting questions: Ferniot, p. 166.

[163] Delegates' reports: *SFIO*, pp. 8–9, 66; Tournoux, pp. 395–8; Ferniot, pp. 173–4; cf. Brombergers, pp. 436–7. Auriol had most influence (cf. last two). Voting: *ibid.* p. 437; *SFIO*, p. 9 (Brutelle) and p. 65 (Lejeune); Ferniot, p. 177; Arrighi, p. 162; all agree the total, 77–74 (except Pado, p. 125) and the executive, 23–18 against; for deputies, Brutelle's figures are mutually inconsistent and other sources are incomplete.

[164] 'Nos affaires se présentent mal, à vous de jouer, tenez-vous prêt': Salan, *Procès Salan*, p. 79.

hours later De Gaulle entered the Assembly to read the shortest investiture speech of the Fourth Republic. During the brief debate the candidate withdrew. In the vote, at 7:35 p.m., he was elected by 329 to 224; 42 Socialists voted for, 49 against.[165] Three weeks earlier, he would not have had a hundred votes.[166]

APPENDIX I: POLITICIANS MILITARY AND CIVILIAN

KEY: *Italic*: by 1961, for *Algérie française* and against de Gaulle.

PLOTS:
1 Cagoulards 1937
2 Algiers riots 6 Feb. 1956
3 General Faure Dec. 1956
4 Bazooka Jan. 1957
5 May 1958 on CSP
5n May 1958, not on CSP

6 Barricades Jan. 1960
7 Putsch April 1961
8a OAS in Algeria 1961–2
8sp OAS in Spain 1961–2
9 Other

ROLE:
a—arrested, or house searched
acq.—acquitted
c—convicted

e—escaped arrest
v—intended victim
?—allegedly involved

CAREER:
d—deputy May 1958
D—deputy Nov. 1958
Dx—defeated Nov. 1958
m—minister in IV Rep.
M—minister of de Gaulle
mx—minister of Pflimlin

s—senator May 1958
S—senator Apr. 1959
Sx—defeated Apr. 1959
pm—premier in IV Rep.
PM—premier of De Gaulle

MILITARY (Generals unless specified)
Allard 5n 7a? i/c Army Corps Algiers
Beaufort 5n 7a?? Gen. Staff.
Catroux m retired
Challe 5na 7c, Gen. Staff.
Chassin Dx 5ne, no post
Cherrières 3? 5ne, retired
Cogny 4?? 5n, no post
Ducasse Lt-Col., 5, on Massu's staff
Ely 5n? Chief of Staff (also under De Gaulle)
J. *Faure* dx (Pouj. 1957) 3 5n 7c, 2 i/c in Germany
Godard Col. 5n 6? 7e 8a, at GG 13 May (Director of Security for Algiers 15 May 1958 to 1960; said to have become police adviser to the Greek junta, 1967)
Jouhaud 5 7e 8c, i/c Air Force in Algeria
Juin Marshal, retired
Lorillot, Chief of Staff replacing Ely
Martin 5n? Staff
Massu 5, i/c 10 Para. Div. (De Gaulle made him Prefect and Corps Commander Algiers to Jan. 1960)

CIVILIANS
Abdesselam D 5
Arrighi dD 4?? 5n
Auriol (Pres. Rep. 1947–53)
Baret Prefect of Algiers 5n
Baudier 2 5
Berthommier d 9c
Biaggi D 2 5ne 6a
Bidault pm dD
Bourgès-Maunoury dDx pm
Brutelle Dx
Chaban-Delmas dD m (President National Assembly 1959)
Chevallier m (Mayor of Algiers 1952–8)
Chevigné dDx mx
Coty Pres. Rep. 1954–8
Debré s PM 4?? 5n
Delbecque D 5
Dronne dD
Duchet sS m
M. *Faure* dD mx
Frey M 5n
Gaillard dD pm

[165] Introduced on the right, he turned back, saying 'J'entre à gauche': Isorni, pp. 166–7. Text in *AP*, pp. 540–1; Pado (pp. 153–6); extracts Arrighi, pp. 164–5 (6 minutes 4 seconds), cf. Ferniot, pp. 179–80 (3 minutes). Socialists: *SFIO*, p. 9; most of the 42 had voted 'never' five days earlier (cf. note 148 above). Lagaillarde tried hard to rally the Poujadists *against* him: Paillat, pp. 17–18. [166] Sérigny, p. 10. Not fifty: Dronne, p. 51.

MILITARY (*cont.*)

Miquel Dx 5n, i/c Toulouse and Operation
 Resurrection (De Gaulle retired him)
Nomy Admiral, Chief of Naval Staff
Petit 5n 7c, Staff (later Debré's military
 adviser)
Prigent Col., i/c Corsica
Salan 4v 5n 7e 8a, C-in-C Algeria (De Gaulle's
 delegate for Algeria 1958, honorific post
 1959)
Thomazo Col., D 3 5 6a 7a, on Allard's staff,
 Salan's Military Governor of Corsica
Trinquier Lt-Col., 5, i/c 3rd Colonial Para.
 Regt. (resigned 1961 when offered
 command of Katanga army but never
 took it up).
Vaudrey Lt-Col., 5n 7ce 8a, 2 i/c at GG on
 13 May

CIVILIANS (*cont.*)

Gazier d mx
Guichard (admin. Sahara 1960)
Jacquinot dD mM
Jolivet 5
Kovacs 3 4e
Lacoste d m
Lagaillarde D 5 6e 8sp
Lecourt dD mxM
Lefèvre 2 5 6acq. 8sp
Lejeune dD mxM
Le Pen dD 5n 6a
Le Troquer d m President National Assembly
 1958
Martel 2 3 4? 5 6e 8a
Dr Martin 1 3? 5n
Mendès-France d pm
Merlo 5
Mitterrand dS m 9v
Moch d mx
Mollet dD mxM
Monnerville sS President of the Senate
Montigny 5
Moreau 5
Morice dSx m
Mutter d mx
Naegelen d m Governor-General Algeria
 1948–51
Neuwirth D 5
Ortiz 2 3 4 5 6e 8sp
Parachini 2 5 6a
Perrou 5
Pflimlin dD pmx M
Piette d
Pinay dD pm M
Pleven dD pm mx
Roseau 5
Schumann dD m
Sérigny Sx 5 6acq.
Sid Cara m D 5
Soustelle dD M 4?? 5
Teitgen d m
Vigier d S

APPENDIX II. SOUSTELLE'S ESCAPE: THE PERILS OF INSTANT HISTORY

The accounts in Arrighi 57–8, Dronne 12, Ferniot 74–5, Pado 68–70, Pajaud 100,
Brombergers 286–92, Paillat 14, agree that he left under rugs on the floor of a
car from which (Arrighi, Dronne, Pajaud, Brombergers) the back seat had been
removed; but on little else.

 A close friend knew a woman in the same building (Pado). He was Soustelle's
travelling companion La Tour du Pin, and she, being the owner's daughter, was
known to the police and allowed to keep her car inside (Arrighi, Brombergers).

The escape was at 2.30 a.m.; the car had been waiting for hours (Ferniot). At 1.30 a.m. she told the police she was ill and a car was coming for her; it came at 2.15 and left at 2.30 a.m. (Pado). Daily before dawn the car took the same route at the same hour (Dronne). Her husband had wanted her to go golfing (Arrighi), but she took out her car (Arrighi, Brombergers) admired by the police and chatting to La Tour du Pin in the front seat beside her (Arrighi); a male friend of Soustelle's drove (Ferniot, Pado, Pajaud). It was 2 p.m. Thursday (Brombergers) or Friday (Pajaud) and the police paid no attention (Brombergers). Their attention was distracted while Soustelle, who had just got home, climbed in (Pajaud). He had returned home long before (Pado). He had stayed in all day, feigning illness (Brombergers, Dronne).

From this car, a Dauphine (Arrighi, Brombergers, Paillat), Versailles (Ferniot), 4 CV (Pajaud), he changed quickly (Arrighi), after a kilometre into a Versailles (Pajaud), on a corner (Brombergers), in a garage (Dronne). The lady was taken to a cinema to prevent careless talk (Arrighi) to see *Sois belle et tais-toi* (Brombergers). He changed cars again in Paris and drove to the frontier in a Buick (Brombergers). The Versailles sped towards Switzerland but he prudently changed cars twice (Pado), twice more outside Paris (Arrighi), four times after Paris (Ferniot). He entered Switzerland at 5 a.m. (Pajaud) after a drive of three hours (Arrighi), eight hours (Brombergers). He reached Geneva at midnight on 15 May and took off from Cointrin on the 17th after spending the 16th trying to arrange for a plane (Soustelle, p. 37). After an argument with the pilot (Pajaud), after 24 hours' negotiations (Brombergers), immediately he arrived at the aerodrome (Pado) of Geneva (Pado, Dronne, Ferniot, Brombergers) or Bâle-Mulhouse (Arrighi), at 9.40 a.m. (Arrighi, Ferniot), the chartered Swiss Viking (agreed) of the Balair Co. (Ferniot, Brombergers, Pado) took off. The pilot had agreed to fly to Tunis and only 'des procédés extrêmement persuasifs' made him change destination in mid-flight (Pajaud, cf. Paillat). The company had exacted 'une rallonge impressionnante' on learning the true destination before take-off (Brombergers). The pilot crossed the French coast (Brombergers) but avoided France and her territorial waters (Ferniot, Pado). He gave his position to no one (Pado), declared himself at Tunis (Ferniot), avoided Tunis (Brombergers).

Next morning the police were still innocently guarding Soustelle's door (Ferniot) and falsely reporting he had a high temperature (Tournoux, 319); but friends who phoned found the telephone cut off (Pado, 66). There were three policemen at the gate (Ferniot), two at the gate with a car near by (Pado, 68), seven inspectors (Pado, 67), seven inspectors and three policemen (Brombergers, 285), ten inspectors (*ibid*. 214), two inspectors with 'abnormal reinforcements' (Dronne), at least two dozen police (Arrighi).

APPENDIX III. LATER INFORMATION

Four books published since this article appeared have added to our knowledge: a few details come from Jacques Soustelle in *28 ans du Gaullisme* (La Table Ronde, 1968); a personal account from an 'ultra' colonel in Roger Trinquier, *Le coup d'Etat du 13 mai* (L'Esprit nouveau, 1962: published too late to incorporate material from it in the article); an academic narrative of events in the most crucial region of France in J.-P. Buffelan, *Le Complot du 13 mai 1958 dans le Sud-ouest* (Librairie générale de droit et de jurisprudence, 1966), whose book was read and annotated by both General Miquel and the IGAME (regional prefect) M. Périllier. Their new material is summarised below (noted as S, T or B respectively). Jean Ferniot produced the best and fullest of the journalists' contributions in *De Gaulle et le 13 mai* (Plon, 1965), which substantiates my version in general and in many details; the main differences, as well as major new points, are recorded here (noted as F).

I. LÉON DELBECQUE

1. He was Chaban-Delmas's own choice and not Soustelle's suggestion (F 130). Lacoste did protest before April at Delbecque's activities but failed to stop them (F 163–4, 189–94). *See above, pp. 134–5.*

2. Salan's telegram was inspired by the Gaullists in Paris and Delbecque gave the generals the first draft (F 219, 223–4). *Above, p. 137.*

3. It was Delbecque who summoned the UTB on the 14th to protect the GG from the tanks supposedly ordered by a loyalist colonel to retake it (F 288, cf. 283). *P. 147, and II.2 below.*

II. ROGER TRINQUIER

1. Trinquier was not in touch with the ultras before 13 May (T 102–3, 121–2). His regiment was not brought back to Algiers out of turn (T 86). Its former commander, Bigeard, still hoped to use it in the Gaullist interest (T 76, 135, 177). *P. 137, n. 26.* ['Raspéguy'—below, p. 192—is modelled on Bigeard.]

2. During the attack on the GG Trinquier was out of touch with his men (T 95) but before they left he had told them not to get engaged alongside the CRS (T 94). *P. 139.* When a loyalist colonel had summoned tanks to retake the GG, they ignored the order; had they arrived the parachutists would have fired on them without warning (T 107–8). *No previous evidence, but cf. I.3 above.*

3. Trinquier and the junior officers tried, directly and through his wife, to persuade Massu to attack Paris and seize power for himself; but he was too Gaullist and too unambitious (T 120, 203–7). *P. 145 and nn. 76–7.*

4. The insurrection was precarious at first because the army, apart from the parachutists, did not join (T 110–11, 119, 134, 155–6, 162, 176, 249). The revolts in Oran and Constantine were instigated by Trinquier and the Moslem demonstration of 16 May organized by him (T 112, 137–8, 140–2, 154–5). The army handed power to De Gaulle because they did not know what to do with it (T 126). *P. 145.*

5. Within the CSP the Gaullists worked for Soustelle and against Massu (whom Delbecque wanted replaced by Jouhaud, T 180); the ultra opposition was organized by Trinquier and Ducasse (T 171–80, 199–201). Trinquier arranged protection against assassination for Massu and himself (T 177–8). *P. 147.*

III. MASSU AND LACOSTE

The three Paris–Algiers phone calls, mentioned by F 258, 262, 270 as referring to firing on the crowd, broadly support the interpretations of the 'don't shoot' story given *above, p. 140 n. 46.*

163

IV. RAOUL SALAN

1. He relied on Trinquier, whose regiment he had recalled because the colonel was anti-Gaullist (F 235, 302–3). *P. 137 n. 26.*

2. He resented being howled down by the crowd in the Forum on the 13th, and so was slow to join the insurgents; Trinquier therefore organized a 'Vive Salan!' claque (T 97, 104, 112). Salan hesitated before crying 'Vive De Gaulle!' to the crowd on the 15th, but he had already said it privately to the CSP (T 133; F 309–11). *P. 144.*

3. Pflimlin confirmed on the 14th the delegation of powers to Salan made by Gaillard the night before—and apparently extended it to all Algeria (implied by F 298). *P. 142 n. 56.*

4. Salan informed the government on the 16th that he would receive either Chevigné, Minister of Defence, or Lejeune, Minister for the Sahara; the unexpected arrival of Soustelle on the 17th destroyed this chance of a settlement (F 343–4). *No previous evidence.*

V. SOUSTELLE AND DE GAULLE

1. The demonstration was to have continued until Pflimlin's expected defeat and only then was the GG to be occupied and a CSP set up; paratroops were envisaged in case there were Communist riots in Paris (F 246, cf. S 144 on the Algiers plans). *P. 136 n. 23.*

2. De Gaulle opposed Soustelle's departure for Algiers but all the Gaullist leaders insisted he must go; so Guichard told him the General had said neither yes nor no (F 244–5). *P. 146 n. 83.*

3. It is 'une contre-vérité manifeste...complètement fausse' to say De Gaulle knew nothing of his partisans' preparations; Guichard and Foccart knew everything and told him everything; the Gaullists asked no instructions so as not to compromise the General's later chances of coming to power legally if they failed this time; 'Mais, évidemment, un ordre de lui, ou un désaveu explicite, aurait tout arrêté net'; there was none (S 145–6). *P. 156 and nn. 146, 147.*

4. In particular the Corsican operation was planned by the Gaullists with the General's knowledge to hurry things up (F 382, 392). *P. 149 n. 95.*

5. So was 'Resurrection'; *see VIII below.*

VI. PUBLIC OPINION IN SOUTH-WESTERN FRANCE

1. The activist demonstration in Toulouse on 13 May was in favour of the 'quartet' not De Gaulle (B 54) whom many of the local CSP disliked (B 97, 98). *Pp. 144–5 n. 72.*

2. Nobody feared De Gaulle would destroy the Republic (B 61). *P. 146 (at n. 80).*

3. In eleven named plants, strike calls against De Gaulle were followed by 75% of the staff in two, 50% in two, and 30% or fewer in seven (B 86, 131–2, 152). Anti-Algiers propaganda was greeted with indifference by workers (details— B 86, 107). Rank and file Communists were against fascism but few opposed De Gaulle (B 86)—though their leader told the Prefect they and the CGT members would fight against a coup d'état, while CFTC and FO leaders said their followers

would not (B 146). Communist support alienated others from the Republican Defence Committee (B 65, 131) and deterred Socialists from demonstrating (B 83). *Pp. 148 and n. 91, 153 and n. 129.*

4. There was equally little enthusiasm on the side of the CSP (B 107; for estimates of pro-CSP numbers 108, of Republicans, 151). *P. 153 n. 130.*

5. On the character and importance of the CSPs in the S.W., especially at Toulouse and Pau, see B 111–16. *P. 155.*

VII. GOVERNMENT SERVICES

1. At Toulouse there were doubts about De Gaulle's cause among a few army staff officers and many air force officers including even the intelligence services (whose telephones were tapped by army intelligence: B 75–6); conversations among officers of the garrison were very cautious (B 87); conscript NCOs who obeyed orders from Republican officers to send statements of loyalty to Coty were disciplined by military security (B 62). *Pp. 151–2.*

2. Miquel, who had served 25 years in Morocco, was recalled in 1955 for openly opposing government policy there (B 91). Périllier regarded Miquel as a moderate in the town itself and saw him daily at this time (B 135 and n.). Miquel denies any contact with Algiers before 18 May (Ferniot repeatedly says he had). *P. 152 and n. 122.*

3. The prefect at Pau could not act against his CSP for fear of action by the army. Threats extended to the wives and children of Périllier, and of Chevigné if he had arrested Miquel whom he summoned to Paris on the 27th but allowed to return (B 135–6, 137). *P. 152 and n. 123.*

4. Disloyalty in the Ministry of the Interior extended to the Corsican telephonists, who at the request of a Corsican official in Algiers allowed Soustelle to use the Ministry switchboard to make his calls to France (S 146, F 139). *P. 152 and n. 125.*

5. At Toulouse the gendarmes and firemen were unreliable and the CRS uncertain. On the 18th the IGAMEs got Moch to call up reservists to form gendarmerie units to replace the CRS who had all been called to Paris (B 109n., 117, 123, 124). *P. 152.*

6. The CSP attack on the prefecture was to give the army an excuse to intervene (B 107, 109, 124) and Périllier thought they would not do so if he could stop the civilians (his comment, B 109n.). *P. 155.*

VIII. DE GAULLE AND 'RESURRECTION'

1. Details of 'Resurrection' given fully in F 397–402, and (read and so confirmed by Miquel) in B 73–5. *P. 155.*

2. Was the strike for the evening of the 27th? Périller learned so, and told Moch, at 10 a.m. on the 24th (B 136). But Ferniot argues at length that this widely believed story was bluff by Algiers (F 437–9)—saying *inter alia* that Miquel denied that date had ever been fixed, and did not send his emissary to discover De Gaulle's wishes till the 28th. But Miquel himself wrote: 'L'opération du 27 mai a été décommandée pour trois raisons principales: 1º Le refus du Général De Gaulle de se prêter à la manœuvre; 2º La certitude de l'absence de réaction communiste; 3º L'annonce du processus d'investiture du Général De Gaulle...' (B 139n.). No

doubt he felt the need to discover De Gaulle's intentions only after the latter's 27 May communiqué; on the reply see B 141 (also F 453). *P. 156 and n. 146.*

3. General Dulac's report of his visit to De Gaulle on May 28 (not 29th as misprinted in my article) is also given by S 147 (and F 451–2). Commandant Mouchonnet who was in the party told Mᵉ Jacques Isorni (once Pétain's counsel) that De Gaulle wanted paratroops dropped on Paris and Colombey and troop landings from Algeria, while the General was telling Mollet and Pinay the opposite: Isorni in court, *Le Monde*, 17–18 January 1965, p. 13. *P. 156 and n. 147.*

4. Wanting to shoot the prefect, mayor and newspaper-owner, the Toulouse extremists were furious at Miquel's refusal to strike on the 31st (B 143–4). When did Salan finally persuade Miquel at Algiers aerodrome to trust De Gaulle? B 145 n. 84 says Miquel claimed this was on 23 June, but in his next note he mentions Miquel's evidence at Salan's trial (*Procès Salan*, p. 217) which specifically denied it was at the later period, and confirmed 2 or 3 June. *P. 159 n. 161.*

8 Moslems and settlers[a]

The Algerian war began just six years ago. In the small hours of a Monday morning, November 1st, 1954, seventy small groups of Arabs all over the country attacked police stations and public buildings and vehicles with their home-made bombs and old hunting-rifles.

Almost everywhere, the raids failed completely; only in the wild Aurès mountains near the Tunisian border, a turbulent area since Roman times, did they develop into yet another local rising. In that region a group of fifteen rebels stopped a bus and shot two passengers, a young French school-teacher and his wife. Germaine Tillion, the ethnologist, was in the mountains at the time; she reports that Moslem opinion unanimously condemned the murder. Only two years later, Moslem children in the Algiers Casbah cheered when the ambulances rushed past to the scene of a successful terrorist out-rage. And after four further years this bitter little war continues to absorb the military strength of France, and to sap the moral credit of the West.

By 1960 the endless conflict was provoking a 'crisis of the French con-science', especially among young men awaiting their call-up. Some *insoumis* went into hiding or exile. A few even (through the 'Jeanson network') offered their services to the Algerian nationalists; twenty of these went on trial in September. A former head of the Algiers police testified in court to the tortures and disappearances against which they were protesting. A manifesto by 121 artists, teachers, and intellectuals justified their motives and excused *insoumission*. And the Cardinals and Archbishops of France, the Protestant Assembly and the Teachers' Federation, while condemning both *insoumission* and torture, all confirmed that the malaise of youth was both widespread and sincere.

These events harmed the Right; but they also brought the Left into dis-repute. At the Jeanson trial, the interminable obstruction of some defence lawyers alienated their warmest sympathisers. Jean-Paul Sartre affirmed that the Algerian nationalists were fighting for French liberties; Francis Jeanson himself, from Switzerland, expressed surprise that they had shot so few French prisoners. These provocative statements brought the popular reac-tion and the official repression which their authors (believing 'fascism' to be the necessary 'prelude to revolution') had probably intended. True to form, the government played into their hands, seizing journals which

[a] From *Encounter*, January 1961; originally entitled *The Algerian Tragedy*.

discussed *insoumission* (even disapprovingly); prosecuting some of the 121 for inciting desertion; suspending civil servants and teachers who had signed; and banning any radio or TV appearance by signatories, or any mention of their names or works. Even Jacques Soustelle condemned this 'mean, petty administrative persecution'.

Opinion was hardening on the other side too.

Abandoning French sovereignty in Algeria is an illegitimate act; it outlaws those who commit it and their accomplices, and places those who oppose it, by whatever means, in a state of legitimate self-defence.

Thus Michel Debré, now de Gaulle's Premier, in 1957. Counsel for the right-wing insurgent leaders of January, 1960 (who went on trial in November), used Debré's words to present them as defenders of republican legality.[b] Meanwhile prominent generals like Salan were demanding drastic action against those who incited disaffection, while themselves threatening to disobey a government whose policies they disapproved. Responsible student leaders feared that the *insoumission* of the generals would encourage that of the next batch of conscripts. They tried to divert their followers by a massive peace demonstration of the entire Left; it was boycotted by the Communists and beaten up by the police. Each side, feeding on the other's excesses, prepared to defy the law. The Gaullists of 1940 and 1958 had denied the legitimacy of previous régimes. Now their own faced a double challenge.

THE 'EUROPEANS'

Algeria is a huge country, nine-tenths of it desert. Even in the inhabited north, only a fifth of the area can be cultivated. But on this land of poor soil and resources, with hardly any industry, live over a million Europeans and nearly nine million Moslems.

Five-sixths of the Europeans were born in the country; thus their roots go much deeper than those of their less numerous opposite numbers in Tunisia and Morocco, Kenya and Rhodesia. Many of their forebears were Alsatians escaping from German rule, or democratic refugees, fleeing from repressive government in France; Pierre Lagaillarde, leader of the right-wing insurrections of May 13th, 1958, and January 24th, 1960, claims descent from a famous democratic deputy killed on the barricades. Others are of Spanish, Italian, or Maltese origin—and the more fiercely 'French' in consequence. The indigenous Jews, who to-day number 140,000, were granted French citizenship in 1871.

[b] These were the defendants who set up barricades in central Algiers and fired, unprovoked, on the gendarmes, killing fourteen.

Only one European in twenty now lives on the land. Of these true *colons*, about three hundred are rich, and about a dozen enormously wealthy. Their urban compatriots have overwhelmingly dominated business, the professions, and (until recently) the public service. Indeed the European minority accounts for three-quarters of Algeria's more prosperous groups, which enjoy an average income rather above that of Frenchmen at home. But the prosperous groups comprise less than a third of the European community; and the income of the remaining 70 per cent is only half the figure in France. These poor whites—the postmen and teachers, clerks and tram-drivers—are, of course, the most afraid of Arab competition. The rich can send their capital to France (and lately have been exporting more than the Constantine Plan brings in). The poor have no such easy escape.

In normal times, the rich have dominated European politics. Most of them have been conscienceless reactionaries, clinging to every privilege and fighting every measure to improve the Moslems' lot. Strong supporters of Pétain during the war, they operated before and afterwards mainly through the metropolitan Radical Party. As skilful lobbyists with large funds, great experience, and a powerful influence on the Algiers administration, they were usually able to impose their wishes on the weak and timid ministries which—theoretically—ruled in Paris.

In times of crisis, however, the European poor have often turned to less orthodox leadership. They were revolutionary in 1871, violently anti-semitic in 1898, often Socialist or Communist after 1945. But well before the 1954 revolt began, class conflict had given way to racial alarms, and most of the reactionary insurgents of January, 1960, came from Bab-el-Oued, a working-class suburb and former Communist stronghold.

Far more dangerous than the Left were the right-wing advocates of fascism and dictatorship. Joseph Ortiz led the Bab-el-Oued workers, Pierre Lagaillarde organised the students, Robert Martel appealed to the farmers of the Algiers neighbourhood. In normal times their movements were tiny; but in a crisis they swelled overnight, as the European population were seized by the fear of betrayal. So, in January, 1960, they became suddenly representative of a fear-stricken population, and even moderate politicians hastened to their defence—among them a Gaullist senator who had only recently warned against the blind folly of trying to repeat the 13th of May.

THE MOSLEMS

The nine million Moslems have for thirty years been among the fastest growing populations in the world. Well over half of them are under twenty, and their numbers are doubling every twenty-five years. Most are Arab-speaking, but about a third are descended from the country's original inhabitants, the Berbers, who have been driven back into the hills by successive invaders. The Berbers live mainly in the rugged Kabyle mountains east of Algiers (parts of which are as heavily populated as Belgium), in the capital itself, and in the Aurès mountains to the east. There seems to be little substance in French claims that Arab–Berber antagonism seriously divides the nationalist movement.

There is no segregationist legislation in Algeria, no separate seating on buses or distinct queues in the post-offices; in so far as the Moslems have worse opportunities than the Europeans, the blame lies with educational inadequacies rather than legal obstacles. About a quarter of the Moslems of working age are engaged in pursuits other than agriculture; in work, their average income (excluding the well-off 2 per cent at the top) is around a third of the French metropolitan average. But a quarter of these Moslems suffer complete or partial unemployment, from which the Europeans are virtually immune.

The three-quarters of Moslems who live from agriculture are nearly all desperately poor. While their average income is calculated to be less than a tenth of the French, one ethnologist's classification—into those who eat twice a day, those who eat once, and the hungry—is more to the point. *The wretched soil of Algeria can probably not maintain its present population, certainly not the ten million more who will appear by 1980.* The only solution is emigration to France; and in 1954, when the revolt began, one adult male in seven was working there. (In parts of Kabylia the proportion was one in two, and is even higher today.)

It was among these emigrant workers that, in the 1920s, nationalist politics first developed; not in Algeria itself. There, the rich Moslem landowners were content with a régime which left them free to exploit and oppress their wretched peasantry. The small intellectual élite ardently desired equal status with the French—a pretension rejected with contempt by both the *colons* and the administration—rather than independence. For Algeria had never been a political entity, unlike the neighbouring protectorates of Tunisia and Morocco with their traditional state organisation, their puppet monarchies and, by 1939, their powerful parties, *Néo-Destour* and *Istiqlal*.

The equivalent Algerian movement was much weaker. It was founded in France by a shoemaker, Messali Hadj, and called the North African Star; repeatedly it was banned by the French and revived under new titles. Its tactics changed as often as its name; Messali co-operated in turn with revolutionary Communists and Islamic reactionaries, with Blum's Socialists and Doriot's Fascists. By 1947 his party, now called the MTLD ('Movement for the Triumph of Democratic Liberties') had attracted Moslem support away from the European-dominated Socialists and Communists. Its chief rival was the UDMA ('Democratic Union for the Algerian Manifesto'), which had been founded during the war by Ferhat Abbas. This appealed mainly to the educated élite which, like Abbas himself, had hitherto favoured assimilation to France; the MTLD recruited from the workers and lower middle-class. The UDMA was mild, secularist, and westernising, the MTLD violent, conservative, and pan-Arab. Messali's following seems, by 1947, to have been at least double that of Abbas.

During the post-war years, nationalist activity took various forms. Disorders at Sétif on VE-Day (May 8th, 1945) turned into an armed outbreak which was savagely put down; the hundred murdered Europeans were avenged by several thousand Moslem dead. (European Communists took an active part in the repression; nationalists have never trusted them since then.) A law of 1947 gave the vote to all Moslems; but both MTLD and UDMA found election after election shamelessly rigged against them by the French administration. Finally, however, in 1953, a genuine chance of constructive progress emerged.

The initiative came from the new mayor of Algiers, Jacques Chevallier, a former reactionary converted to liberalism. He invited the MTLD municipal councillors to join his administration and co-operate in his spectacular re-housing programme. The party's Central Committee accepted his offer; Messali, who was interned in France, was furious at this capitulation to reformism. A bitter quarrel broke out, with fighting for the party's physical and financial assets, rival congresses and mutual expulsions. In the midst of this struggle another group made its appearance.

The new body originally called itself the CRUA, 'Revolutionary Committee for Unity and Action'. Most of its leaders had formerly belonged to the 'Secret Organisation' (OS) of the MTLD, a direct-action body which the French broke up in 1950. They were younger and poorer than the established politicians; most of them were peasants by origin, extremists by temperament, and professional revolutionaries by occupation. The soil had been prepared for them by the repression of the Sétif outbreak and the rigging of elections; organising work had been started by the OS; and their opportunity came with the MTLD split. For now they could offer to the party activists, disgusted with fratricidal strife, a way to end nationalist dissensions overnight: an armed rising against French rule which would render all the old divisions obsolete and force every Moslem to choose his side. Moderate nationalist intellectuals, corrupt stooges of the administration, middle-class assimilationists, reformist city councillors, even the old patriarch Messali dictating terms from his Vendean exile—all would be swept aside once the stark alternative was posed: for the freedom fighters or against them? *Thus the revolution was directed against the Moslem politicians no less than against the French.* Its first handbill, issued on the first day of the rebellion, proclaimed:

Our National Movement, prostrated by years of immobility and routine, badly directed, was disintegrating little by little. Faced with this situation, a youthful group, gathering about it the majority of the wholesome and resolute elements, judged that the moment had come to take the National Movement out of the impasse into which it had been forced by the conflicts of persons and of influence and to launch it into the true revolutionary struggle...

REBELS, NATIONALISTS, TERRORISTS

The rebels, who soon took the name of National Liberation Front (FLN) were determined to monopolise the representation of Moslem opinion. Their method was to eliminate or intimidate those who contested their claim. Rival nationalists were even more obnoxious than Francophiles, for one day France might try to negotiate with them as she had in Tunisia. But, as a leader in exile wrote to a commander in the *maquis* in 1955:

France as well as the trashy politicians will be sadly disappointed. The vigilance of the combatants will, in Algiera, nip Bourguibaism in the bud...

Several nationalist (especially UDMA) leaders were sentenced to be assassinated during the outbreaks of August 20th, 1955; though most escaped, Ferhart Abbas' nephew was killed. Abbas himself was one of the designated victims. But he soon made his peace with the FLN, and joined them in Cairo in April, 1956. In 1958 he became head of the 'provisional government', a position of more prominence than power. Many other moderate politicians have similarly 'taken out insurance' by vigorous criticisms of the French, or even by going over to the FLN; most have been treated with contempt. In September, 1955, the FLN publicly warned those who

now think they can climb aboard with us...But the people will not forget that these men, instead of helping them, helped themselves...their eleventh-hour speeches cannot ward off the punishment that awaits them.

The FLN is thus determined to monopolise Algerian nationalism. Naturally it is strongly opposed by the original nationalists of Messali's party, now called the MNA ('Algerian National Movement'). In Algeria these have almost been wiped out except for a few pockets; their armed bands were attacked by both sides, their civilian sympathisers deterred by terrorism (the worst example was the massacre of the three hundred male inhabitants of Mechta Kasbah, near Melouza, in April, 1957) or discredited by being driven to accept French protection. But the MNA survives among its original adherents, the Algerian workers in France. Here the two movements wage a savage war: *over five years, an average of two Moslems a day have been killed in France, and four more wounded, by their co-religionists.* (Thus one emigrant in forty has been a victim.) The MNA trade union has had six leaders murdered. Workers are attacked for holding the wrong views, or for not paying the stiff levy demanded by FLN (about ten shillings a week; merchants, of course, pay much more). The FLN is said to raise £500,000 a month in this way within France; in Algeria its 'taxes' bring in a similar amount. There, most of the Moslem rich, and many Europeans, protect themselves by heavy contributions.

In Algeria itself, terrorism against Europeans has usually been indiscriminate—attacks on isolated victims, or bombs timed to explode at peak hours in cafés and dance-halls, at football grounds and bus-stops. Moslems sometimes suffer from similarly indiscriminate violence, such as the inexplicable attack on a school bus at El Marsa (25th November, 1959), in which four Moslem children were killed. But more commonly the Moslem targets are such designated victims as local councillors, candidates at elections, 'tax' defaulters, smokers (the FLN banned tobacco), or participants in the French land reform scheme. About six Moslems a day (till recently, eight) are still being assassinated by terrorists in Algeria.

Terrorism cannot simply be explained away as the brutal but understandable elimination of 'quislings'. For instance, Senator Chérif Benhabyles, who (with an unlucky passer-by) was shot dead in Vichy on August 27th, 1959, had denounced the excesses of French repression, condemned integration, avowed his continued friendship with Ferhat Abbas—and refused French police protection. He had recently made several trips to Switzerland, undoubtedly to meet FLN representatives. His murder was plainly meant by the extremists as a warning to any moderate, on either side, who was thinking of the compromise peace for which Moslem opinion unquestionably longed.

It would be absurd to accept the official French contention that the FLN are a mere handful of criminals without popular support; if they were, they would have been destroyed long ago. But it seems hard to maintain that a movement which uses terror for so long, on such a scale, represents the true wishes of all its people—those of El Marsa, for instance. One should not make too much of the 180,000 Moslems under arms on the French side, some six times more than the FLN forces ever had. For the latter could probably multiply their numbers if they had more arms, while the former include village self-defence groups which often reach a live-and-let-live agreement with the local FLN band, and auxiliaries (*harkis*) who willingly accept a well-paid occupation in a land where unemployment is rife. Yet it is worth noting that desertions, frequent among Moslem troops in 1956–7, are negligible to-day; and this although the *harkis* include many *ralliés*—ex-FLN soldiers who have come over, voluntarily or after capture. (According to *Officiers en Algérie*, a 'stop-the-war' pamphlet by three returned officers, prisoners who join the French forces number between 10 and 15 per cent of all the FLN casualties, and the proportion is rising.) Many French officers go out on patrol night after night with a section entirely made up of former FLN fellagas.

The FLN thus meets hostility from its bitter enemies who have everything to lose from its victory: all the *ralliés*; some of the *harkis*; a few rich friends of France; the families of the victims of terrorism; the villagers who have supported the French because their neighbours and traditional enemies were pro-FLN; the surviving followers of the MNA. Yet the groups committed to France are no doubt a much smaller minority than that actively supporting the FLN. The majority, as in most civil wars, passively endures the exactions of both sides and longs for the return of peace.

As FLN terror has won some Moslems to the French side, so French repression, often blind and undiscriminating, has been the rebels' strongest weapon. Villagers from the hills, numbering a million and a half, have been 'regrouped' in new areas where they could be better protected and controlled —but only a third of these re-groupments were economically viable; most suffered hardship, sometimes even starvation. In the towns, any Moslem with a primary education is likely to have been in an internment camp. These naturally function (as in Ireland in 1917) as nationalist universities; in one of the best managed, where the authorities hoped most of the inmates would cast votes at the 1958 referendum, the turn-out was 2 per cent. The system is neither as efficient nor as ruthless as is often supposed—the murderer of Senator Benhabyles has just been freed after a short prison sentence (in France) for illegally carrying arms. But conditions vary widely. A Red Cross inspection commission reported in December, 1959 that, while conditions in over half the camps in central Algeria (*Algérois*) were bad, in two-thirds of those in the west (*Oranie*) and east (*Constantinois*) they were good or very good.

The French have some ground for complaining of their bad press. Charges of torture, like the cases of Djamila Bouhired in 1957 and Djamila Boupacha in 1960, invariably and properly receive wide publicity, both in the Paris opposition press and abroad. Understandably, the critics demand a higher standard from the French than from the FLN. But the picture they present is often incomplete. Thus a respectable American professor, in an academic work, can denounce French infringements of civil liberties without once mentioning FLN terrorism (Edgar Furniss in *France—Troubled Ally*). The

New Statesman's account of the Red Cross report gave a quarter of its space to describing the worst camp of all, without bothering to say that the Commission, on its second visit a month later, had found the place transformed. No one pointed the contrast between the French, who invited Red Cross inspections (though not publicity for the results), and the FLN which, up to June, 1960, refused every Red Cross request for access to prisoners or even for a list of their names.[c]

There is, however, no doubt that torture is still all too common. Some commanders have made genuine, sometimes even effective efforts to stamp it out—though punishments, in accordance with French tradition in cases of abuses committed in the public service, are never publicised. But, only too often, the authorities have preferred to cover up outrages by denouncing those who reveal them, or pointing to the FLN terrorism which may explain, but does not excuse, French brutality and sadism.

THE MEN BETWEEN

The ordinary Moslem is caught between the violence, arbitrary or deliberate, of both sides. His dominating wish is for an end to the nightmare. Yet the profound changes made by the war have not all been evil. Psychologically, since Algerian Moslems are affirming their nationality in arms, to accept western values no longer seems a symbolic capitulation; where French modernisers could not induce Moslem women to renounce the veil, or men to abandon their right to divorce their wives at will, sociologists now report that these changes have spread rapidly under FLN sponsorship. Materially, French attempts to win Moslem allegiance have brought substantial improvements. Land reform has been begun, industrialisation encouraged, civil service jobs opened to Moslems, local government brought under their control, education greatly extended.

These belated measures seem unlikely to fulfil their political aim. Too many of the beneficiaries regard them as by-products of the revolt, and give their gratitude to the FLN. Moreover, the repression, striking blindly, causes the whole Moslem community to feel endangered, and reinforces its solidarity —from which the FLN profits. Even Moslems who detest FLN methods cannot help feeling pride in men of their race who have defied the French army for six years. While the war continues, few Moslems can repudiate their own folk under arms.

But afterwards? Psychologically, everything would be changed once the terror and repression ended—though the Moslems' thirst for human dignity could no doubt be slaked only by the grant of independence. Materially, those who give the FLN credit for provoking the French into constructive reforms

[c] See note on p. 184

may well doubt its capacity for carrying them out itself. Many who know the Moslems well, therefore, believe that, with peace, the elusive third force might at last come to life. For the mass of *attentistes* are not without views on their country's future; they are *cross-pressured*, like those voters in western democracies who are slowest and most hesitant in making up their minds. In Algeria, where the conflicting pressures are so much more terrible, the uncertainties are magnified. Numbers of Moslem families are divided against themselves. Mme Germaine Tillion, who knows the Moslems as well as any westerner, believes that while 90 per cent of them favour the FLN, 60 per cent want friendship with France. The left-wing authors of *Officiers en Algérie* record similar impressions.

To Moslems who want *both* independence and links with Paris, *both* the FLN and the French, de Gaulle has long been the one man capable of making peace, and the only leader who could fulfil their aspirations. 'Their confidence in de Gaulle is total, startling,' wrote one of the *Officiers*, referring to 1958. An 'Algiers letter' in Mendès-France's monthly *Cahiers de la République* (June, 1959) spoke of their 'immense hope [in de Gaulle] which you can scarcely conceive'. During the January 1960 insurrection anti-Gaullist European territorials at Mostaganem, in Oranie, clashed with Moslem demonstrators shouting '*Down With Massu!*', '*We want work!*', and '*Vive de Gaulle!*'. Later, in the anti-Gaullist *L'Express* (February 11th, 1960), Claude Krief reported that 'At Algiers. . .(de Gaulle) could be acclaimed by virtually the whole Moslem population', and Mendès-France agreed that his 'measures have brought, as all witnesses confirm, a profound response among the Moslems'. And on June 1st, *Le Monde's* correspondent recorded that 'the anti-Gaullism of the FLN has practically no hold on the Moslems, even the nationalists'.

THE FRENCH ARMY

Besides the Europeans and the Moslems there is a third political entity in Algeria: the French army. It cumulates the powers of all armies in countries at war, with the immense *civil* administrative authority conferred by successive governments, from 1956 to 1960, on the only force capable of running this chronically under-administered territory. This transfer of power was at first warmly approved by Mendès-France and his friends, who rightly much preferred the army to the settler-ridden administration and police. Even Moslems welcomed it as a lesser evil.

The consequences have been mixed: neither black nor white, or rather both black and white, for in Algeria the contrasts between neighbouring zones or sectors are often startling. The army is not a monolithic unit, and its conduct depends on the standards and outlook of individual generals—

and second-lieutenants. Moreover, there are many divisions within its ranks. The 'activist' officers have always been concentrated in the Algiers command; Oran and Constantine have never been in their hands—just as civilian extremism has always been far stronger in the capital than in the two regional centres. There are distinct differences of outlook between professionals and conscripts; between the parachutists (who get all the glory and publicity) and other regulars; between different paratroop divisions; between the politically minded staff officers in the Algiers hot-house and their fellows out in the *bled*; between the powerful, strongly integrationist psychological warfare enthusiasts, and the 'SAS' officers directly administering Moslem villages and towns.[d]

Yet on two points the great majority of officers are agreed. First, the unity of the army must be maintained; the political split of the second world war must never be repeated. Secondly, they will not put up with another defeat imposed by the politicians. They have no desire whatever to take over political power, and loathe the thought of making and unmaking governments like a 'Mexican army'. But they will not tolerate a capitulation in Algeria. Some may fear the loss of comforts and privileges. Others are alarmed at the likely effects in France itself of the return of an angry army and a million furious settlers. None will concede defeat in a war which they believe they are winning, or again abandon to nationalist vengeance, as they did in Indo-China, natives who had trusted in French promises to remain.

The army's political role has been more that of a lobby, trying to influence the government, than that of a conspiracy to replace it. Few officers are prepared to plot—though their numbers might swell rapidly if a capitulation seemed imminent. Their attitude is more like that of Gough's cavalry officers who, in 1914, resigned their commissions rather than coerce Ulster—and so in effect vetoed certain possible lines of policy. But this analogy conceals a crucial fact: *the French army in Algeria is pro-Moslem and anti-colon.* For, to compete with the well-entrenched FLN clandestine organisation, the army has been forced to behave almost as a political party, paternalist in outlook yet progressive and even revolutionary in aim.

The insurrection of January, 1960, with which the troops then in Algiers plainly sympathised, should not mislead us. These were Massu's paratroops, partly recruited from the city and based there for three tense years; in contrast, the troops who replaced them (another parachutist division) were furious at having to abandon their operations in the *bled* to deal with Lagaillarde. Yet even Massu's entourage was described by a left-wing journalist (Jean Daniel in *L'Express*, February 11th, 1960) as advocating 'rural

[d] SAS: *Sections administratives spécialisées.*

socialism'. The soldiers hoped to counter the 'myth' of independence by the rival myth of modernisation, equality, integration—a 'Kemal revolution' sponsored by France. Thus, though ashamed of French neglect of Algeria in the past, the army—despite all its bitter critics—is proud of what it is doing there to-day, enthusiastic in its efforts to improve the living conditions of remote peasant villages which have never before seen a doctor or a schoolmaster.

'For the very first time in my military career I have an entirely clear conscience', I was told by a general distinguished for his liberalism and humanity. The junior officers in the SAS often voluntarily prolong their military service to continue with their task of social reconstruction. These constructive activities cannot compete for publicity with charges of torture. But in fact, once more, the black and the white exist side by side.

SELF-DETERMINATION?

Yet the policy of self-determination by referendum—accepted officially by both de Gaulle and the FLN—arouses no enthusiasm in the army, despite military sympathy for the Moslems. For it is a procedure, not an objective; and, as one officer put it, 'you can't commit yourself to a question-mark'. The army knows that France cannot remain in Algeria without Moslem support and co-operation; the Moslems know what happened to France's friends in Morocco and Tunisia after independence. How can any self-respecting officer, out in the *bled*, encourage a village leader whom he likes and trusts to risk his own life and his family's by becoming mayor of his hamlet—unless the Frenchman can honestly promise that no scuttle in twelve or eighteen months' time will deliver his friends into the power of the FLN?

The practical problems of self-determination, too, are enormous. Can there be a fair vote in a primitive country torn by the passions and hatred of six years of bitter civil warfare? A spokesman from Ortiz's balcony, in January, put the point brutally:[e]

If no one takes the Moslems to the polls, they will stay at home. If the army takes them, they will vote for France; if the FLN takes them, they will vote for independence. So what's all this nonsense about self-determination?

No doubt the two sides might agree to regroup their forces and keep them out of the referendum campaign. Even so, the verdict would reflect the sum of local positions of strength rather than any genuine popular wish. Moreover, de Gaulle has demanded a long delay between the cease-fire and the

[e] Joseph Ortiz was, with Pierre Lagaillarde, one of the rival leaders of the January 1960 'barricades revolt' in Algiers.

vote. But if the military contest were merely transformed into a political one, would passions really cool off as the crucial vote approached? Would the rival armed forces really withstand the temptation to intervene surreptitiously where things were going badly for their side?

This is not all. Even if no one interfered improperly with the campaign or the poll, the vote would be profoundly influenced by the result the Moslems *expected*; once convinced the FLN was going to win, every *attentiste* would hasten to make his peace with them. Experience in the North African protectorates has shown that a compromise line cannot be held more than a few weeks (in Morocco) or months (in Tunisia) because of the rush to get on the victor's band-wagon. Thus the first sign of French recognition of the FLN—however informal or unofficial—would consolidate their hold on Moslem opinion, and give them the representativeness which they have always claimed, but might not find it easy to retain once peace was signed. *Once recognised as representative, however, they will become so.*

This is why the FLN long refused to discuss peace terms until France had agreed to concede both Algerian independence *and* their own status as a provisional government. They abandoned these explicit claims after de Gaulle's offer of self-determination on September 16th, 1959. But they still hoped to reach the same ends by an indirect approach. For their insistence that military talks on a cease-fire must be accompanied by political negotiations on the guarantees of a fair vote (fully justified by the history of French-managed elections in the past) was accompanied by a rejection of round-table discussion with other tendencies of Algerian opinion. These, whether European or Moslem, must express their views to and through the French government—which would thus have to accept a *tête-à-tête* with the FLN. And to ensure that the lesson sinks into Moslem minds, the FLN wanted an early meeting between General de Gaulle and Ferhat Abbas.

Thus a truly free vote, without physical or psychological coercion, will be very difficult, if not impossible, to obtain. Much left-wing opinion, and perhaps some Gaullist opinion too, holds that the one way out is through *a referendum of which the result is predetermined by negotiation between the contestants*, both sides campaigning for an affirmative answer to a solution previously agreed between them. The FLN would accept no such solution unless their claim to independence was conceded. But, today, a state can be independent and yet remain within the French Community.[f]

There are two strong arguments for 'pre-determination'. The first is the impracticability of a truly free vote. The second is that, even if this were practicable, it would leave the Europeans and the pro-French Moslems

[f] The Community ceased to exist later in 1961.

wholly without protection. The Algerian economy is utterly dependent on the Europeans, who employ more than 90 per cent of those working in industry and commerce, account for 92 per cent of gross business earnings, and provide 92 per cent of the country's private investment; a vote for independence without safeguards would inevitably provoke a panic exodus, disrupting the economic life of Algeria—and the political life of France. Only by negotiations with those who have the prestige to accept unpopular concessions, and the authority to carry their followers' consent, can any sort of guarantees be obtained. But the word 'guarantees' arouses only scepticism. Stages and safeguards, time-limits and precautions have been utterly discredited by developments in Morocco and Tunisia. *The exodus will not be prevented by paper promises which no European will trust; it can be averted only if the French army remains in Algeria for a decade after the cease-fire.*

ALTERNATIVES

Even last summer a settlement on these lines still seemed possible. France badly needed one, both to regain influence in Europe and to retain her ties with the new African states of the Community. And the FLN needs one too.

For the French held some strong cards. The military situation has been moving steadily in their favour. Though the FLN keeps strong forces in Tunisia and Morocco, fewer arms have been getting through to its troops within Algeria; they are broken up into much smaller bands than a year ago; their morale seems to be lower (the proportion of prisoners is rising); and they are finding more difficulty in recruitment. Whereas in 1958 the *maquis* leaders were thought to be much more intransigent than the exiles in Tunis, by 1960 the roles were reversed.

Next, the French could impose what the FLN most dread: *partition*. No one can stop them from setting up a 'new Israel' along the coast from Oran to Algiers, and denying to the nationalists the principal cities and most fertile lands in Algeria. Both sides agree that this would be disastrous to the country's welfare—but if the war drags on a few more years, it might then seem less ruinous than an endless struggle. The choice before the FLN—and the French—might well lie between a negotiated settlement in 1961, and a *de facto* partition in 1963 or 1965.

Thirdly, Moslem opinion in Algeria is passionately anxious for the nightmare to end. Extreme intransigence by the FLN might in the end have forfeited Moslem goodwill. Tunis was beginning to fear this last February, when de Gaulle's firmness against the European insurgents had sent his prestige soaring among the Moslems.

Fourthly, the alternative for the FLN is dangerous. China is prodigal with offers of aid; but the benefits are dubious, the reluctance of the Tunisians evident, the risks of acceptance manifest. Their cautious acceptance of de Gaulle's overtures in June, and their refusal finally to break off talks after the first unsatisfactory meetings, suggested awareness that they stood at a cross-roads, and reluctance to follow the highway to the east.

Moreover, in the last resort a link between France and Algeria is even more important to the Moslems than to the French. Not only do Frenchmen provide capital and technical skills, but France offers an indispensable outlet for Algeria's leaping population. As French citizens, the Algerian Moslems have free access to the French labour market—unlike the Tunisians and Moroccans, only one of whom works in France for every ten Algerians. These immigrants send much of their earnings home, and keep alive at least a million-and-a-half (some estimates say three or even four million) of their fellow-countrymen. If Algeria were wholly severed from France, most nationals of each country would soon return home, voluntarily or under compulsion. Economically, the exchange (and the loss of Saharan oil) would bring minor inconvenience in France. Algeria would suffer immediate catastrophe.

An agreed settlement clearly meant hard bargaining, with the FLN manœuvring to obtain implicit recognition and the French to deny it, the French trying and the FLN refusing to give the negotiations the outward appearance of a capitulation. It would have faced hostility from the Europeans and the army, both determined to resist concessions beyond a certain point. But experience did not seem to bear out the gloomy views expressed by the *New Statesman* when the Fourth Republic fell:

De Gaulle is a 'Wooden Titan'…The *colon* extremists…do not expect much resistance from this ageing prima donna who owes his Indian Summer of power entirely to their efforts. De Gaulle's slogans may be vague…but…it is Soustelle and Massu who will do the interpreting.

And again,

There is no doubt that the new régime will be dominated by the French in Algeria …General de Gaulle can play the role of a Neguib, but if he tries to carry out his personal policy he will soon be replaced by a Nasser.

THE GENERAL

For two-and-a-half years, General de Gaulle had survived these dangers by skilfully blurring the issues and bewildering his opponents. His seemingly incomprehensible zigzagging policy had gratified and discouraged each side in turn. In January he delighted the Moslems by refusing to compromise with Lagaillarde; in March he bitterly disappointed them by his reassurances to the army; in June he swung back so far that the FLN, for the first time, agreed to send an emissary to Paris—only to confront the emissary with conditions so rigid that no one can have imagined they would be accepted. Where, if anywhere, was he going?

The answer, I think, is to be found in his past career. De Gaulle has twenty years' experience as a politician, and his strategic method has not varied. Against Churchill, against Giraud, against the Communists in 1944 and the Committees of Public Safety in 1958, he has played for time, confused the issue, conciliated everyone a little and no one completely, and created a fog around his real intentions in which he could forge steadily ahead towards his objective. When he came to power, he would neither repudiate integration nor commit himself to it. But by 1960 integration was dead. The army had swallowed, without reacting, first the dissolution of the Committees of Public Safety; then self-determination; finally, instead of *Algérie française*, 'an Algerian Algeria linked with France'. And even while the war goes on, this Algerian Algeria is coming into being. Power is passing quite rapidly into the Moslems' hands. Nearly 200,000 of them have been armed by France; a predominant share in new administrative appointments is reserved to them; local government is under their control; their integrationist representatives have nearly all swung over to supporting *Algérie algérienne*. De Gaulle has given an irrevocable answer to one crucial question: in a few years' time Algeria will be a land ruled by Moslems, not by Frenchmen. A second crucial question remains open: will its rulers be friendly or hostile towards France?

De Gaulle hoped that his concessions on the first question would ensure a favourable answer to the second. 'France', he had said in 1957, 'dislikes half-measures which turn against her. She likes great concessions which bring everything back to her...The more the Algerians are free the more they will be united to the French.' For this happy ending he needed time—to win back the army, to master the Europeans, above all to convince the ordinary Moslem voter (through economic and educational reforms) of the advantages of the French connection. As they found these advantages working in their daily lives, he could begin to build up a Moslem-controlled Algeria—keeping a place open for the FLN, but denying them exclusive control.

The FLN might well refuse to come in. For, on both sides, war is now routine, and peace a leap into the unknown. Negotiations would threaten French unity; but they would also terribly strain the cohesion of the FLN, as they broke Sinn Fein in 1921. If the FLN did refuse, the new Algeria would be built without them—subjecting them to growing pressure to join. If they agreed, this would mark the defeat of the extreme wing by Abbas and the moderates, who could then co-operate with the 'third force' nationalists in facing the desperate problems of reconstruction.

Early in 1960 it seemed de Gaulle might be granted the time he needed.

In France his popularity was unimpaired. Among the Algerian Moslems it soared after the January 1960 insurrection—which alarmed the army by showing how isolated it was from both Moslems and Frenchmen at home. Abroad, both the great powers were courting the General, and thus wary of the FLN. So at Melun, in June, France confronted the FLN emissaries with rigid terms. Most observers thought this a prelude to tough bargaining; none, however pessimistic, expected the FLN to break off the talks.

Yet a turning-point came, if not at Melun, at de Gaulle's press conference of September 5th, when the world waited in vain for the balancing move towards peace. For all the President had to offer was this: 'People sometimes say: de Gaulle is the man to settle the Algerian problem—if he cannot, no one can. Then will they kindly let me get on with it?' The answer was No.

The General's assets began to fall away alarmingly. Khrushchev, for reasons of his own (Berlin? China? U.N.?), gave *de facto* recognition to the 'Provisional Government of the Algerian Republic'. His press began printing violent criticisms of France; FLN visitors in Moscow (whose presence in the past had been concealed) were given a state welcome. Ferhat Abbas returned from Peking to answer de Gaulle's invitation to 'peace if they lay down the knife' with a defiant 'we will lay down our knives when we have planes instead'. The United States had at last to choose whether to back France against the Afro-Asian bloc, or to help the FLN so as to keep them from the Communist embrace. Back in 1957, one American senator had outspokenly condemned the former course. His name was John F. Kennedy.

De Gaulle's collapse was equally sudden in North Africa. Hopes had been raised and then dashed once too often. 'Moslem Gaullism is stone dead', wrote a journalist who had formerly insisted on its importance. The Moslem politicians reflected the widespread disillusionment. Most of them, elected under army auspices as integrationists, had rallied to de Gaulle when he defied Lagaillarde's insurgents; now they were demanding political talks with the FLN. Even President Bourguiba of Tunisia, who had so often preached moderation to the FLN leaders, publicly doubted whether de Gaulle could solve the problem, or whether he himself could any longer prevent Communist arms from flowing through his country.

In France, too, the position was deteriorating fast. The active minorities on both sides were growing, as we have seen, in numbers and extremism. But the masses, too, were affected; Grenoble became the first provincial city to receive the President of the Republic frigidly. His increasingly personal conception of his power drew heavy fire from both Right and Left in Parliament and the press. Centre politicians dared to attack him in public, and even the devoted Guy Mollet went into formal opposition. As General Salan emerged as the spokesman of *Algérie française*, tension built up again in army circles.

De Gaulle knows he must quickly regain the initiative. On November 4th he promised the nationalists their Algerian Republic. For the Right, Bidault denounced his policy: 'execrable, worse than ever.' But the Left did not abate its distrust of *pouvoir personnel*. Confidently monarchical, the President continued to evoke the popular faith in himself which he had so far rekindled after each disappointment.

The State will not permit the claim of those who enjoy some personal standing—political, trade union, military, journalistic, or other personalities—to influence the guidance of France. The guidance of France belongs to those upon whom she has conferred that duty. Therefore it belongs above all to me.

NOTE (see text, pp. 174–5)

'The French have some ground for complaining of their bad press...There is, however, no doubt that torture is still all too common.' These two sentences, in this form, were quoted in an attack on contributors to *Encounter* (where Chapter 8 was originally published) which appeared in 1967. The reader who checks pp. 174–5 will see the grounds for the French complaint set out in the omitted passage—including the *New Statesman*'s treatment of a Red Cross report. (Red Cross reports were sent privately to the French government, so that improvements resulting from them were not just adjustments to bad publicity. The report mentioned above leaked subsequently to *Le Monde*.)

The author of this revealing example of selective quotation was Mr Alexander Cockburn of *New Left Review*; it appeared in the *New Statesman*, 19 May 1967.

9 Algerian conversations[a]

Early in April I spent a week in Algeria, talking to civilians and army officers, Frenchmen and Moslems and foreigners, policy-makers and professional men and unemployed workers. I detected no military conspiracies. But I did discover something of the mentality behind them.

The frustration of the army is understandable. After twenty years of defeat, they have at last won a war—yet it is ending in the loss of everything they have fought for. No wonder they are bitter against civilian opinion which 'hasn't understood', against allies who have let them down, against political leaders who— they think—have squandered all the fruits of their efforts and sacrifices. Not that they proclaimed these feelings at once, spontaneously, as they sometimes did even eighteen months ago. Their first reflex was one of resigned, reluctant obedience. But it didn't take much probing to discover the bitterness seething beneath the surface.

Two weeks ago I was talking to a captain of the French army in a small town about forty miles from Algiers. He had been showing me round the *regroupement*—the new village built to house the peasants who had chosen voluntarily (as he stressed) to move down from the exposed hills to live in the plain under the protection of the French army. Of the various *regroupements* I saw in Algeria, this was easily the best organised. The officer had been there from the start, four years ago. For an hour and a half he had been talking schools, roads, doctors and crops. His devotion to his job and to his villagers was evident.

It was nearly time to leave. I asked my last question. 'And what about the political outlook, captain?' There was an embarrassed pause. 'Well, first of all the Moslems want peace, that's for sure.' Another pause. 'We try not to think about it. That way we hope to exorcise the bad dream.' He turned, walked away, came back. 'They don't talk. They don't say a word. It would take a really clever man to know what they are thinking.' 'They are waiting to see who wins?' I suggested. 'Of course,' he replied. 'And if one terrorist— just one—can promenade through this village with his sten-gun, the lot of them will decide that the FLN have won, and they'll go over as one man. Do they realise that in Paris?'

I asked whether he thought things could have been different. Again he

[a] From *The Guardian*, 29 April and 2 May 1961. The military putsch in Algiers had lasted from 22 to 26 April.

hesitated. 'I'm like the centurion, you know—come and he cometh, go and he goeth. Politics are no concern of mine.' Pause. 'But if you want my personal opinion, yes certainly it could have been different.' He turned his back, scuffed at a stone, walked round and came back to us. And suddenly it all poured out. 'What's going to happen to my harkis (Moslem soldiers) if we scuttle? What's going to happen to these villagers who chose to seek the protection of the French army? I promised them we would never desert them. I told them what my chiefs told me. Now if they get their throats cut, it's me—me—me who will be responsible.

'Can I trust my own men, now? There's been no sign of trouble so far. But suppose they decide they'd better make their peace with the FLN? They never talk about what might happen—but don't imagine they don't think about it. And so do we.

'Well, if that's the way it's going to be, if the FLN are going to come in they needn't expect any more Constantine Plan money. We can use it in France, you know—the peasants in the Ardèche are no better off than the ones here, and it's about time we paid our teachers decently. And then you'll see. First you'll have chaos in Algeria. Then Communism. Doesn't Kennedy see it? By deserting the Belgians and the Portuguese he's handing Africa over to the Communists. And after Algeria, France will go Communist next. And then how long do you think England will resist?'

The day before, I talked to another young officer, this time in a combat unit—commanding harkis engaged in guerrilla fighting in the Kabyle mountains. 'Peace talks?' he snorted. 'Won't make any difference to my chaps. They will go on with the war on their own as long as they can, and then they will try and get out, to France. Self-determination is all very well, but in my sector we've 130 harkis and only twenty "fells"—what about self-determination for them? No, I've no dealings with the civil authorities—that all goes on over my head. But I'll tell you this—we never see any of them out in the bled. And my men can't understand why we, who live among the people and understand what's going on, have to take orders from these chaps sitting behind their desks in the towns. We're not political. We took no part at the referendum. That's not the army's job. But I myself saw the Moslem mayor of the village stuffing the ballot-boxes. As for the riots last December—my harkis saw what happened on television. They couldn't understand how French troops could just stand by while demonstrators marched around with the FLN flag.[b] What do I think? Well, my

[b] When de Gaulle visited Algeria in December 1960, his European opponents demonstrated against him in the cities (which he avoided). Moslem counter-demonstrations, originally organised by the Gaullist authorities, soon turned into massive expressions of support for the FLN, which greatly impressed opinion in France.

class at St Cyr has already lost twenty officers in this war. That's not something we can forget easily.'

The European civilians, unlike the officers, were more worried by the political nightmare than by the personal engagement. 'We could get on fine with Ferhat Abbas', said a doctor—'but he wouldn't last six months in an independent Algeria. The Communists really control the FLN, and the Moslems are getting scared of them. I have heaps of Moslem friends— because I treat them like human beings—you've seen for yourself that I'll have no segregation in my hospital. I'm a local councillor—elected by a 100% Moslem ward—and I've never concealed my belief in *Algérie française*. And I tell you, my Moslem friends who were for independence six months ago are getting cold feet now they see Ahmed Francis dashing off to get his orders from Moscow.'[c]

The doctor was a kindly, rational, travelled man. He had little in common with the extremists who explode plastic bombs—yet he defended them. 'What do you expect? There's no liberty. The press is censored, the authorities talk only to those who tell them what they want to hear, people are shipped off to internment camps without trial.' 'Hasn't that been happening to the Moslems for years?' I asked. 'Yes,' said the doctor. 'But it was wrong then and it's wrong now. Stop people saying what they think, and they will find other ways to show you.'

There are other reasons for the bomb campaign, of course. Some Europeans, regarding independence as inevitable, thought the only way to make the FLN take their interests into account was to use the FLN's own methods —if bombs made de Gaulle listen to Ferhat Abbas, bombs would make Ferhat Abbas listen to them. Others went further. They were willing to blow up Algiers rather than let the FLN take it over—and the bombs were to show they could do it. One tract I saw in Oran, put out by the fascists of *Jeune Nation*, called for all-out war against the FLN, invasion of Tunisia and Morocco—*and* for reducing military service from 27 months to 18! Another quoted Pétain's alleged remark on entering his prison cell, 'They will have to raise this ceiling. The next occupant is much taller than I am.'

A liberal-minded priest[d] told me, 'The Europeans are in an ugly mood. News of negotiations with the FLN was received by the Moslems with unrestrained joy—by the Europeans with resignation. They thought it was all over. Then came the bomb campaign, and hope revived among them—but

---

[c] The doctor rightly thought that Colonel Boumédienne would emerge as the real power in an independent Algeria—but quite mistakenly thought him a communist. Ferhat Abbas resigned as President of the Constituent Assembly (an honorific rather than a powerful position) and was expelled from the party in August 1963—thirteen months after independence.

[d] He has stayed in independent Algeria and won local office by a huge majority in a contested election.

a nasty kind of hope. Yes, they are delighted (the poor more doubtfully than the rich, for they are utterly fed up with the war). I was dining with some wealthy friends when we heard a bomb explode—and the whole family cheered. When they saw I didn't approve, they said "But it's for keeping Algeria French, and we know there will be no victims". If only that were true.'

'And yet', he went on, 'they are fine people. You think I'm bound to defend them because they are my flock—not a bit of it, I have furious rows with them every day of my life. Still, most of the time they are fine people, brave and generous—but in a panic they are capable of the most horrible cruelty. Yet before the war they got on well with the Moslems. Now they are afraid. But they could still be won back—if it weren't for the local press, which plays on all their worst instincts.' He was silent for a moment. 'I don't wish harm to any man', he said—'but when I think of Alain de Sérigny' (former editor of the chief Algiers paper) 'I have my doubts. That man bears a frightful responsibility.'

Yet the Europeans had some excuse for bitterness. It was not only the press that misled them. For five years after the outbreak of the war, official propaganda went on asserting that Algeria was as French as Brittany and that the Moslems, other than a handful of terrorists, were devoted to keeping it that way. Even in late 1959 this line was still being put about by official spokesmen, especially military ones. By 1961, however, this note was no longer being sounded. The myth had perished in the riots of December and the vote of January.[e] I found some soldiers (even a colonel) who accepted the fact and regarded independence as inevitable. And the civilian officials—a remarkably able group—had drawn all the conclusions. They had no time for the tame Moslem 'beni-oui-oui' (their Moslem contacts were all nationalists), and they tended to be impatient with the soldiers for their narrow views. Said one of them cheerfully, 'You know what the military are like. They'd clear up the war in short order if one or two trivial preliminaries could be arranged for them—like eliminating Tunisia, and Morocco, and the UN, and international opinion. And on those terms, no doubt they could.'

The same man arranged for me to meet the brother of an FLN leader. Elsewhere, another told me 'This is an old nationalist area—only thirty per cent voted at the referendum, one of the lowest figures in the country. The Moslems have been nationalist ever since we gave French citizenship to the native Jews, back in 1870. But don't imagine they want the FLN in power. They are traditionalists, and bourgeois, and they have been *attentistes* for

---

e The referendum on self-determination in January 1961, when the Europeans voted No, the rural Moslems Yes and the urban Moslems stayed at home.

a long time—and there is no minister from this region in the GPRA.[f] Because of their past they think they should have a leading part in running independent Algeria—and they are not at all sure the FLN will give it them. The FLN do try to adjust to the local climate—for instance, hereabouts they are against foreign innovations, such as women abandoning the veil. But their links with Moscow have really frightened the old nationalist leaders in this town.'

In another area, I asked a thoroughly liberal young official about the RDA (a group of Moslem deputies and senators who have recently come out for the FLN). 'Rightly or wrongly', he replied, 'everyone—even FLN supporters—thinks they are simply saving their skins. Everyone. The movement has been a flop here—only two of our members have gone over, and their influence has collapsed since they did so.' 'Then the deputies do have some influence?', I asked. 'Oh yes', he replied. 'They may have represented nothing at first. But in a few years they soon build up a clientele—unless they are imbeciles, *on est idiot à vie*. But most of them are pretty shrewd politicians.'

He had previously served in a prefecture in France. 'It's very different here', he said. 'It takes some getting used to. If you refuse a favour to a local bigwig, he'll abuse and denounce you in the most hair-raising terms—and when you meet him next day he'll be as friendly as ever, and astonished if you remind him of the things he said yesterday. That's the trouble with trying to administer this country decently', he went on. 'No one wants the rules applied fairly—everyone wants exceptions made in their favour. If you say no, they think—he won't do it for me, but he'll do it for *Y* next door. And if you convince them that you won't do it for anyone, they simply conclude—he doesn't have the power, we must go elsewhere to find the man who does.'

'The contrasts in this country are astonishing', said another administrator. 'In this city we are trying to organise some social work with a young fellow—a nationalist, of course, he's been arrested two or three times—who says, "No uniforms. If any officers take part, they must wear civilian clothes." Yet, out in the bled in the east, another nationalist said to me, "Whatever happens after independence, the SAS officers must stay to carry on reconstruction in the villages."' I asked him whether there were any Moslems of standing willing to work with the French, and again referred to the RDA. 'Worthless', he replied. 'Time-servers. Only one or two of them have any real influence. You know the conditions in which they were elected. It's a great weakness that the Moslem parliamentarians are such a poor lot. But the local councillors are far better—and there are others. *X*, for instance,

---

[f] The Provisional Government of the Algerian Republic. This conversation took place in Tlemcen.

whom we offered to make a prefect. He refused. Said he could be of more value in politics after independence, as a voice for reason and moderation, if he didn't compromise himself with us now. And he was quite right.'

The whole problem, said this administrator, has changed completely in character. The trouble-centres now are not the mountains but the towns. And here, it must be said, the French army is reaping what it has sown. Though in the bled officers have often worked devotedly to improve the conditions of the Moslems, in the cities the army fought against terrorism by a ruthless police counter-terror. General Massu's victory in the 'battle of Algiers' destroyed the nationalist hope of winning the war militarily— but by means which ensured their ultimate political victory.

I had several long conversations with a brother and sister whom I met by chance. I found out very early on that they were FLN supporters. ('Of course. We are Moslems.') But not for some time did I learn that their father and two other very close relatives had been killed or imprisoned by the French, for acts (my friends claimed) that they had had nothing to do with. Their stories of tortures and arbitrary executions were numerous, circumstantial, horrible—and four years old. 'Then it was terrible. Things got better after 1958, but they were still grim as long as Massu was here. It hasn't been so bad since he left.'

I asked about the fraternisation rallies of May 1958. 'A fraud. The soldiers rounded our people up by force.' Did *no* Moslems go voluntarily? 'Yes, a few.' What proportion? 'Oh, ten per cent. Maybe a quarter. No, nearer ten per cent.' And last December? These demonstrations, they said, were spontaneous—provoked by Europeans who invaded the Moslem quarters to get the people out to shout for *Algérie française*. The boy had lost his job for taking part. 'The big companies only take on Moslems who are on their side. And lately, since the referendum, they've even been sacking those.' He had tried to go to France, or to the oilfields, or to eastern Algeria—but you needed your father's permission. And their father had been arrested three years ago. They did not know whether he was alive or dead. 'We think perhaps they have sent him to Madagascar.'

I asked them how many Moslems had been killed in the December demonstrations. The official figure was a hundred; they reckoned a thousand. (The liberal priest, whose views repeatedly confirmed theirs, estimated 800 at least.) What did they think were the chances of peace? 'Not much. The French want the Sahara—for the oil, and as a testing-ground for their bombs which are spreading disease all around. The war will go on for years—three maybe, or even five—before independence.'

'And after independence, what will you do with it?' The answer was instantaneous and intense. 'Educate ourselves. Educate our children.' The boy complained bitterly of having to leave school at fourteen. I suggested that the French had made a real effort to expand education in the last five years. 'That's right', they replied. 'In the last five years. When they wanted to bribe us away from independence.' Their brother had taken correspondence courses, but he lost his job and had to drop them; the books were too expensive. (Their enthusiasm was typical; I was told of one lycée in a medium-sized town[g] where the standard is rather higher than in a good lycée in France, and the sons of French officers in the area find it hard to keep up with their Moslem classmates.)

I asked about the Europeans after independence. 'Those who want to be bosses will have to go', they replied. 'But the rest can stay on as our equals—no more, no less. We aren't savages—we don't want to drive them out. In fact, we get on all right with the French. The real troublemakers are the capitalists—the Spaniards and above all the Jews. There are some decent Jews, of course—we aren't racists. But not many. Massu's a Jew, you know—born in the Congo. And so is Soustelle—his real name is Ben Soussain. What, don't they know that in France?' (This story was spread by the European ultras in Algiers when Soustelle arrived in 1955 as a 'liberal' governor appointed by Mendès-France.) And Mendès-France?, I asked. 'He's a good Frenchman.'

They spoke with respect and affection of the French liberals, especially the murdered lawyer, Popie.[h] 'They are criminals, the ultras. We wept when we heard he was dead. Fourteen stab wounds!—and they call us savages.' I suggested there had been horrors on both sides. There was the outrage at Boufarik, when a second bomb was placed to blow up those who were treating the victims of the first. 'Boufarik! Anything is understandable there. That place was a slaughterhouse—Lagaillarde's slaughterhouse.' And the two European women burned alive at Oran last December? 'Yes, that was terrible. The Moslem is a decent fellow until he gets in a rage. And then he is capable of any horror—anything.'

The priest had used almost the same words about the Europeans.

[g] Tizi-Ouzou.

[h] He had defended accused Moslems, and was killed by the European terrorists who later organised the murder squads of the OAS (the Secret Army Organisation). The shop owned by my Moslem friends near the Forum was the scene of the OAS's first indiscriminate attack in September 1961, when five customers (mostly children) were killed.

10 The army and its putsch[a]

'Algeria', wrote the left-wing editor of *L'Express* early in August, '... is the one political problem over which, in France, men are ready to die... On the Right and on the Left are only weariness, resignation, a kind of fatalism and shrinking into oneself. But over Algeria there does exist a category of Frenchmen ready for the last sacrifice. And what a category! Those who control physical force, the Army.'

Before the second world war the French officer corps had been mainly drawn from social and religious groups which were hostile to the existing political regime. Yet the army, despite Republican suspicions, remained obedient and loyal, *la grande muette*. The defeat of 1940 shattered that tradition. After General de Gaulle's appeal, honour and discipline (to quote Colonel Argoud, a leader in last April's putsch) were henceforward on opposite sides and every soldier had to choose. At the trial of Major Denoix de Saint-Marc for taking over Algiers with his regiment in the putsch, a priest who had gone through Buchenwald with the defendant appeared as a character witness. 'For our generation', he said, 'there are no fixed values.'[1]

Indo-China and Algeria completed the alienation of the army. The state of mind of the most rebellious element, the parachutist officers, is well portrayed in Jean Lartéguy's semi-documentary novel, *The Centurions* (Hutchinson). The author, himself a former officer in a parachutist regiment, follows a group of his old comrades from Dien-Bien-Phu to the 'battle of Algiers' in 1957. Most of his characters are left-wing types: Raspéguy the Basque colonel, proud of his peasant origins and loathing General Franco; Esclavier the son of a *Front Populaire* professor, who joined the Resistance at sixteen and was tortured by the Germans; Pinières the former FFI leader; Merle, the youngster in revolt against his dreary provincial bourgeois family, who is always proclaiming that he is really a civilian who hates the army; Dia the jovial Negro doctor who acts as a confessor to them all. In Indo-China they find 'a useless squandering of heroism, suffering, weariness and death, while corruption, rackets and general staffs were doing well'. At

---

[1] This and other quotations and evidence are from the 'barricades trial' (November 1960 to March 1961; also two long letters arising out of it from Colonel Broizat to *Le Monde*) and the 'putsch trials' (June to August 1961). Colonel Argoud's evidence at the former, given in camera, was published (with comments) by the left-wing Editions de Minuit under the title *Sans Commentaire*; its authenticity has not been denied, and the government has seized (most) copies.

[a] From *Encounter*, December 1961; originally entitled *The French Army*.

home, military secrets were being leaked to the anti-war press; political parties were raising funds through the currency racket; hospitals in France were promising donors not to use their blood for soldiers wounded in the 'filthy war'. Cut off from their own people, the army reacted bitterly to the humiliation of defeat. And in this mood they went through the Viet-minh prison camps and the experience of Communist indoctrination. They were forced into unwonted introspection. 'At Dien-Bien Phu, Julien had met officers who said they were in the war simply because those were their orders. It took the defeat to make them look retrospectively for their reasons...dismissing for the first time that myth of discipline which the defeat of 1940, the Resistance and the Liberation had emptied of all its meaning.'

Looking for the reasons why they had lost to a weaker army, Larteguy's officers pointed to the Communist success in mobilising against them the energies of a whole people. Then, personally subjected in their prison camps to the pressures of Communist re-indoctrination, they discovered for them-selves a new military technique. They emerged convinced that they alone understood the enemy who threatened the comfortable existence of their unheeding compatriots. 'Yes,' says Esclavier, 'our development has been going out of touch with our country—and for the first time it seems to me that we, the soldiers, are ahead—for the first time for centuries.'

Returning to France, they were plunged almost at once into the Algerian conflict. Convinced that they alone had grasped both the stake and the methods of this new form of war, they set out to create an entirely new kind of revolutionary force from the mutinous conscripts under their command. One of the most interesting passages in the novel describes the combination of physical isolation, intensive training and active propaganda used to enlist the men in a kind of militant sect—a unity because the officers lived and slept, worked and suffered alongside the troops.[2] 'In Indo-China', says the "political commissar", 'we felt ourselves rejected by the nation. We don't want any more of that. We must form a popular army through which we can recover communion with the people. That's why you conscripts are infinitely more important to us than the volunteers who are more or less mercenaries.' Yet the first stage to this communion with the people was to turn the people's sons against civil society and civilian authority. And the result was a state within the state. As one real parachutist officer has put it, 'We like war and we are tooled up for it; we have our chaplains to bless us

[2] 'The only officers who were really close to their men were those of the parachute regiments', wrote an officer in *France-Observateur*, 4 May 1961. And, 'The best of our comrades are excluded from the army. The command will go to the most mediocre and conformist generals and colonels... who have never won any battles except battles for promotion...the 1939 army, only worse.'

before the battle and to put us underground after it, our toubibs [doctors] to treat us, our quartermasters to feed us and our courts to judge us if we don't behave according to the laws in force among us.'³ Last July in Metz, after two parachutists were killed in a terrorist raid, hundreds of their fellows beat up all the Moslems they could find, killing several; much later, the police arrested the real terrorists. According to an official statement ninety per cent of the troops involved were conscripts.

The Centurions ends with the 'battle of Algiers'. Bombs at the bus-stops and in the big stores were reducing the city to chaos; lynch-mobs were out and a violent clash between the communities was imminent. The 10th Parachutist Division was brought in, and told to use 'every means'—without legal or moral restrictions—to break the terrorists. 'Repressing those out-of-date notions which at once make Western man great and prevent him, nowadays, from defending himself', they did as they were told. But after the danger was over, they were condemned by politicians who had willed the end but preferred not to know about the means.⁴ 'Whenever a minister or a deputy came to HQ', says Raspéguy, 'I told them, "It's done round the corner. It's disgusting, it's heart-rending, but we do it because your government has ordered us to." Some of them pretended not to understand or to think I was joking—others replied with an unctuous little wave of the hand, "It's for France's sake". And now these same swine want to haul us in front of their courts.' Esclavier explodes, 'Let Rome beware of the wrath of the legions.' And the book ends with one of them remembering a phrase from his schooldays, 'They became the Emperor's pretorian guards until they began to choose Emperors from among their own ranks. And that was the end of Rome.'

Many of the same problems are discussed from an opposite viewpoint in P. H. Simon's much slighter *Portrait of an Officer* (Secker and Warburg). Jean de Larsan is a Bayard-like figure, who comes of an old military family, has never imagined himself following any profession but soldiering, and believes that twentieth-century warfare can still be conducted with chivalry. In Indo-China he again meets Brahim, his devoted Algerian sergeant and friend of the Tunisian and Italian campaigns, now a second-lieutenant, conscious of racial discrimination and unhappy about the war. Brahim is persuaded by Larsan not to resign the commission of which he had been so proud; four days later he is killed. When his son Kadour decides to join the army, Larsan takes him as his driver and regards him as a son. But their

---

³ From Claude Dufresnoy, *Des Officiers Parlent* (Julliard).
⁴ The chairman of the official 'watchdog committee' to protect civil liberties told a colleague of Argoud (he says in *Sans Commentaire*): '...send us up good files, even find us false witnesses, but cancel, for heaven's sake cancel that directive' authorising summary execution of prisoners.

relationship is poisoned by the war. Larsan will allow no torture in his unit; his superior, Dhagondange, reproaches him for being a 'high-class soldier' but an 'indifferent and troublesome officer' who produces no information. On orders, Larsan arrests all the males of a village where a murder was committed; he reports them not guilty, but still they are interned. Next time, he refuses to arrest innocent suspects; Dhagondange, pointing to 'the soldier's golden rule of obedience', asks, 'If you intend systematically to refer your actions to the arbitration of your private conscience...do you think you have the right to command a unit on active service?' Returning to his battalion, Larsan finds that his popular second-in-command has been killed and horribly mutilated in a supposedly friendly village, and that his furious subordinates have slaughtered half the inhabitants (there is an almost identical episode in *The Centurions*[b]). Appalled by the massacre, Kadour deserts and delivers a truckload of arms to the FLN; he gives himself up rather than kill Larsan. On the day of Kadour's execution, Larsan resigns his commission. We hear the echo of a real captain, Branca, in the putsch trials, lamenting 'the collapse of my soldierly ideal'. But Branca regarded resignation as 'an egotistical solution'.

One major problem of personal conduct is hardly touched upon by either Lartéguy or Simon. This is the responsibility of the officer to the local people whom he has sought, on instructions from above, to recruit to his side. The French knew—none better than the army—that they needed Moslem co-operation if they were to stay in Algeria. They enlisted soldiers (200,000 Moslems were armed by them) and persuaded civilians to take responsibility for running their own local affairs. Out in the bled, SAS officers engaged in purely constructive activities, bringing roads and schools and doctors to primitive areas which had never had them, had a good conscience about the work they were doing and the merits of their cause. But Moslems who co-operated were threatened by the FLN. The French officer who told them (as instructed) that France would never betray them was bound to feel that he had contracted a personal obligation. What could he say to the municipal councillor who, when reproached for paying FLN taxes, replied 'We all know you Frenchmen will soon be deserting us. We who have compromised ourselves with you, we shall stay here. My house will be burned, not yours; my children will have their throats cut, not yours.'[5] He could only swear to himself that this must never be allowed to happen. And he would swear it all the more forcibly if, like so many of the defendants

[5] Quoted by Raoul Girardet, *Algérie 1960* (articles from *Combat*). For a fascinating picture of operations in the bled and the problem of confidence as seen by a sophisticated and liberal officer, see Georges Buis's novel *La Grotte* (Julliard).

[b] It is based on fact, and occured at Palestro in 1957.

in the putsch trials, he had already once, in Indo-China, given his own word and his country's to local friends of France who were soon to be abandoned to the reprisals of the Viet-minh.

To the personal problem of responsibility was added a practical problem of confidence which again impinged on politics. No sensible Moslem would work with the French unless he believed they really meant to stay. To give him that confidence was a political problem; to leave him without it made the army's task hopeless. So the greatest of military handicaps was political weakness; and the soldiers greeted the 13 May revolution with delight because it might at last settle the problem of confidence. Surely the Moslems would be convinced of French determination now that in Paris there was a strong government under a general they greatly respected, and in Algeria full powers of civil administration were concentrated in military hands. The referendum of September 1958 seemed a golden opportunity to obtain an expression of this confidence through the integrationist slogan of *Algérie française*; the soldiers threw themselves enthusiastically into the campaign. But a series of disappointments followed this triumph. First, de Gaulle did not commit himself to integration. Then he insisted (though ineffectively) on elections in which all shades of Moslem opinion could express themselves. And in September 1959 he revived the problem of confidence and jeopardised the results of the referendum victory by promising another referendum on self-determination (his critics called it 'no determination'). One activist, Colonel Broizat, lamented this 'victory for the FLN'. Another, Colonel Argoud, conceded that 'no sensible person and certainly no officer' believed France could hold Algeria by force against a hostile people (except by Budapest methods which she would not use), but argued that though self-determination was right in principle, while the war lasted it was disastrous, for it made Moslems fear that one day France might desert them.[6] And 'men won't die for a question-mark'.

The 'barricades' insurrection of the Algiers Europeans, in January 1960, gave a chance to put pressure on the government to reverse its policy. Both Argoud and Broizat warned their superiors that they would disobey (and tell others to disobey) an order to fire on the demonstrators. Broizat's paratroop regiment, moving at a crawl, arrived late at the square where the crowd had just shot down the gendarmes Broizat was supposed to be supporting. The insurgents had found complicities among officers who had not done their duty, said General Crépin; among the parachutists, complained the Algerian-born General Coste, 'an order is no longer an order, it's a basis for discussion'. But the group which meant by military disobedience to enforce a change of political policy was as yet small, and they failed to win

[6] See note 1, above.

over the commander-in-chief, General Challe. After a critical week, the President made a decisive broadcast; Argoud himself admitted that the army in the bled was impatient with the tolerance shown to the insurgents of Lagaillarde and Ortiz. Remembering the bitter wartime clashes in Syria and elsewhere, he and his colleagues resolved not to shatter the army's unity by openly defying the government.[7] But he was soon to regret his decision.[8]

For during 1960 the slide downhill became a headlong rush. In June the government agreed to talks with the FLN—thus losing, the ultras believed, a splendid chance to obtain the military surrender of half the rebel army (the 'Si Salah affair'). In September, 121 (later 200) prominent writers, teachers and entertainers publicly excused the defendants in the 'Jeanson trial' who had organised desertion from the army and assistance to the enemy. In November President de Gaulle conceded the principal FLN war aim, promising 'the Algerian Republic'; in December, the Moslem city masses came out to demonstrate openly for the FLN—and when the army command wanted to call in the parachutists, the civilian authorities (who had by now recovered their old powers) kept them out and tolerated the seditious demonstrations. At home, their political allies suffered crushing defeat at the referendum of January 1961. Talks with the FLN were about to be resumed without the previous cease-fire on which France had always insisted. The last straw was the press conference of 11th April, at which the President of the Republic, renouncing the nation's civilising mission, said that if negotiations failed France would stop pouring money down the Algerian drain; and if other Powers came in to take her place, 'I wish them joy of it'. The great patriotic cause in which men like Challe had so heavy an emotional investment was reduced to a sordid profit and loss account. To Boisfeuras in *The Centurions*, 'Algeria was the ball and chain attaching France to her great power role and forcing her to behave with more greatness and generosity than a Switzerland of today, a nation of merchants and fat bourgeois.' Now the wrong choice was being made by the very leader they had themselves chosen to ensure the right one. The putsch followed ten days later.

The men who made it were of very different types. Challe and his close associates 'jumped on a moving train' after 11th April; but it had been set in motion much earlier by the five colonels, Argoud, Broizat, Gardes, Godard and Lacheroy. Broizat had links with the far Catholic Right. But Argoud called himself a left-wing revolutionary,[9] while of Lacheroy and Godard

---

[7] See note 1, above.
[8] Interview (Argoud) and articles (J. Planchais and Lieut. X) in *La Nef*, July 1961.
[9] See note 8, above.

(whose first command was in the famous Glières maquis) it was said that they 'spit on the extreme Right, they are fascinated by a Tito'.[10c] Among the generals, Jouhaud was Algerian-born; Zeller, an activist with no Algerian contacts, thought of himself as an old Republican from Alsace. Salan, the time-server with the left-wing past, was willing to use the Fascist OAS (which had already murdered a few political opponents and threatened hundreds of others, with their families, both in Algeria and in France itself); Nicot, who thought that de Gaulle's was the only possible policy and that the putsch was bound to fail, feared that it would end in bloodshed if Salan and the colonels were left in control of it. Petit had won over the Algiers commanders to de Gaulle on 13 May; Challe (a wartime Gaullist who was thought to be politically leftish) had in January 1960 persuaded his subordinates to obey the government on the strength of assurances which later proved false; both supported the self-determination policy, but both now felt an obligation to those they had unwittingly misled. On the other hand Faure, whose arrest seems to have scotched any putsch in France itself, had been first an ardent Pétainist, then the first general to plot against the Fourth Republic, later a Poujadist candidate, and now a close ally of the colonels.

The aims of the leaders differed as much as their backgrounds and temperaments. There is no reason to doubt either the assertion or the reservation in Challe's assurance to the court that there was never any intention, 'as far as I was concerned', of seizing power in Paris. The colonels, however, could not have achieved their aims without doing so, and had no scruples about obedience to the civil power to restrain them. Though there is some evidence that an airborne invasion was planned, it is uncertain whether they could have spared enough parachutists even if they had not been obstructed by loyalist defiance at the air-bases; they seem, however, to have depended mainly on a putsch by the troops stationed in France (or Germany).

Theirs was at least an understandable policy. But what could Challe hope for if he did not mean to attack Paris? He claimed that in three months he could win the war and present a pacified and loyal Algeria to a startled government and a grateful country; eventually Algeria would no doubt become independent—but in conditions infinitely more favourable than the present ones. When the prosecutor asked him his reasons for believing that he could achieve in a few weeks a result that had eluded him in as many months as commander-in-chief with the full support of Paris, he had no arguments to give. His programme cannot be taken seriously: yet he was a very serious and sober man. It seems hard to avoid the conclusion that he

[10] As a Gaullist officer told Jean Cau: *L'Express*, 27 July 1961.

[c] But Godard is now said to be advising the Greek military regime and organising its police operations at home and abroad.

acted on what he believed to be the imperative demands of personal honour, and then rationalised his conduct into a political programme bearing no relation to the facts of the situation. But when a man of his reputation, intelligence and international experience declared it possible, his juniors were delighted to believe him. For it was his appeal rather than that of the extremists which attracted support in the army; his assurance that his aims were 'non-political' and confined to Algeria was quoted again and again in the trials, while Argoud brought in many of his recruits on fairly innocent pretexts such as 'taking part in a demonstration', avoiding any mention of a seizure of power.

Those who responded to the leaders' call, therefore, were rarely Fascists.[11] A few even shared Nicot's doubts and fears; on the very first morning Captain Carreté told a police officer he was protecting from a Fascist mob, 'I shall be in jail within a week. But meanwhile I can give my men orders that will prevent bloodshed. If others replaced me they might act differently.' More typical in his expectations, if outstanding in his personality, was Saint-Marc. His men were devoted to him (one lieutenant gave as his sole reason for joining the putsch, 'I'd have been a miserable wretch to desert Saint-Marc'). As divisional press officer he had won affection and respect from the journalists, French and foreign, Left and Right. After the Resistance and Buchenwald he had served in Indo-China, seen the villagers in his area abandoned and massacred, and lost his native wife who was murdered by the Viet-minh. In Algeria, he told his judges, 'I have never thought I was fighting for any kind of colonialism, which I condemn, but for a just and humane cause.' It was only on the evening before the putsch that Challe asked him to join; Saint-Marc, once he had assured himself that it was 'neither a Fascist *coup d'état* nor an action tending to racialism', agreed wholeheartedly. It was his unit which seized the main government buildings. Later, he was asked to release the fellow-legionnaires who had murdered the liberal lawyer Popie; he refused (however, they were freed by Godard). At the end he stood by Challe in preventing bloodshed and stopping Salan from loosing the OAS on the city.

Against men like Saint-Marc, all too many of the loyalists and especially the generals (notably excepting the commander-in-chief, Gambiez) cut a poor figure.[12] Gouraud, at Constantine, wavered from side to side; when a colonel phoned for instructions he was told 'Be patient, we're thinking about it'; when he arrived in person and asked for orders, the general replied 'What are your intentions?' 'To carry out your orders', answered the colonel—but he was left to decide for himself. Another general (Autrand) told his officers, 'Go if you wish, stay if you wish—I'm off to bed.' Of those

[11] See note 8, above.   [12] See note 2, above.

who refused to join the putsch, few said flatly that they were loyal to the government; most merely objected (rightly) 'It won't work', 'You can't succeed', or 'It will get you nowhere.' And even among the firmest loyalists, some who had been through the internecine battles of 1941–2 could not bear to think of another. General Simon said he had three times ordered Frenchmen to fire on Frenchmen and would never do so again. Colonel Darmuzai, who had fought in Syria, thought he might be ordered to Algiers to attack the mutineers. Like Paget at the Curragh, he would not give his officers (especially those born in Algeria) a command they would feel bound to disobey. 'We shall get our orders tomorrow', he told them, 'and then you must make your choice.' The regiment left that night to join the mutineers. 'Knowing your views', wrote his second-in-command, 'we all agreed not to inform you.' And Gambiez himself agreed with Challe's comment that 'if we took the town in an hour and a half, it was because the doors were opened to us.'

Those who made the putsch were a minority. But among them were very many of the best officers: the least careerist, the most capable of decision, the ones enjoying the highest respect from their colleagues and subordinates.[13] They were also the most determined, for many who did not join them were with them at heart. There was little firm support for the government's policy in the army, for the government had done little to obtain it. Like its predecessors, it had used its army for the most diverse and disagreeable tasks, engaged its officers in personal responsibilities, and then changed course without explaining the reasons to those who had to pay (or watch others paying) the price for mistakes. 'My only political action', said Captain Estoup at his trial, 'has been in obedience to my orders: colonialist up to 1956, paternalist in 1957–8, "fraternalist" in 1958–9, opportunist since. They never taught me at Saint-Cyr to arrange for a town's food supply, follow up a police investigation, do the job of Prefect of Police, organise a polling-station, or suspect my fellow-officers.'

Ministers did not always seem to remember that, as General Beaufort said at the trials, 'We have no trade union in the army. We have to give orders which send men to die. Policy must give commanders sufficient grounds to justify such orders.' Hardly anything was done to make these grounds clear. Radical and Socialist ministers in the Fourth Republic spoke of holding out for the last quarter of an hour, or blamed their failure on the ill-will of the foreigner, or on the unpatriotic conduct of those journalists who in 1956 or 1957 still upheld the principles and policies which those same ministers had so ardently defended at the previous general election. The Fifth Republic did little better. The army was allowed to commit itself (and its protégés)

[13] See note 2, above.

to *Algérie française*, only to find the objective changed to self-determination. The shift was not explained but explained away—a mere diplomatic manœuvre to win a debate at the United Nations. Colonel Gardes was told to continue his psychological warfare activities based on the old objective. In the week of the barricades, officers who sympathised with the insurgents were officially reassured that the government's policy was still 'the most French solution'. In his *tournée des popotes* a few weeks later, President de Gaulle himself told them that a military victory would precede the political settlement. Within three months he was opening negotiations with the FLN. Then what had their fellows been killing and dying for since 1955? 'The Army's first duty is to obey the government', said a regular major (who accepted de Gaulle's policy); 'but the Government's first duty is not to sacrifice the Army in useless wars for causes that are lost in advance.'[14] Saint-Marc put it more bitterly: 'Fifteen years of hope have turned out to be fifteen years of fraud.'

Six months later the President announced the advent of the Algerian Republic. 'The Army no longer understands', said another pro-Gaullist regular major. 'We have to adopt the attitude of mercenaries and obey whatever the orders—above all, not try to understand.'[15] 'Why is the victory thrown away when we have won the war?' demanded Colonel de la Chapelle at his trial. 'In a few months an evil force outside the army has destroyed the fruits of all the sacrifices.' The president of the court questioned the imminence of victory, adding, 'Besides, there are international considerations beyond your competence.' 'But', protested the colonel, 'no one has ever mentioned them to us.' When de Gaulle himself thought to please the army by telling them, 'Militarily, the war is won', many officers inferred a corollary: 'Now leave me to my job of losing it politically.'[16]

These complaints were sincerely felt, particularly in the lower commissioned ranks. But from the army's political opinion-makers, especially the psychological warfare specialists and the 'activist' staff colonels, they were partial and specious. For in 1956–7, as one officer honestly admitted, 'we had a real *gouvernement introuvable* in Paris—a ministry headed by the Socialist party leader which beat the Right on its own ground'.[17] And in 1958 the army imposed a President of its own choice. Where the Fourth Republican ministers had compensated for their left-wing allegiance by patriotic bombast, de Gaulle sought national unity through masterly obscurity. But if neither ever explained frankly the limits to their freedom of action this was largely because both were so assiduously 'intoxicated' with warnings that the army would revolt rather than accept a policy it disapproved. The

[14] See note 3, above.   [15] See note 3, above.
[16] See note 10, above.   [17] See note 8, above.

psychological warfare specialists had put its loyalty in doubt long before it was subjected to the machiavellian treatment in which their colleagues in the field found understandable cause for rancour. De Gaulle had to move slowly, step by ambiguous step, because he feared (probably rightly) that the alternative was a clash between the nation and its armed forces in which, whatever the outcome, democratic liberties would almost certainly succumb.

Moreover, in blaming the government for losing the war the activist officers had found a defence mechanism enabling them to overlook their own responsibility. The charge of ineffectiveness was perhaps ultimately harder to bear than that of acting like criminals. For to the latter they had ready answers. Those who were devout Catholics could get from chaplains like P. H. Simon's Father Legouey, of the type Lartéguy describes as 'priests in uniform who swear like troopers and dream of holy war', the reassurance the heads of their Church denied them. Or they could persuade themselves that the critics were all perverted, masochistic intellectuals, blind to the crimes of the enemy. Why, asked Colonel Broizat, is there a committee protesting at the torture of Djamila Boupacha ('which if it happened I reprove') and silence about the four young Moslem nurses lately killed in an FLN ambush? (Did he really not see that patriotic Frenchmen might feel responsible for deeds done in their name, and reluctant to have their army use the methods of a terrorist gang?) But above all the activists, 'ahead for the first time for centuries', knew that they knew what was at stake. 'We are like doctors', said Colonel Argoud, 'talking of a deadly illness and a change in his way of life to a client who, in his ignorance, doesn't believe a word of it.'[18]

It was harder to face the haunting fear that the crimes and the sacrifices, the devotion and the horror had alike been futile; that psychological warfare had been waged and villages regrouped, new roads and schools built, comrades killed and suspects tortured—all for nothing. The activists had assumed that their army could move among the people like a fish in water, like Mao Tse-tung's, although the people was not their own. They had talked revolution without making one. They had adopted the Viet-minh's techniques without their political driving force. They had thought words could be a substitute for deeds. The one triumph of their psychological warfare had been in consolidating their own illusions. And their harsh and arbitrary repression had lost them the people they knew they had to win. The Casbah, which had been controlled by FLN terrorists, obeyed Colonel Godard after the 'battle of Algiers'—willingly, Broizat maintained, because in that battle ninety per cent justice was done. In December 1960 the FLN demonstrations gave the answer to the colonels' claims. But that conclusion was intolerable.

[18] See note 8, above.

Therefore the blame must lie elsewhere—on foreign intervention, Allied betrayal, Munich-minded civilians, the 'treasonous press', or the 'government of scuttle'.

So the duty of unconditional soldierly obedience was challenged both from Left and Right, as it had already been challenged for nearly five years—in literature by Larsan and the Centurions, in life by General Faure plotting to seize power in Algiers at the end of 1956, and by General Paris de la Bollardière publicly denouncing the repression at the beginning of 1957. They soon had many imitators. But the leaders of the 1961 putsch, like so many of those who debated the army's crisis, were amazed to find that a man with no commission might still have a conscience. The conscripts (whom Captain Branca quaintly called 'the mutineers') were eager to follow any officer who stayed loyal. But disobedience is contagious; when the commissioned ranks rebelled or hesitated, the men took matters into their own hands, so that while lieutenants were busily arresting generals with his full approval, Captain Roquefeuil was horrified to find himself arrested by privates. When the insurgent Major Robin told his subordinates 'to obey traditional discipline, that is to say myself, whatever their problems of conscience', he inevitably undermined traditional discipline. In 'trampling under foot the notion of service to the State which is fundamental to an army', as Gambiez put it, the insurgents had themselves destroyed the force they wanted to save. (Rather than admit it, they blamed those Communists whose influence in the army they had for years—and rightly—estimated at nil. Challe himself, the prosecutor said, 'saw red everywhere'.)

Men of the Left were often no less self-righteous. After condemning the arbitrary regime of *pouvoir personnel* and excusing desertion and aid to the enemy, they were soon clamouring for the *tribunaux d'exception* of the detested regime to put to death the imprisoned leaders of the putsch—the very ones who had ensured that it was liquidated without violence. Fortunately, some at least of the 'Fascists' had been less willing than the professional humanitarians of the Left to spill French blood. But they offered exactly the same defence for their actions.

'Conscience prevails against the law. The law is no excuse.' Whose words? *France-Observateur*, *Témoignage Chrétien*, Larsan answering Dhagondange? No, an OAS journal addressed to officers in the army in Algeria, entitled: *Les Centurions*.

PART IV

LEARNING FROM HISTORY?

11 Gaullist grandeur: myth and reality[a]

The French President not only makes history, he rewrites it; and among his many roles the boldest is surely that of distinguished historian. No one reading his pronouncements since his return to power would conceive of the celebrated seer's bitter resistance to post-war decolonization, or realize how preposterous are the claims that he offered self-determination to the colonies at Brazzaville in 1944, gave independence to Syria and Lebanon in 1941, or favoured a real new deal in Algeria after the war. In reality the disasters in Indo-China and Algeria, which the great statesman out of power so successfully exploited against his pygmy successors, were directly traceable to policies that he had adopted and men he had appointed to implement them. Yet, in spite of his performance after the war and as head of the RPF, President de Gaulle has shown he is no Bourbon: he forgets nothing but he does not fail to learn.

In his own words, 'logic and sentiment do not weigh heavily in comparison with the realities of power; what matters is what one takes and what one can hold on to', for States are 'the least impartial and the most partisan bodies in the world' and a strong ally is only one degree less dangerous than a strong enemy. De Gaulle knows that France alone cannot play her former role. But since she is acceptable because of her universal vocation, and powerful because she wields the Bomb, she can speak for a Europe in which Germany is disqualified for leadership by history, and Britain by her own choice. But on three conditions. First, no political integration: the process of bargaining between several independent but indispensable partners, which he condemned as a recipe for paralysis when the units were French parties, becomes the one realistic way to arrive at a coherent policy when they are western European States. It follows, secondly, that the other partners, above all Germany, must—out of bad conscience or good Europeanism—always accept French demands. German ministers have to risk a farmers' revolt at the polls so that French ministers can escape one; President de Gaulle sternly champions the German *status quo* when talks between Washington and Moscow are in the air, but blandly looks forward to reunification prepared through Franco-Soviet agreement. The President, like a European

[a] Originally published as a book review in the *Journal of Common Market Studies*, 5.3 (March 1967). Two paragraphs of comment on the books have been replaced by two new opening sentences, and subsequent references to the books have also been deleted.

John Foster Dulles, tries to manipulate his German puppet while denouncing America for satellizing her allies. For the third condition, of course, is the exclusion from Europe of the United States: an indispensable protector as long as Russia threatened, she has become the more pressing danger now that Soviet attention is diverted by the quarrel with China. Gaullist policy therefore works to stimulate local nationalisms against both the super-powers, and busily fosters the revival of American isolationsim which it professes to fear.

A strong France dominating Europe is the central Gaullist objective and all the rest is contingent—even anti-Americanism, for the undermining of NATO was a second-best policy, adopted only because of Washington's stubborn and foolish refusal to admit Paris to a privileged status within the Atlantic alliance. Other aims are equally changeable. Germany was to be dismembered in the forties, kept divided in the fifties, perhaps reunified in the seventies once the super-powers have gone away. Soviet Russia was the partner in a fine and beautiful alliance in 1944, the carrier of the world's most intolerable tyranny soon afterwards, but in time was reinstated as the traditional friend of France (i.e. of mankind); while the wretched yellow multitudes of 1959 were to inherit, five years later, the ancient treasures of Oriental civilization. Decolonization, belatedly adopted when the vain attempt to cling to empire was weakening France throughout the world, had become the proudest feather in the General's progressive képi.

Frequent changes of objective are the response of a great realist to new situations; they are also a convenient cover for the failure to attain concrete results. Gaullist intransigence and German good-neighbourliness have indeed brought notable benefits to French agriculture; and in Africa France keeps her cultural and economic dominance over her former dependencies. While in Algeria France buys political influence with soft words and hard cash, the methods are cruder farther south: when the corrupt dictator of Gabon was overthrown by revolt, it was the champion of non-intervention in the internal affairs of small nations who sent paratroops from Paris to restore him to his throne. Elsewhere there is not much to show. In Latin America France pursues a policy of gestures, varying from the sublime— de Gaulle's tour—to the ridiculous—the enthusiastic visit to revolutionary Cuba of a bunch of notably reactionary Gaullist deputies. The gestures have one thing in common: ineffectiveness. Fourteen months after Gabon, the U.S.A. intervened in the Dominican revolution: France condemned her in words but did not venture to recognize the popular government of Colonel Caamano.

However, the applause from the Left is loudest where Gaullist policies have only symbolic significance. Yet even the symbols are ambiguous.

Nothing better illustrates the skill of the conjurer—and the character of the audience—than the fascinated applause of world progressive opinion for this friend of Spanish and Portuguese dictators; this supplier of arms to South Africa; this open champion of force and despiser of international organization; this financial conservative who champions the gold standard and the rich nations' Group of Ten; this recent tester and principal proliferator of the Bomb. For all their moral absolutism, few left-wingers withhold their admiration for the hero who flouts their principles, but also the United States.

Yet if the President's world-view is ambiguous, his objectives bewildering and his methods insufferable, his triumphant exploitation of limited resources to project himself and his country on the world stage becomes all the more extraordinary. One reason for his success is a singleminded decisiveness of which few other leaders are capable. Once convinced that Algeria was 'blocking every road', he boldly capitulated to every FLN demand—a solution within the reach of the dimmest Fourth Republican premier, but one from which only a political genius could have drawn a psychological fillip, instead of a new humiliation, for frustrated Frenchmen. Who else, again, would continue subsidizing the rulers of free Algeria and tolerating their repeated outrages against French interests and dignity, in the calm and justified conviction that their friendship insures him against any African or Arab criticism and thus guarantees him a sizeable block of votes to wield for higher objectives at 'that Thing' in New York? Then the grounds on which he challenges his opponents are shrewdly chosen, for he is careful to take up genuine problems which are already causing widespread concern—but which others smother out of short-term considerations of prudence. Thus he earns respect by saying aloud what others privately think on a whole series of problems: the working of the UN, the dollar problem, the absurdities of the MLF,[b] the credibility of American nuclear protection for Europe. Furthermore, his chief opponents regularly play into his hands. The crudities of American policies and leadership in Europe helped to shape his own mentality in the past; repeated today in Latin America or South-east Asia, they contribute to his audience. But his greatest asset would still exist even if the great powers always behaved with circumspection and finesse, for the Gaullist critique feeds on resentment of power itself.

Nothing is more striking than the way the President is applauded everywhere by people and countries with little, and ignored by those with much ability to influence the course of events.[c] Appropriately, his warmest admirer of all is the 'socialist' prince of Cambodia, who publicly berates the American presence in South-east Asia while privately praying he will never be left to

---

[b] The 'multilateral force' once much favoured by one school of Washington policy-makers.
[c] No longer (early 1969) true of Germany.

face the Chinese alone. But when de Gaulle tries to detach other countries from Washington he meets everywhere with a blank negative—in Bonn as in London, in Moscow as in the capitals of Latin America. His attitudes have provoked an American response which reinforces German influence and bargaining strength. His policies have prevented the emergence of the only power which might have influenced United States conduct—a united and friendly Europe. Yet in compensation for the lost influence she might have had in Washington, France has not acquired the least capacity to persuade Moscow or Peking. In his deeds, the President can offer no alternative to the international systems he so successfully wrecks; and his gestures arouse dangerous echoes beyond his frontiers. Gaullists justify the French nuclear deterrent by claiming that proliferation makes peace more secure—as if no one was listening across the Rhine. 'The Bomb for all—but not for Bonn' is a policy unlikely in the long run (if there is a long run) to enhance General de Gaulle's reputation for profound historic vision.

Yet whatever impression his foreign policy has made abroad, it has proved a triumphant success at home, repeatedly enabling him to silence or out-manœuvre his domestic critics. The wide support for it in France needs stressing in Britain, for a long history of myth and misunderstanding has provoked discord between the two countries. Even in method, his sulky obstructionism merely employs to greater effect a tried Fourth Republican technique; while in purpose Frenchmen and Englishmen look differently at many matters of policy, and at the roles the two countries, and Europe as a whole, should play in the world. Perhaps this is not just because France is out of step with all her allies: even in Britain de Gaulle has more admirers—from blimpish old Tories to 'with it' Young Liberals—than might appear from the respectable portals of Chatham House. But in attracting followers everywhere by his spectacular defiance of the strongest power, he naturally delights his own compatriots by winning international applause for his 'policy made in Paris'.

'As was only human, [Roosevelt's] will to power cloaked itself in idealism.' The President's scathing irony is for others; for all his culture and realism he can proclaim without a shadow of doubt in 1944 and again in 1962, 'that what was to the advantage of France was to the benefit of all'. No French-man will dissent from this General Motors philosophy of history. Some of his countrymen (notably farmers) welcome the concrete benefits won by his policy. Nearly all applaud the gestures which soothe their inferiority complexes and convince them that France is again playing her proper role in the world. To restore a nation's self-confidence after generations of doubt is no mean achievement. It is more than all the wizardry of two Harolds has achieved for Britain.

12   Vietnam: America's Algeria?[a]

The President had inherited his war from a previous administration—and soon found himself under fire from his predecessors. The first spokesman of the doves to make any electoral impact was widely admired for his courage and honesty, and was credited with introducing a new political style— especially among his large student following, who thought him much more radical than he really was. But before long he was replaced as leader of the Left by a politician who had, at the outbreak of war, been the minister responsible for law and order, and whose reputation for ruthless opportunism was offset by his many contacts with political bosses both radical and con-servative. In contrast to these vocal opponents, the man who had carried out the first major escalations—by sending hundreds of thousands of draftees, and by extending the war across a frontier—thought that his share of re-sponsibility debarred him from criticising the President over Algerian matters. For the President in question was Charles de Gaulle, not Lyndon Johnson, and the three dissenters were not McCarthy, Kennedy and McNamara, but Mendès-France, Mitterrand and Mollet.

Such parallels may amuse but they do not illuminate. No two historical situations are identical, and the differences between the Algerian and Viet-namese wars are both important and obvious. Politically, Algeria had been under French rule for over a century; a million Europeans were settled there, and 400,000 Algerian Moslems worked in France. Militarily, the French won the war on the ground—but they never subjected the 'privileged sanctuary' in Tunisia to sustained attack. Psychologically, many French civilians had close ties with Algeria; and French officers were willing to obstruct or even rebel against policies they disapproved. So the similarities are only partial, and false analogies can be dangerous. Yet if the highly questionable similarity with Munich has been allowed to influence the policy and the public opinion of the United States, there may be something to be learned from the last prolonged war fought by a Western power in an undeveloped country.

During the Algerian war, military and political hawks in Paris judged the international situation in familiar terms. 'Their' National Liberation Front was not officially Communist, but was regarded as an agent of the inter-national Communist conspiracy. If Algeria was lost, the rest of North Africa

    [a] From a talk given in the U.S.A. in April 1968; unpublished.

was expected to follow quickly and other Arab and African states in due course, as the early stages of the gigantic pincer movement by which Lenin had long ago proposed to encircle and isolate Western Europe. In view of these risks to the western alliance, whose common interests they claimed to be defending, the hawks of Paris could not understand why their NATO partners denied them active support.

These unsophisticated views found no echo in Washington. But France was not treated by her allies as the United States is treated today. As a weaker country, she invited less jealousy—but more pressure. Her partners observed diplomatic forms, paying embarrassed lip-service to the French cause (as Britain still does to the American). But when in February 1958 the French air force carried out its first and only punitive raid across the Tunisian border, the American and British governments promptly intervened with a 'good offices' mission to restore the peace—through French concessions. A resentful French Assembly at once overthrew the government and opened the political crisis which was to bring de Gaulle to power.

The incident illustrates a second similarity between the hawks of the Seine and those of the Potomac: their common conviction that their troubles were essentially, or even exclusively, due to foreign aggression. Concentrating their attention on Cairo or Tunis or Prague (the source of the Communist arms with which the guerrillas supplemented those obtained by capture) the French hawks were often inclined to overlook their lack of any real popular base in Algeria itself. They were probably right in thinking that many (at the start, perhaps a large majority) of Algerian Moslems were indifferent or hostile to the National Liberation Front. But vigorous and effective opposition came only from a few conservative landowners, and from the European community, privileged foreigners and infidels (like the militant Catholics from the north of Vietnam) who alienated rather than attracted support. Moslem opposition to the NLF never found effective political expression. Declining in numbers, aggrieved by European predominance and intimidated by NLF terrorism, dissident Moslems (and even some Europeans) attempted to reinsure against the future by clandestine contacts with the enemy. The French had on their side many unreliable Moslem soldiers (the harkis), some uneasy Moslem administrators, but little or no active support among the people. Yet their regime had to appear legitimate to their allies and to their own citizens. So elections were organised to show that it represented the popular will: the results looked almost excessively satisfactory, and were taken seriously only by those convinced already. At best, they demonstrated to policy-makers elsewhere that, at least by day, the army controlled more territory than the guerrillas. But even this short-term gain for the hawks turned into a liability later in the war, when the

Moslem representatives originally chosen with the goodwill of the French army began to reflect the outlook of their constituents and to move towards a nationalist position.

This political development took place in spite of the French army's military success. For the third (and fundamental) error of the hawks was their belief that superior fire-power could compensate for inferior politics. In Algeria (unlike Vietnam) they attained the ten-to-one ratio then considered essential to defeat a guerrilla offensive; they built frontier defences which reduced infiltration to a trickle; they succeeded in pacifying most of the country—and in doing so they lost the war. This was not because the French army was composed of ruthless reactionaries, savagely exterminating the heroic defenders of the poor and oppressed. Few French soldiers had any sympathy for the wealthy settlers, and many of them were far more conscious than the politicians at home of the need for reforms if 'hearts and minds' were ever to be won. In the SAS (Special Administrative Sections) young French officers worked devotedly at civilian reconstruction jobs; and when the schools they had built were burned down, or the Moslems who had co-operated with them in entirely non-political village improvements were slaughtered by the NLF, they noted with bitterness the silence of the anti-war liberals who were so alert to condemn French misdeeds.

In pointing out the liberals' double standard, the hawks could claim a moral case. But politically their critics were right in dismissing it as irrelevant. Justifiably or not, the sufferings inflicted by the weak had less impact than those imposed by the strong—especially torture in Algeria, napalm in Vietnam. The problem for the French was to bring to battle a worse-equipped but elusive enemy who knew the terrain better than they. His movements could not be traced without information; information could not be had without security—that the informer would not have his throat cut for giving it; security—for 24 hours a day, seven days a week, fifty-two weeks a year—could not be guaranteed without identifying the enemy. So, at the village level, the temptation was overwhelming to counter fear by fear, and extract information by torture. At the command level, the temptation was overwhelming to reduce the scale of the problem by moving the peasants out of their exposed villages into fewer, larger, better-protected, more strategic hamlets; the 'regroupment camps'. The worst of these settlements were virtually concentration camps, but some were even preferable to the original villages; none, however, allowed for peasant attachment to their own land and family graves.

In the cities, especially Algiers, the nationalist organisation was strong, and in 1956 its terrorism was very effective in intimidating the population and breaking down the fabric of daily life. But that winter, in a ruthless campaign of systematic torture, the French parachutists succeeded in shattering the NLF apparatus in the Casbah. Like the bombs and shells in Vietnam, the violent repressive measures in Algeria did not discriminate very successfully in their selection of victims. Symbolising the power of a rich, white, alien people, they created a solidarity among the weaker Algerian community which had not previously existed, and from which the NLF benefited as the one group which was effectively fighting back. This superior power, used without political imagination to win military success, led directly to political defeat.

In Algeria it did so, not only by throwing the Moslems into the arms of the NLF, and by discrediting the French cause in the international arena, but also by provoking a bitter division within the French people themselves. For a fourth miscalculation by the hawks was to misjudge what their own compatriots would stand. Opposition to the war began as an expression of moral indignation against torture: not very widespread, most common among minority groups such as Jews and Protestants, but felt increasingly in the churches and above all in the academic community. The most extreme of the student protesters identified themselves with and worked for the NLF; a much larger number engaged in organised or individual draft resistance. Their official union defied the government by continuing fraternal relations with the Algerian students. (The government retaliated by victimising some of the leaders, and encouraging the growth of a rival 'non-political' body. Later when the Gaullists decided it was legitimate after all to deal with Algerian nationalists, they were embarrassed to find that the 'non-political' student association they had favoured was really controlled by their deadly enemies of the far Right.) Student protest aroused passionate feelings on both sides. It could not be explained in customary political categories, for the revolt was inspired by the ablest and most civic-minded of the country's future leaders. Its impact indeed owed a good deal to the social origins of the objectors: some of the top Gaullist ministers and officials found their own sons and daughters sitting down in the Place de la Concorde to demonstrate against the war.[b]

Opposition spread well beyond the academic community, and moral outrage was not the only basis for it. Moderate liberals were at first reluctant to condemn their own government in wartime. They had fewer illusions than their juniors about the character of the other side, and were more aware of the dangers of playing into the hands of the right-wing extremists. Yet as the war continued they became increasingly concerned, both by the

[b] In the longer term, the protest movement against the Algerian war was to develop into the great student outbreak in May 1968 when the Government, having successfully weakened the students' union, could find no one with authority to negotiate with them.

apparently pointless human suffering in Algeria and by the growing political damage in France. They were disturbed by the alienation of the new generation's leaders and alarmed at the persistent threat to civil liberties (during the war, freedom of speech, of assembly and of the press were curtailed far more severely in France than they have been in the United States). Later, radical and liberal objectors were joined by millions of disillusioned citizens who had lost faith in the repeated predictions that the 'last quarter-hour' of the war was at hand. In the supposedly secure cities of Vietnam, the Tet offensive revealed to many Americans that the Viet-Cong's military capacity had not been broken; in those of Algeria, the Casbah demonstrations of December 1960 convinced Frenchmen that the NLF's political influence remained intact. On the spot, neither necessarily proved (as some claimed) 'what the people really felt'. But at home, both confirmed the suspicion that the authorities had misled the country, and perhaps themselves, about the real state of the war.

Thus, though their origin and course was quite different, the two wars had one central feature in common: the attempt of a strong western power to overcome a revolutionary and nationalist guerrilla force by the large-scale commitment of its own well-fed, well-equipped troops. Their massive presence concealed from some critics the existence of a large if ineffective indigenous fighting force on the same side (in Algeria the harkis, soldiers under French command; in South Vietnam, a distinct army under—or over —the Saigon government). The extra purchasing power of the foreigners overwhelmed the local economy, stimulating the artificial boom occasionally celebrated by some particularly insensitive official spokesman, in France as in the United States. Their immense fire-power could all too easily obliterate the towns and villages over which the combatants fought. The unequal character of the struggle, however, was just what gave the political advantage to the military underdog: for within the country itself it exasperated nationalist feeling against the rich Western intruders; and with most of their allies, and many of their own people, it cast doubt on the benevolence of their intentions. Paris and Washington therefore faced somewhat similar political problems if they determined to continue the war; it does not follow that they could choose to end it in the same manner. Nevertheless, the later stages of the Algerian story may also in some respects be suggestive.

De Gaulle, unlike Johnson, had owed his initial electoral triumph in 1958 to the nation's hawks. But he too soon disillusioned his former supporters by his search for a middle way between the dangerous or impracticable panaceas clamoured for by what he called the 'two packs' (ornithology is less developed in France than in the United States). His attitude was not always reflected in that of all his subordinates; the President took account (and advantage) of their reactions, and in any case, he himself had no intention of giving away any more than necessary. His early speeches were deliberately ambiguous, and his initial peace offers—mostly spurned, but once (in June 1960) accepted in a first contact which quickly broke down—seemed designed to improve France's international posture, offering the NLF merely an opportunity for honourable capitulation in conditions (such as 'the white flag of parley') which would have made the NLF appear to be suing for peace. Such peace proposals were a continuation of the war by other means: if the mass of war-weary and politically indifferent Moslems were once convinced that the NLF had accepted defeat, they would hasten to seek the favour of their future masters; as they turned away from the NLF its bargaining power would decline and France could enforce a more favourable settlement. Conversely, negotiations which seemed merely the prelude to an NLF takeover would swell its ranks with every fence-sitter in the country, demoralise the Moslem administrations and harkis, and enable the nationalist leaders to dictate their terms. Behind the apparently trivial squabbling over questions of face, there were real considerations of political advantage.

As the war dragged on, however, de Gaulle became convinced that time was no longer on his side, and in November 1960—a month *before* the Algerian 'Tet offensive'—he announced a change of course, promising 'the Algerian Republic which will exist one day'. Yet in his increasingly anxious search for a way out, he could never forget that an open French defeat might provoke a serious reaction in the electorate (and above all in the army). Only after he had overcome the Algiers military putsch of April 1961 could he begin serious bargaining with the other side. By then he was impatient to be free of a conflict which was weakening France economically, paralysing her internationally, and violently disrupting her domestic unity. But it was not until March 1962—twenty-one months after the first abortive contact, sixteen months after his change of course—that France at last signed the Evian treaty with the NLF.

On their side, the NLF also made concessions. For years they had been utterly unwilling to negotiate seriously. Now they had taken some severe military knocks—yet at the same time they knew their political strength was growing, and they believed that peace talks would increase it further by undermining the other side. Moreover, as power came to seem no longer far away but almost within their grasp, they began for the first time to think of the constructive problems of governing an independent Algeria—and to realise their need for the economic aid France was prepared to offer them. And when de Gaulle defeated the military hawks, he established his credibility in nationalist eyes. Thus, the NLF became much more conciliatory just when France's former protégés, sensing defeat, were moving towards total intransigence. Refusing to face reality and help France bargain for the best terms she could get them, the Europeans (and the Moslems most compromised with the French) turned to the new Secret Army Organisation of officers on the run, the OAS. Its campaign of terrorism in both Algeria and France quickly exasperated public and official opinion alike, and even before Evian there were signs of a startling reversal of attitudes which was soon to become a reversal of alliances. When the OAS was bombing and machine-gunning Moslems and Gaullist Frenchmen equally, the military and civilian servants of the French state were driven into tacit co-operation with the nationalists they had fought for so long. Over the transition from peace in March to independence in July there presided a coalition administration, in which French officials sat beside 'neutral' Moslems with no organised support, and friends of the NLF with no formal credentials—while around them the country descended rapidly into chaos.

Now that it was too late the NLF, convinced at last of de Gaulle's goodwill, were anxious to reassure the Europeans. Thorough paper guarantees for their survival and equal treatment were written into the treaty. But these promises were never to be tested, for the Europeans were totally sceptical, and by the OAS terrorist campaign they transformed their most gloomy predictions into a self-fulfilling prophecy. Their own acts ensured that they could not remain in Algeria; and within a few weeks the entire community (and the Jewish community too) had fled the country.

This outcome of the war, as so often in politics, left each school of thought claiming it had been vindicated. The hawks could point out that the negotiations were, as they had always argued, a false solution; for talks could succeed only when France had made up her mind to accept defeat and discuss 'the cosmetics of capitulation'. The reality was again (as in Indo-China) the abandonment to exile or massacre of those who had believed the repeated assurances that France would never leave the country. Many hawks had also prophesied quite accurately that before long an independent Algeria would be ruled by the army under Colonel Boumedienne—but had quite mistakenly added that this would certainly mean control by 'international Communism'.

The doves had always foreseen that in the long run it would prove impossible to govern Algeria without the support of most of its people, and that the attempt to maintain control by military force would merely drive more Moslems into the arms of the intransigent nationalists. They had rightly condemned reliance on the militant Europeans as bound to alienate Moslem opinion, and warned that the fruitless search for a middle way would merely postpone (at a huge economic, political and human cost) the inevitable discussion with those against whom France was fighting. But their suspicion of their own leaders made many doves remarkably starry-eyed about the nationalist 'underdogs' they championed so generously. Their expectations about independent Algeria were pitched so high that the reality (though the government of the NLF was no worse than average) came to many of them as a painful shock. For no one was the awakening more disastrous than for the young idealists of the very far Left who had identified themselves with the Algerian cause, and chose to live in the new Republic to help in reconstruction—only to find when Boumedienne came to power that they were vilified, imprisoned or exiled as interfering and presumptuous paternalists.

In France itself the settlement did not provoke the political crisis that many observers (including the author) had expected. Yet in some ways the circumstances seemed to point straight to disaster. The Evian treaty managed to save France's face and obscure the reality of defeat, but it collapsed within three months of signature. By July Algeria was ruled by the NLF leaders, 800,000 penniless European refugees were swarming into France, and it could not be concealed that France had lost yet another war. (Whether this is psychologically more painful than losing your first war is not clear.) There were, however, a number of favourable factors. The extreme Right was powerless, and totally discredited by its unsuccessful resort to force. The economy was booming, and the government had both the authority and the will to intervene actively in settling the new arrivals—who were not entering a country in the grip of an acute urban and racial crisis. Ordinary Frenchmen (and even the refugees themselves) were desperately anxious to forget the whole nightmare and make a fresh start. An immense mood of relief dominated the country; and fortunately for France, a political leader of genius was able to make the most of it. And the indispensable key to his success was his decision, once he had changed his policy, to pursue the new course wholeheartedly: no more nostalgic regrets, no more haggling over details, no more crude or cunning manœuvres to put the other side in a false position, but a bold determination to stake everything on making the new departure a success.

By signing the treaty of peace, the President closed his yawning credibility gap (except for observers on the extreme Right). Other Frenchmen were eager to believe that they had arrived at a new beginning, rather than an end; and de Gaulle told them that at last, freed from what Lord Salisbury once called 'the carcasses of dead policies', France could begin to tackle her urgent domestic problems and play her proper role in the world. By showing financial generosity and psychological understanding to the new masters of Algeria, he contrived to present himself to the Third World as the great emancipator —while selling arms to South Africa on the side. By convincing Frenchmen that the recognition of necessity was really a free choice of a noble and generous role, he turned a political defeat into a psychological fillip, and conjured away their national inferiority complex—while incidentally snatching an electoral triumph from a settlement which would have ruined anybody else. However insufferable French national self-confidence often seems today, it is fundamentally healthier than the old, bitter internal vendettas, the minority attitudes of self-flagellation or xenophobia, which reflected contradictory feelings of national shame or frustration on both Left and Right. Adopting the new policy without hesitation or compromise, proclaiming the virtues of decolonisation for all the world as if he had believed in them all his life, de Gaulle persuaded both Frenchmen and foreigners to look to the future instead of the past.

Index

Index

Index

Index

Germany, 11–12, 21, 25–32, 48, 61 n, 70–1, 152 n, 155, 160, 168, 192, 198, 207–10
Gestapo, 5, 80, 122
Gillet, P., 73 n
Girardet, Raoul, 195 n
Girardot, Capt., 40–42 nn, 45–6, 48
Giraud, 182
Glières, 198
Godard, Col., 95, 139 n, 160, 197, 198 n–199, 202
Gohier, Gerald, 79, 117–18
Goldey, David, 9 n
Good Friday, 17
Gough, Gen., 177
Gouin, Félix, 37 n
Gouraud, 199
Goutailler, 136 n
Gouvernement-Général, 130, 136 and n, 138–41 nn, 143 and n, 161, 163–4
Government of Public Safety, 132, 135–8, 143
'Grand O', 132, 144 n
Great Train Robbers, 98
Greek Church, 3; — junta, 160, 198 n
Grenoble, 183
Grévy, Pres. Jules, 19
Gringoire, 6, 28 n, 59 and n
Gross, John, 48 n
Grosser, A., 13 n
Group of Ten, 209
Gstaad, 81
Guibaud, Gen., 79, 83, 86, 123 n
Guichard, 145 n, 148 n, 149 n, 154–6 nn, 159, 161, 164

Hachad, Ferhat, 13
Hadj, Messali, 170–2
Halévy, Daniel, 29
Hamon, L., 146 n, 154 n
Harding, W., 4
Hardy, René, 5, 38 and n
Hassan II, 78–9, 81, 83, 87, 92, 97, 108–11 and n, 121
Havana, 79, 118
Hayot, Me, 60–1, 63, 79, 101, 105
Henry, Col., 21
Herriot, Edouard, 22, 29
Hervé, Pierre, 73 n
Hirsch, 64
Hiss, Alger, 48, 50
Hitler, A., 18, 28 and n–30, 70
'Hokum', Gen., 25
Housseini, El, 78, 81, 107, 112
Hug, Me, 91
Hugues, André, 57, 62 n
Huguenots, 11
Humanité, L', 47, 53 n, 131 n, 151 n, 156 n
Hungary, 132, 138

IGAME (*Inspecteurs-généraux de l'administration en mission extraordinaire*), 152 and n, 163, 165
Imperialism, 12, 14, 24, 151, 199
Indo-China, 6, 12–15, 38–9, 42, 44 n, 47–8, 50–2, 55 n, 59, 60, 71–2, 132, 155, 177, 192–6, 199, 207, 217; communists, 38, 42, 192–3; piastres affair, 5, 15, 45 and n, 47
insoumis, 167–8, 214
Institut des hautes études de défense nationale, 39
Internment Camps, 174–5, 184, 190, 193
Ireland, 13, 15, 75, 174
Islam, 170
Isorni, Jacques, 130–1 n, 134 n, 143 n, 145 n, 150 n, 152 n, 158–60 nn, 166
Istiqlal, 170
Italy, 9, 11, 29, 50, 168

Jacobins, 8, 25
Jacquet, Marc, 51, 66–7
Jacquier, Gen., 79, 83, 90, 93, 94–6 n, 100, 119, 123 n
Jacquinot, Louis, 145 n, 161
Jaurès, Jean, 24
Jeanson, Francis, 167, 197
'Jeanson network', 167
Jeune Nation, 187
Jews: French, 20–21 and n, 24, 29, 61 n, 152, 214; Algerian, 168–9, 188, 191, 217
Joanovici, 5
Johnson, D., 15 n
Johnson, Pres. L. B., 211, 215
Jolivet, 141 n, 161
Jouhaud, Gen. Edmond, 131 and n, 135 n, 136 n, 137 nn, 144 n, 156 n, 158 n, 160, 163, 198
Journal d'Alger, 138
Journal Officiel, 72
Journalists, *see* Press
Jouvenel, Robert de, 17
Judiciary, 3, 5–8, 15–16, 54, 59–61 n, 69–71 n, 102–3, 120, 123
Juin, Marshal, 68, 152, 160
July Monarchy, 9

Kabyle, 156 n, 170, 186
Kadour, 194–5
Kahn, 114
Kasbah, Mechta, 172
Katanga, 161
Keeler, Christine, 3
Kemal revolution, 178
Kennedy, Pres. J. F., 99, 183, 186
Kennedy, Sen. Robert, 211
Kenya, 168
Kerr, Walter, 130–1 n, 151–2 nn, 155–6 nn
Khrushchev, N., 183

226

Index